30 YEARS OF 'MISSING' A-Z INTERVIEWS

By Andrew Cassidy

Printed by City Print Derry

ISBN: 978-1-3999-9437-8
ISBN-13: 978-1-3999-9437-851299

CONTENTS

FOREWORD

Thanks for buying the book and continuing to support the club and the match programme, CityView.

I first took over as editor of CityView in 2015, and a regular feature of the programme from day one was the A-Z interview. Over 250 programmes later and we've managed to get interviews from nearly every player during that time period. Fans of the A-Z will know that there are two sets of questions, and some players have done both.

I've always been glad that the players themselves know the A-Z interview at this stage and look forward to reading their team mates' responses and look to reply to get their own back during their own interview!

Over the years of asking these questions, I've often wondered what players that I would have grown up watching would answer to the A-Z interview. It was then that I got around to thinking of doing a one off feature length programme spin-off in the form of a book, featuring all the 'lost' A-Z interviews that I never got to do with players that were long gone by the time I arrived.

Over 30 players were interviewed in total, and it's been a great journey speaking to so many club legends and past players and something that I thoroughly enjoyed since taking the project on.

I'd like to thank every player who took part as well, I didn't have one refusal from any of the club legends that I approached and it was great to hear that every one of them still keep the club close to their hearts.

I hope you enjoy reading their A-Z interviews as much as I enjoyed chatting to each and every one of them.

Thanks!
Andrew Cassidy

DENNIS TUEART

SPONSORED BY
JOHN BROWN

A IS FOR ANNOYING...

Which of your former team mates was the worst to sit beside on the bus for long away journeys?

Well, I always used to sit behind the bus driver. That was always my seat wherever I played. I would have to make sure he wasn't going the wrong way!

B IS FOR BEHAVIOUR...

Which of your former team mates was always the most likely to get booked?

Don't have to think long about that one! Asa Hart-

ford!

C IS FOR COSMOS...

What was your time at New York Cosmos like, and what first attracted you there? Do you think it's similar to players going to Saudi Arabia now?

It was a fabulous experience at the time!

Soccer in America was booming at the time. Pele had gone there, Carlos Alberto, Franz Beckenbauer, Johan Neeskens... it was just boom time in America, you know?

They were the trend setters for what's happening in the global football world now, so it was a fantastic experience. And, well, yeah, it's similar in a way to the situation in Saudi Arabia in recent times. Very similar in terms of the players attracted there, but what I would say about the Cosmos was that it was the right strategy, the right place for it, but unfortunately the wrong time. I just think America wasn't ready for it at that stage, but the game in America, and it's grown again since then and it's attracting the players it used to attract.

D IS FOR DERRY CITY...

Do you still keep an eye on the Derry City results?

Yeah, I still keep an eye on things to see how it's going. They're still selling out the Brandywell which is good to see, and I was keeping an eye on developments to the stadium as well. I have great memories of the Brandywell being packed and people are standing on the hills overlooking the stadium because they couldn't get in, so it's always been crying out for expansion, even in my day!

E IS FOR ERA...

Big money included, would you prefer to have played when you did, or in modern football?

No, I'd definitely would prefer to be playing football when we did!

F IS FOR FUNNY...

What was the funniest thing you remember from your time in football?

That's actually a pretty tough one to think of!! Can I pass?!

G IS FOR GOAL...

I have a feeling I might know the answer to this one, but what was the best goal you've ever scored?

Well, obviously when you win something the goal can mean more, you know? The most famous as you say was in the 1976 League Cup Final when I scored the overhead kick against Newcastle.

That was my hometown team and so it was very emotional day, but the fact that you've won it, you've won a trophy for your family, for the club, it's supporters and for your teammates. It's important, you know? You don't get many chances to take trophies when you retire, but thankfully every club I've played for I won a trophy.

H IS FOR HOME FARM...

What do you remember about the first home

game back in the Brandywell in 1985 against Home Farm?

Well, again, what I mentioned to you about the fact that I remember that the Brandywell was absolutely jam packed! I couldn't believe it!

You know, they were queuing around the stadium to try and get in even when the game was about to kick off!

I IS FOR INFLUENCE...

Who would you say was the biggest influence on your footballing career?

Probably my first coach. Well, one of the first coaches I had anyway called Alan Brown in Sunderland.

J IS FOR JOKER...

Who was the biggest practical joker you've met in football?

Probably Joe Royle! I'll not go into any of the stories!

K IS FOR KIT...
What has been your favourite football kit that you've ever played in or owned?
I'd probably say the Cosmos kit you know. It was just something a bit different to what we were used to in England at the time.

L IS FOR LIFE AFTER PLAYING...
Did you have a plan for after your playing career ended? Was management something you ever wanted to do?
No. I never imagined management. I was more into business.
There wasn't the money in the game in those days to keep you going for life after you retired. And once you finished playing, you had to have a plan, you know?

M IS FOR MEMENTO...
What is the one football memento you own that you'll never give away?
I think it has to be the F.A. Cup winners medal that I won with Sunderland.

N IS FOR NIGHT OUT...
Which team mate was usually the first to initiate a night out?
Probably Asa Hartford again!

O IS FOR OPPOSITION...
Which opposition did you always look forward to playing the most in your career?
Manchester United! The old rival!

P IS FOR PASSTIME...
Outside of football, what keeps you occupied now in your spare time?
What, now? I don't have any spare time! I've had a video conference production business for 30 years. I had a retail travel agency for 12 years. And I've got a small property company as well, so I'm kept going anyway!

Q IS FOR QUIZ...
Which former team mate would you definitely not want in your team if you were doing a quiz?
Peter Barnes! I didn't have to take long to think about that one either!

R IS FOR RESULT...
Which result stands out or meant the most to you in your career?
I think probably in my New York Cosmos first season, because when I went into New York Cosmos, I was bought to replace Pelé., which was no easy task! He'd won the championship the season he retired, and I came the next season and I was happy to win the championship as well, the North American Soccer League Championship in my first season. We beat Tampa Bay Rowdies 3-1 in the front of 75,000 people, and I scored two goals. So that was a big one for me to achieve after coming in to replace him.

S IS FOR SIGNING...
Do you remember the story of you signing for Derry City came about?
Yeah, it was through Eamon McLaughlin who I played with at Sunderland and, I even went and had a holiday with him on my off season when I was still a player. And then this opportunity came when he was speaking to me and I had been retired by six or eight months or so, and he said that Derry City had been accepted to the League of Ireland and would I play a few games and he kept bothering me because I was having to

11

get the plane across on a Sunday morning for games. I was picked up at Belfast airport and brought down, so it was a bit of a job!

But I played about eight or ten games, I think, in the end. And then, they changed the manager. Jim Crossan was the manager then and I knew his brother John from Man City and he played for Sunderland as well.

Noel King arrived then and quite rightly he wanted to start planning for the rest of the season because I was only on a game to game basis, he asked me if I'd sign until the end of the season, but it was becoming too difficult. The travel was becoming too difficult. So I just said, no, I'd rather not.

T IS FOR TEAM MATES...

Who is the best player you've ever played with?

Has to be Franz Beckenbauer!

U IS FOR UNPARALLELED...

Who is the best player you've ever played against?

That's difficult! Not really an individual player, but the best team would be the Liverpool team of the mid 70s. They had players like Kevin Keegan, Tommy Smith and they just had a real, fantastic system and way of playing, and, yeah, they'd be the hardest team. The Liverpool team of the mid '70s.

V IS FOR VANITY...

Which team mate spent the longest in front of the mirror?

Rodney Marsh!

W IS FOR WISHES...

Is there anything you'd change about your career if you could do it all

again?

No, not at all. I was quite happy with what I had.

You know, the three clubs I played for Sunderland, Manchester City, New York, Cosmos, I won a major trophy each time, I played for England six times.

You know, I can't grumble about that. I think I made the most of what I had!

X IS FOR EXPERIENCE...

What's the best atmosphere you've ever experienced as a player?

Probably going to play at Anfield.

Y IS FOR YOUNG...

What is your earliest memory of going to a football match?

When Newcastle United won the F.A. Cup in 1955, and they came back to St. James's Park and my dad, I was only six at the time. Five or six. My Dad took me to St. James's Park and to welcome the team home.

Z IS FOR ZONE...

Did you ever have any pre-match rituals or superstitions to get you in the zone?

I had a few, yeah! Always have a nice warm bath to stretch the muscles out. And I always put my shorts on last, and I always follow the number ten out on the pitch!

TONY O'DOHERTY

SPONSORED BY
MARTIN BRADLEY

A IS FOR ANNOYING...

Which of your former team mates was the worst to sit beside on the bus for long away journeys?

There's never any doubt about that one! By a country mile it's Paul Kinnard!

B IS FOR BEST...

You played with George Best didn't you? What was that like?

I did. Several times. Well, the man was unbelievable. What George would do on todays pitches is anybody's guess! I mean, I saw George playing on mud heaps against teams like Spain, Russia out in Moscow, etc. You know, at that time, N.Ireland didn't have a great side and George was amazing on his own. I mean, the man was a genius, end of story!

C IS FOR CAUTION...

Which team mate was always the most likely to get booked?

Probably Paul McLaughlin! Now, you're saying team-mate, but I'm obviously going for Paul from the time I was the manager!

D IS FOR DERRY CITY...

Who is the best player Derry City have ever had?

You can't answer that in a simple sense because people from different eras you can't really compare like for like, but I mean the the list is endless. Take your pick! Jobby Crossan, Liam Coyle, Felix Healy, you know the list of great players in the past, and now we have the likes of Patrick McEleney etc. You can never... I think you can't name a player because of different eras. Those are the guys who stand out, but as I say, I could list a load more!

E IS FOR ERA...

Money aside, would you prefer to have played

when you did, or in modern football?

That's a good question. You can never put a value on a lifetime of memories so... I mean someday in the future, and I'll be long gone, somebody will be asking players today the same question! Football moves on very fast, you know. So I think it's a bit like trying to compare players from two different eras of football, you can't. So I'm saying... I enjoyed my time, simple as that, and and I have a lifetime of memories. It's not something we give up lightly.

F IS FOR FINN HARPS...

You won the FAI Cup twice, one with Harps and one with Dundalk, which was meant the most to you?

Well, probably the Finn Harps one, because it was an incredible occasion. An incredible occasion, you know. It was in Dalymount Park and there was an incredible crowd up from Derry and Donegal. I think there was 17,000 at the match and I could honestly say that about 12,000-14,000 of them were Finn Harps fans. And and that included half of Derry because remember at that time, there were no other teams in Derry that people supported, so they used to travel to watch Harps. An incredible occa-

sion though. Absolutely incredible.

G IS FOR GOAL...

What was the best goal you've ever scored?

I was fortunate enough to score a free kick for Coleraine against Derry City that I think was one of the best. Jimmy Hill was the Derry manager at the time and he was so annoyed because I wasn't really known as the goal scorer! He was so annoyed Eddie Mahon that he dropped him for the next game! That's true!

H IS FOR HOME FARM...

What do you remember about the first home game back in the Brandywell in 1985 against Home Farm?

I remember it rained all that week! I met Dennis Tueart that morning at the Everglades and trained with him across the road in Prehan and then just that day there was intense heat! I remember the intense heat and the occasion, to a large extent overshadowed everything. It just flew by, the memories of the match are little or none! You know, you you're playing the game, but you were more in awe of the size of the crowd! You kept just looking at the crowd and thinking, this is unreal, you know!

I IS FOR INTERNATIONAL...

Do you remember how you got your first International call-up?

Yeah, it was a nice and simple one... England! At Wembley! Just the 100,000 people there! Billy Bingham was the manager and I just got a call to come in training and it went from there.

J IS FOR JOKER...

Who was the biggest practical joker you've met in football?

Paul Curran! Without a shadow of doubt! No question!

K IS FOR KIT...

What was your favourite football kit that you've ever played in?

Finn Harps had a nice kit one year. It was donated by West Brom. Johnny Giles was the then manager of West Brom, and he was actually trying to get me to sign. It was supposed to be part of the deal, the kit, but the tansfer never happened. It was a lovely kit though. Even today it's still the same West Brom kit that you see today on TV. Lovely kit. Really nice.

L IS FOR LIFE AFTER PLAYING...

Did you have a plan for after football? Was management something you always wanted to do?

No, I never wanted to be a manager. Never, ever, ever! I just fell into management as opposed to planned it. Had Roy Coyle stayed on that time, I'd have never been involved in management! I think I was a bit of a crisis appointment you know. I was maybe an easy and cheap option, you know. I did it more to help and fill a hole until they got somebody proper, you know.

What was your original plan for after football?

Nothing really. Maybe working on the coaching side more than the management side, so I would have done a bit of coaching, which I did on a few occasions.

M IS FOR MEMENTO...

What is the one football memento you own that you'll never give away?

I don't have any. I gave every football momento I have away. I don't keep any.

I don't believe in keeping them. I think they're lovely for, you know, the history rooms within the club and stuff like that, but on a personal level I never bothered.

N IS FOR NIGHT OUT...

I have a feeling I know the answer to this one, but which team mate was usually the first to initiate a night out?

You know who I'm going to say for that one that one!

Paul Curran?

Yep! Paul Curran! Dear God, he's serious!

O IS FOR OPPOSITION...

Which opposition did you always look forward to playing the most in your career?

I would have to say Sligo. Even though they beat us in the Cup Final, I always enjoyed playing Sligo.

P IS FOR PASSTIME...

Outside of football, what keeps you occupied now in your spare time?

More football!! No, I do a bit of community work. The community work keeps me going.

Q IS FOR QUIZ...

Which former team mate would you definitely not want in your team if you were doing a quiz?

Again, dead simple! Paul Kinnaird! He never knew what day it was never mind taking him to a quiz!

R IS FOR RESULT...

Which result stands out or meant the most to you in your career?

Probably because of it's significance I would have to go with the first match against Home Farm. I mean, we didn't win anything, but the significance of that match can never be lost. And I would advise younger fans and readers, it's on YouTube, if they get their hands on that video of that match and the crowd coming to it, you should watch it and remind themselves of what football is all about and how much it means to this City.

S IS FOR SIGNING...

Do you remember the story of you signing for Derry City came about?

Yeah, it's very simple. I was the coach at the time. I had no intention of playing. And one of the players in the squad had come up from the intermediate team, and he had decided that it wasn't for him or whatever. He didn't fancy the training, which in fairness to him was tough at the time, but he couldn't commit anyway and he pulled out, so the manager Jimbo Crossan came to me and said, 'Do you fancy playing?' So that's how I signed for Derry! Instead of being coach I ended up playing!

T IS FOR TALENT...

Who is the best player you've ever played with?

Undoubtedly George Best. But by the same token, I've been lucky enough to have played with some of the absolute greats locally, Jobby Crossan, Liam Coyle, Felix Healy... Incredible footballers! Incredible footballers in any era!

U IS FOR UNPARALLELED...

Who is the best player you've ever played against?

Probably Colin Bell at Man City. In them days we played inter-league all the time. We played against the English league a good bit. I mean, you can imagine the English leagues sides at the time and the players they had. But Colin Bell was some-

thing else, you know.

V IS FOR VANITY...

Which team mate spent the longest in front of the mirror?

I'm trying to think who? Out of pure badness, he actually wasn't too bad, but out of pure badness I'm going to say Pizza! if you speak to him tell him I owe him one as payback for Cork! *(We did ask Pizza on Page 44!)*

W IS FOR WISHES...

Is there anything you'd change about your career if you could do it all again?

No, definitely not. Nope. I'm happy enough with the career I had and I would consider myself very fortunate.

X IS FOR EXPERIENCE...

What's the best atmosphere you've ever experienced?

I would have to say despite the fact that I've played

some of biggest arenas in the world, nothing match the Brandywell for Linfield games in the Setanta Cup! It was something else!

Y IS FOR YOUNG...

What is your earliest memory of going to a football match?

Well, my father was a football fanatic, so I was going to football since I was two or three. So in some ways I was always destined to be involved in football somewhere, you know? Yeah, I was only two or three but I still have memories of that.

Z IS FOR ZONE...

Did you ever have any pre-match rituals or superstitions to get you in the zone?

No, I never had no. I've had team mates with superstitions and if it works for them well and good, there could be something in it alright, but it's just not for me.

OWEN DA GAMA

SPONSORED BY
KEVIN MCDAID

A IS FOR ANNOYING...

Which of your former team mates was the worst to sit beside on the bus for long away journeys?

I would say Kevin O'Neill! He was always so quiet! He wouldn't speak a word! So it would be quite a boring trip if it was quiet all the way to where we're going!

B IS FOR BOOKING...

Which team mate was always the most likely to get booked?

I'm just trying to think who that would have been. It

must have been Raymond McGuinness! He was tough! He'd kick and smack the guy at the same time! And get away with it most of the time as well!

C IS FOR CITY...

Do you remember the story of how you signing for Derry City came about?

Yeah, I was playing in Belgium at Beerschot in Antwerp and I was still considered a rookie over there and they had a lot of internationals at the time. So I think I was one of seven international players from

outside the country and they could only play three at the time I think the rule was. They'd given me a lengthy five year contract because they obviously were thinking of the future, and I was only a young player that they maybe seen a future in. But Noel King was playing in France at the time, and he was about to retire and he had got the job at Derry as a coach. So he came up and he watched us play a couple of games and then he asked if they could loan me to Derry City and they spoke to me and I was on and off in the first team there because

17

the more senior players like the goalkeeper, the defenders, they were players that they had to play. I did make some appearances for the first team, but it was going to be very hard because as I said, it was more the senior players that got to play. The captain was also a foreigner, from Holland, so it was going to be very tough for me to get consistent game time if they were only allowed to play three at a time. So they spoke to me and told me Derry was an option. It was not a forced situation or anything, they were asking me did I want to rather than telling me I was going. So I thought to myself, 'well, let me go and see what it's like in Derry, and let me go and play.' I just wanted to play, that was the most important thing. So I spoke to Derry and Noel King really convinced me of the possibilities of moving forward with my career in Derry and so on, and my mind was made up and I signed. So that's how I eventually got to Derry.

D IS FOR DERRY...

Do you ever keep an eye out for the Derry City results?

Yes, I do! Every week! And they've been doing exceptionally well this season! I saw recently that somebody just equaled my record after 30-something years! One of the strikers. I think it was fastest to reach 10 goals or something. So I hope he goes on and breaks that record next season! It's no good equaling it, he must go on and break it!

E IS FOR ERA...

Given the money and technology involved now, would you prefer to have played when you did, or in modern football?

I never played football for the money, to be honest. It was never about money. It was my passion, you know? I'm a coach now as well. I've been coaching now for a couple of years in South Africa and I always tell my players that if you put your football in front, the money will follow. If you put money in front of you, the football sometimes stays behind, so I've never been somebody that played for money. So for me it would be the same even if I played now. But then as long as I'm driven by my passion, I think that's the most import thing.

F IS FOR FAN CLUB...

You had your own Fan Club at Derry! Did you ever expect that level of fame?

No, I did not to be honest with you! Even in Belgium, nobody had a fan club! And I mean Belgium has quite a big league. So, yeah, I was really surprised with regards to the passion of the people in terms of football and the liking they take to players, so it was exceptional. It really, really surprised me and it's something that I will cherish for the rest of my life.

G IS FOR GOAL...

What was the best goal you've ever scored?

There were too many to mention! But for me, every goal is the best goal. Because you can score a great goal and it's only the first goal in a 5-0 win, or you can score a simple goal in the last minute of an important game and it's only a 1-0 win, but that goal means more. And so for me, I would never have a goal that I would say was the best goal in my life. All the goals are equally as important as far as I'm concerned.

H IS FOR HAHA...

What's the funniest thing you've seen happen in your time in football?

The funniest thing I saw in football was when I was playing in Belgium when the referee gave the linesman a red card! That, to me was absolutely the funniest! We couldn't believe it! The linesman said it was offside and the referee disagreed. I mean, the referee's got the right to overrule the linesman anyway, but the linesman persisted and he actually threw his flag on the ground and started shouting in the referee's face! So the referee's reacted and took out his red card and sent him off! That, to me, was truly funny! It's like something you'd see in a comedy movie and think it's made up if I hadn't actually seen it happen myself!

I IS FOR IRELAND...

What were your initial thoughts of Ireland and

the League Of Ireland?

Well, my father was a politician and he never wanted me to mix politics with sport. He was a highly educated man and he raised me properly in never mixing the two when I started playing football in South Africa. But when I told him about the move to Derry, he made me aware of the political situation and the sectarian situation within Northern Ireland and Ireland. So, before I even arrived, I had a pretty good idea as to what the political situation was about, but I was still very, very cautious about the situation. To be honest with you, because I had done a little bit of reading as well about it all, I was very sympathetic towards the situation faced by the people, and that also convinced me to go and play there because I was going to be part of a great cause, you know? Because I think football unites people and sport in general unites people, and it calms the political and sectarian tension, even just for 90mins. So for me, I thought that moving forward I would be part of a very good cause within the city. So when I went to Derry it was really something very new to me. Even though I personally lived in a country where there was apartheid and, you know, bad treatment of its citizens. So because I too grew

up in a in a very bad situation politically, I was very sympathetic because I think Ireland was the first country that had a goods embargo with regards to South Africa. So they banned all trade with South Africa because of the way they were treating their citizens. So, to me it was very sympathetic and I understood that, and I was very happy to be to be part of that, although I didn't get involved in politics or anything. I just put my football ahead of everything else and thankfully, I never experienced any trouble.

J IS FOR JOKER...

Who was the biggest practical joker you've met in football?

I would say Kevin Mahon! He was one of the senior players at the time, but he was very, very funny! He would make fun of people, but in a very serious manner! You had to understand the way he was though. You had to be very smart to understand his humour. He had humour at a level that I've never come across! He was just unbelievably funny, but always with a straight face!

K IS FOR KIT...

Did you get to keep your Derry City kit? And do you still have it?

Unfortunately, when I left I donated the kit to a charity that helped a lot of people.

19

I'm happy that I did that, but at the same time I'm so sorry that now I don't even have one Derry City jersey! I just have my photos and so on. But I always meant to go back to Derry and try and get one of the latest jerseys, just to keep as a memory. Unfortunately even my blazer with the club crest on it, the day after the cup final when we were at the Guildhall, on the second floor there, and there were like, thousands of people there beneath the balcony, I actually took off my blazer and I threw it in the crowd! I ended up standing there just in my underpants in the end up! Somebody got my shoes, my tie, my trousers, my shirt, everything! I actually walked out afterwards in just my socks and underpants and somebody borrowed me a coat so that I could get home! But, yeah, I gave a lot of my stuff to the people there because you know, they treated me so well and with so much love that I just had to share whatever I had with everybody around me.

L IS FOR LIFE AFTER PLAYING...

Did you have a plan for after football? Was management something you always wanted to do?

My plan was actually to go into business. I wanted to go into business outside of football, but I never planned to retire at the age of 30 due to a bad knee injury! So I wasn't ready at that stage! I mean, guys used to kick the hell out of me when I was playing! I was very fast, so the only way to stop me, they discovered, was just to kick me! I wasn't so fast when I was injured! So I ended up with a very bad knee injury. I had two operations and it was so painful to me both physically and emotionally because I never thought I would stop playing at that age. So it really was terrible, because I had not planned for it at the time. So, I went on for a year still trying to do rehab and trying to strengthen after my injury, and the team that I was playing for at the time actually extended my contract. A team called Moroka Swallows. One of the top teams in South Africa. They actually gave me a two year extension. That's how much they wanted me still to play, but after a year when I saw no real improvement, I just thought, no, your time is up now, so I went back home. My parents had a farm, which I now actually run, but we had a farm so I started working there and went into farming in a very big way just to get my mind right and to sort of, it was like a cooling down period after football. I al-ways wanted my own business though, so I started a sports bar in Pretoria and it was very successful, but it was very strenuous. The working hours were terrible and it was just getting too strenuous. So I sold that and I got into the computing business. I was running my own computer company, but the whole time I knew I was missing football. Eventually the bug just got to me and I had to go back. I was approached by a club called Dynamos in Johannesburg. They were in the Second Division and they wanted me to come and assist them. So I sold my business, actually I sold it to my sister and she still has the business, but I sold it to her and then I went into coaching and in my first season we promoted the team to the to the Premier League here in South Africa. After that I just became a full time coach. So I've promoted four teams already to the Premier League. Two teams from the Third Division, and three teams from the Second Division to the Premier League. I also coached for a while in the Premier League. I think it was 2016 that I won South African Coach of the Year. So yeah, the bug just caught me and ever since that I've been coaching. So, managing wasn't ever something that I set out to do, it just evolved over time.

M IS FOR MEMENTO...

What is the one football memento you own that you'll never give away?

I've got a picture of Derry City framed on my wall at home in our red and white striped kit and that is honestly my prized possession! I've got coaching certificates and things framed in different places as well, but they don't come near to that. I did very well academically as well and I have those certificates framed, but all those things count for nothing at the end of the day. My most prized possession is my Derry City picture. That brings me more memories and joy than anything else in those frames.

N IS FOR NIGHT OUT...

Which former team mate was usually the first to initiate a night out?

Oh, there were too many!

The guys liked to party! But it was so professional because our night out was always the night after the match. We would normally go to the hotel. What was it called? The Everglades? We will go to the Everglades in our in our blazers and suits and then after that some of the more senior players would go on home and then some of us would make arrangements and say we're going to the Point Inn, you know? I don't know if it's still there, but we would usually go to the Point Inn and that could be the only time that we would go out. After a game. Apart from that, never. So it was very professional. When we played away, we would come back very late, so we would just go home, so there wasn't really any big nights out apart from after a home match.

O IS FOR OPPOSI-

TION...

Which opposition did you always look forward to playing the most in your career?

Well, I always liked playing against the biggest teams at the time. Like, in South Africa there was Kaiser Chiefs, in Belgium it was Anderlecht, and in an Ireland it was Shamrock Rovers. I mean, they dominated the league at the time. They were the best by far for many years, so it was always nice to play in those games. And I remember my last game against them. We played in Dublin and I scored two goals. That was my last game against Shamrock Rovers so it was it was always nice to play against the bigger teams and big opposition. And in Belgium as well, in the Champions League we went to play in Moscow against Spartak Moscow, and that to me was a great thrill as well. Getting to play in the Champions League.

P IS FOR PASSTIME...

Outside of football, what keeps you occupied now in your spare time?

I read a lot. I always try to be a better person, to know more, and I try every now and again to learn a new passion and something new to learn about. But I think reading is, for me, something that I just love doing.

Q IS FOR QUIZ...

Which former team mate would you definitely not want in your team if you were doing a quiz?

Let me see… If we're doing a quiz… I know quizzes were a big thing in Derry. I remember I used to go for pub grub a lot because I was single at the time and it would save me cooking! But there were always quizzes on in the pubs, so I know it's a big thing in Ireland and enjoyed them, I learned such a lot. But a teammate that was no good at quizzes… Paul Caryle maybe. I remember he had a nickname. Storkey wasn't it?! He was very funny actually, so I wouldn't say him because he was a he was a smart guy. I'd say maybe Declan McDowell! Because he was also a very shy guy!

R IS FOR RESULT...

Which result stands out or meant the most to you in your career?

Yes, as a player we played against the top team in South Africa called the Sundowns. Mamelodi Sundowns. They were one of the richest teams in Africa. They had all the star players in the league. They had players from Argentina and from all over the world. So we played against them in the in the Cup final, the Bob Save Cup Final as it was

known then, and we beat them. That was probably the best match of my life. I scored a hat trick and it was an amazing experience. There was 80,000 people in the stadium and it was the best game of my life. And even up until now, people remember me in South Africa for that Cup Final.

S IS FOR SOUTH AFRICA...

You made the move back to South Africa after Derry City missing out on the treble. How did your move home come about?

Yeah, what happened is that there was actually a deal done with Figueres in Spain, near Barcelona. They were a second division team at the time. I think now they've

gone defunct. The owner of the team was actually at the Cup final when we played in Dublin. That was my last game for Derry City. We lost 1-0 in that final, but the owner was there and I met the owner. Jim McLaughlin introduced me to him. And by the way, please include my condolences to Jim McLaughlin's family. I just heard recently that he passed away. He was a great, great man. But, yeah, Jim McLaughlin, may he rest in peace, he introduced me to the chairman of the club and they were very excited to have me there. I actually went to Manchester where the Spanish embassy was and I applied for my visa to work in Spain. They gave me, like, a visiting visa for one month and so I went to Spain and then we did the further applications and all that when I was out there, but in the end up, my visa was denied. It was just because of the political situation in South Africa. There was a sports embargo against all South Africans at the time, so I said 'But I'm the one who's suffered because of it.' But they said no, they're just banning every South African. There was even a golf tournament around that time and the South African golfers were all banned and they had to withdraw from the tournament. But, yeah, it was denied on that basis. They kept on trying, but unfortunately the chairman, like in most European countries, the chairman is the guy with the finances and he passed away in that very same year and so the club actually went bankrupt and defunct not long afterwards. I think they came back 2007 under a new name. They came back and now they're in the 4th Division or something. But yeah, it didn't work out because of the sports embargo, so Jim wanted me to come back to Derry City. But because I was under contract to Figueres, and they were still trying for about seven months to get my visa even through, it didn't work out. We even came up with a plan that I would live in Corsica, which was an island belonging to

France. So I was going to go to Corsica and then from there travel into Spain, but it never worked out. I remember at the time, South Africa was banned from FIFA. We couldn't enter into FIFA because of the political situation here, and more countries were banning South African good and services, so I had a fear that even going back to Derry, an issue could arise there as well and I'd be out of football for another 6 months. But I knew that I could come and play in South Africa without any issue, you know? So I actually just came back and then I started as a player coach for a team called Durban Leeds United. The owner and founder was a big Leeds United fan! We were in the Premier League in South Africa, and that's how I ended up back here. I just wanted to play, you know? But I remember Jim just contacting me saying 'come back, come back and play, come back', but it never transpired. I eventually just remained in South Africa because I had bought a house in Durban and my girlfriend didn't want me to leave the country again. So it just went from that situation where I thought maybe I was going back just for a while to play until we get something sorted, to me being permanently in South Africa.

T IS FOR TEAM MATES...

Who is the best player you've ever played with?

The best prayer I played with would actually be a toss-up between Alexander Krstic and the captain we had at Derry City at the time, Felix Healy. I think Felix was a superb player, you know? An unbelievable player. And a great singer as well!

U IS FOR UNPARALLELED...

Who is the best player you've ever played against?

Let me just think… My head is so full of names! No, actually, I'll tell you who it was. It's Jean-Pierre Papin! He went from Brugge to Marseille I think, and had a great career from there. But, yeah, Jean-Pierre Papin was a fantastic player. And then there was another guy, a Senegalese player in Belgium called Jules Bocandé. He is probably one of the best strikers I've seen in my life. He was unbelievable.

V IS FOR VANITY...

Which team mate spent the longest in front of the mirror?

I would say Kevin O'Neill! I actually bought him lipstick as a present one day to tease him because he was so into himself! He was always with the hair, you know? Always

combing his hair! Very neat guy!

W IS FOR WISHES...

Is there anything you'd change about your career if you could do it all again?

I've got no regrets, no. I just think that everything is as it should be. You must live by the consequences of your actions, and you learn by that. And whether you've made mistakes or not, you just move on in life, because it's no use looking back. So I just look forward. But if I had one wish, I would have wished to have stayed at Derry City, and even concluded my career there and lived in Derry. It was definitely where I was very happy, and if I'd known the way the transfer away would go I wouldn't have left, but as I say, my actions and decisions have led me to where I

am now, and I'm very happy.

X IS FOR EXPERIENCE...

What's the best atmosphere you've ever experienced?

It's a toss-up between that Cup Final against Sundowns in South Africa, and the Derry City final where we beat Finn Harps 4-1. I remember in that game, I think there was about 5 or 10 minutes remaining in the game or something, but after I scored the penalty to get my hat-trick, the people just stormed onto the field and the referee couldn't do anything about it. There was still some minutes left but the referee blew the end of the game. That for me was unbelievable. Every player was great, and every player was carried by the fans. That's what an atmosphere is all about. It's not about one player, it's about the team. Even the manager. The whole team was carried. To me, that was an unforgettable experience.

Y IS FOR YOUNG...

What is your earliest memory of going to a football match?

I think I was eight years old. There was a team in Pretoria called Arcadia Shepherds. They were the top team at the time, and my father took me there go and watch some games. That's when I

started understanding what football is about. We'd go every Friday night and that's where my passion started as a youngster. Then I went and played for Arcadia Juniors U10s and the U12s, and so on. And that's where I started my footballing career.

Z IS FOR ZONE...

Did you ever have any pre-match rituals or superstitions to get you in the zone?

Not really, no. I mean, prayer was always part of my day. Every day is the same for me. I don't have special rituals for before a game or anything like that. Every day for me has got to start with a prayer and every day has got to end with a prayer. So I was very consistent in that. I always remember a friend of mine who had a specific pair of pyjamas that he wore before the game, and it became a big thing because whenever he didn't have his pyjamas with him, he would have a bad game! He was a very successful guy though. He went on to be a doctor. But, no I didn't want to have anything to tie me down, you know, in case I couldn't do it and in the back of my mind, it would affect me. So, I always just maintain that, just a prayer every day, be consistent in it, and that's all you'll need.

FELIX HEALY

SPONSORED BY

MENSWEAR CO.

A IS FOR ANNOYING...

Which of your former team mates was the worst to sit beside on the bus for long away journeys?

To be honest, I always used to sit on my own if I could! There was a fella played for Port Vale though called Brian Sinclair. He was a Scouser. And he never shut his mouth! And his jokes were filthy! He was funny at times, but he was mostly annoying! And he's still annoying me, because there's actually a photograph of Port Vale that keeps appearing and it says my name on the team list at the bottom and it's actually Brian Sinclair in the photograph! So a lot of people keep sending me the photograph and I have to see him again! People keep saying 'that doesn't look like you at all' and I have to say 'Aye, because it isn't!'

B IS FOR BEHAVIOUR...

Which team mate was the most likely to get booked?

Paul Doolin! Or Roy Mc-Cready either actually! One of the two! Take your pick!

C IS FOR CHAMPI-

ONS...

You won the league and the cup both as player and as manager. Which meant more to you?

Winning the league as manager was the biggest triumph for me, yeah. That was, for me, the Holy Grail. It doesn't happen very often. So winning the league as a player was brilliant, but, yeah, I'd say winning it as manager would be the best one.

D IS FOR DERRY CITY...

Who is the best player Derry City have ever had?

That's a tough one because

25

there's been a lot of players over a lot of years. I think, the likes of Liam Coyle would be a popular choice, and he'd be up there, definitely. As would a lot of others. But for me, I think Paul Hegarty wins you leagues. Paul was always the kind of player you wanted in your team. I played with Paul and had him there when I was manager as well and I was glad to have him!

E IS FOR EUROPE...

Which team was your toughest European opponent?

I think the likes of Benfica would be the first one that comes to mind, but thinking about it, there was a team called Lokomotive Leipzig

that we played when I was at Coleraine, and they were just filled with great players at the time. I remember in between the home and away legs, six of their players were on international duty and played against France and won. They beat us 5-0 in the second leg and went on to draw AC Milan in the next round and beat them as well 2-0.

F IS FOR FAI CUP...

What are your memories of that FAI Cup final in 1989 that wrapped up the treble?

I remember just being glad it was all over! I was injured as well and probably shouldn't have played. I played 90mins the week

previous to it with an injury too, so another memory was how sore my leg was during the game! But, no, obviously it was an unbelievable feeling to finally get it over the line as well and the pressure was off and we could finally celebrate. There's one or two pictures I have of my youngest fella on my shoulders with the cup with brilliant shots of the crowd behind us. He was mascot for the game as well, so that was a special moment. My main memories of the game itself would obviously be the goal. You get a serious adrenaline rush when you score the winner in a cup final and I was able to run like I was able to run 10 years before! But, yeah, the main memory as I say was just the relief when it was finally over.

G IS FOR GOAL...

What was the best goal you've ever scored?

I played at Bradford City one night for Port Vale and I hit one from about 30 yards and it absolutely flew into the back of the net. That was at the old Valley Parade ground a few years before the tragedy. And I scored a goal in the cup final against Linfield at the Oval where I turned the center back and ran from the halfway line and smashed it across the 'keeper. But that one at Valley Parade always sticks out for me. There was one I hit on the half volley as well from about 30 yards against Linfield for Coleraine on Boxing Day one year. We beat them 2-0. That was a serious strike as well. There were some great team goals

that I was involved in too, but the one at Valley Parade and that one against Linfield are the ones that stick out.

H IS FOR HAHA...

What was the funniest thing you remember from your time in football?

Funny, I was talking about this recently to someone! I was playing a game at Sligo, and the kit when we played for Sligo was a very, very old kit! I mean, the socks could barely be pulled up over your calves, and the shorts were short! But this one match, the late Seamus 'Shakes' McDowell was playing and on several occasions his... 'meat and two veg' were dangling out all over the place! It was hilarious! Another one that made me laugh, there was also there was a fella called Johnny McIvor who played for Coleraine and Johnny

made the mistake of going into the wrong dressing room at half time! He did it at Larne and not only walked in, but he actually went in and sat down and looked around him! But that was just the first time! He actually did it twice! He did it again at some other ground as well! But, yeah, there was a lot of funny things down the years, but that day with Shakes running around the pitch with everything on show always springs to mind! I think a lot of people were in stitches that day! It was hard to keep our composure when something like that happens!

I IS FOR INTERNATIONAL...

Which was better, your first international call-up, or your call-up to the World Cup squad?

Oh, that's a tough one... Well, I suppose I could say that getting called up against Scotland would be the better one for me because getting named in the World Cup squad would never have happened without that Scotland game getting me in the door, so to speak. I got the call to join up with the squad to play Scotland at a team dinner after we lost the Irish Cup Final. And it obviously came out of the blue for me and it was a massive achievement.

But then, you know, when Billy Bingham tells you walking off the pitch in Wales that you're going to Spain to play in the World Cup, that's almost like a different level completely. So that was really pleasing because, you know, I'd done OK against Scotland, and I did really well against Wales and I was literally told there and then after the final whistle in Wales that I was going to be playing in the World Cup. I mean, the fact that I'm able to recall it as well as I can shows just how much it meant to me.

J IS FOR JOKER...

Who was the biggest practical joker you've met in football?

There was a boy called Gerry Keenan at Port Vale that was a funny lad. He was always up to something.

There was another guy Bob

Delgado. He was best mates with Terry Owen, who was Michael Owen's father. They were funny boys as well as a double act! At Derry, Ryan Coyle was a funny boy. Really, really funny sense of humour. Really silly jokes, you know? He was good craic!

K IS FOR KIT...

What was your favourite football kit that you've ever played in?

I always think the Argentina kit, which we wore as the away kit was a nice kit. There was a kit as well when I managed Derry, the yellow one. That was the away kit the year we won the league. I remember fans nearly wore more of that one than the red and white that year! That was a popular kit as well. But if I was to pick one from the past to go again next year, I mean, you can't go wrong with the sort of Argentina

look.

L IS FOR LIFE AFTER PLAYING...

Did you have a plan for after football? Was management something you always wanted to do?

No, it wasn't. I mean, when I when I finished playing, I was working with Guinness. I was always singing as well, so it was never a plan to get into management. I was happy enough, you know. It's just the way that things actually turned out. It was just a number of life events just all happened at the right time and you were dealt a certain hand, and that's the way that it actually turned out. The plan was never really going to into management. It was one of those where, I had a full time job and I was singing away, and I was happy enough. But I count myself lucky to have done it though.

M IS FOR MEMENTO...

What is the one football memento you own that you'll never give away?

Actually, the one memento that I had that was more from the club than my career, and funny you should ask about giving it away because there's a big Derry City supporter actually has it now, but it the pennant from the Benfica vs Derry game in Benfica when I captained the team, and it was actually my birthday as well. I was actually 34 that day, and so the club gave me the pennant to keep. As I say though, I've actually given it to a friend of mine. He's a big Derry fan, but it's a great thing to have. I'm sure that he's taking good care of it for me. But in terms of something I have myself, I've actually got a photograph of the treble team at home and it's framed with the three metals inside it as well. Which is another great thing to have. And I've got a photograph of the World Cup squad from '82 as well framed.

N IS FOR NIGHT OUT...
I have a feeling I know the answer to this one, but which team mate was usually the first to initiate a night out?

Aw, that'd be Curny! Paul Curran without a doubt!

O IS FOR OPPOSITION...
Which opposition did you always look forward to playing the most in your career?

Linfield. I always like to play the Blues. It was always one of those where me as a boy, you know, going to the Brandywell and you always knew when Linfield came to town because it took over the whole ground back in the day. And they're a massive club and always were. Obviously somebody from my background playing against Linfield was, you know, often at times more than just a football match. Sadly, it was more than just about football. But yeah, I used to enjoy playing the Blues. Particularly at Wind-

sor Park.

P IS FOR PORT VALE...
How did your move to England come about with Port Vale?

Well, what actually happened was, I had been out of the game for a year or so, and I signed for Finn Harps and I played against Everton in a friendly and did quite well. But the following week, there was a fella from Liverpool called Danny Maher, who was the chief scout of Port Vale, and it just so happened that he came then to watch Finn Harps playing Sligo because The Vale were looking for a left back, and Graham Fox was an English fella who was playing left back for Sligo and they thought he was a decent player, so they come over to have a look at him, but he saw me play in that game and obviously recommended me to the manager and, yeah, it was quick. It was only two or three days later that I ended up signing for the Vale.

Q IS FOR QUIZ...
Which former team mate would you definitely not want in your team if you were doing a quiz?

Well there's quite a few to pick from there! I'll say Pascal! Not because he's stupid or anything though. He probably just wouldn't understand the

finally went through. And I think Derry paid… I'm not sure, ten grand or whatever it was. You know, I was 32 years of age at that stage and coming towards the end so it was a good deal for Coleraine, but when it finally went through, like everything else, I was relieved at the time that it finally happened because, as I say, I tried to get there the year before, but it never happened. But it was, it was a combination of Noel, Jim and Bertie Peacock coming to some sort of arrangement.

question! Or he'd let on he didn't understand it anyway if he didn't know the answer!

R IS FOR RESULT...

Which result stands out or meant the most to you in your career?
Well, I'm not too sure about result-wise, but I think the result against Benfica and the Brandywell. I mean, we lost 2-1, but the one thing that you're always worried about, particularly when you play at the Brandywell and you play someone like Benfica, is that you don't want to be left embarrassed, you know? And although we lost, I think it was a good result at 2-1. But you also have the likes of the Cup Final that went to extra time in Belfast when I scored four in extra time. That was quite a result as well. But definitely that game against Benfica was a great result. On anoth-

er day we could have gotten a bit of a hiding, so to speak, so we did well.

S IS FOR SIGNING...

Do you remember the story of you signing for Derry City came about?
Well, what actually happened was; I'd been at Coleraine for seven years. There was a lot of talk that I was going to sign for Derry the previous year and it didn't go through, and then it was one of those where, after that, it was always kind of on the cards. I think Bertie Peacock who I was always very close to at Coleraine talked to the Coleraine board and said 'look he's been here for seven years, we've got good service from him, and he wants to finish his career back at his home town club'. So, I think that it was only through Bertie's intervention that the thing

T IS FOR TEAM MATES...

Who is the best player you've ever played with?
The most gifted was Liam Coyle. I would say, International-wise, Norman Whiteside was a top, top, player. Paul Doolin's end product was serious as well. And as I say, Higgsy as well. Higgsy was part of the treble squad. He won the league with me when I managed. I mean, Paul Hegarty to me was like a Roy Keane type of character. He was an 8 or a 9 out of 10 every week. There was a lot of players who could be a 9 or a 10 most weeks and then the following week it was a 2 or a 3, but Higgsy was always consistent. So, yeah, Whiteside was a really top player, but Liam Coyle talent-wise would have blown most people away.

U IS FOR UNPARALLELED...

Who is the best player you've ever played against?

There was a guy called Kenny Dalgleish that I played against many times, he was a fantastic player. There was actually a guy as well that I played against in the World Cup when we played Honduras. He played for Real Valladolid and he was the captain of Honduras. He was a big fella called Gilberto. He was just a machine! And Ricky Villa at Spurs as well, another serious talent.

V IS FOR VANITY...

Which team mate spent the longest in front of the mirror?

It wasn't Storky anyway!! Well, the first that comes to mind, there was a fella that played for Coleraine called John Shannon, and John, had a bit of a perm going on back in the day, you know? So he'd be full time looking after his hair with his wee comb!

W IS FOR WISHES...

Is there anything you'd change about your career if you could do it all again from the start?

The only thing I ever look back on is that I should have signed for Luton after the World Cup. I could have gone and the offer was there, but I didn't want to go. Luton at that time were in what the Premier Division is now. I probably should have gone and not thought about it too much. It's the one regret that I would have was not signing for Luton. And I should have stayed in England and played longer over there and looked for clubs there when I was over. But again, it was life events or circumstances and everything else that led to those decisions. But, yeah, knowing what I know now, and as you say, if I could do it all again from the start, I would have definitely signed for Luton Town.

X IS FOR EXPERIENCE...

What's the best atmosphere you've ever experienced?

Well I was nearly involved in the Spanish match at the World Cup. I was sitting in the dugout with Billy Bingham and he called me to warm up and I was going on, then I wasn't going on, then I was again, but then Mal Donaghy got sent off and I ended up not going on! But the atmosphere in the ground that night was just unbelievable.

by the hand when I was very young, to a Linfield match actually! I was probably about 6 or 7 years of age. Just at the end though when the big gates opened. You know the big games that open to let anyone out that's leaving? So I would have got in to see the last 15-20 minutes of the game. But other than that, the first real full match that I can remember going to was the Cup Final in 1964 against Glentoran. I was at that match as an 8 year old and I have great memories of Derry winning 2-0. I still remember it vividly!

Z IS FOR ZONE...

Did you ever have any pre-match rituals or superstitions to get you in the zone?

No, not particularly. There was no real superstitions. I think sometimes when you get a good result, you tend to maybe wear the same thing the next time; until it doesn't work that is! I'm sure there were small things like that I always did, you know, but it wasn't a hard rule or anything. Looking back on it now, you tend to think, 'I wore that particular jersey the day we won, so I'll wear that again today', or that shirt and tie, or whatever it was. I'm sure there was always something small that I maybe did back at the time.

The night I played against Everton at Goodison Park park the atmosphere was amazing, and I have to say White Hart Lane as well. The atmosphere was terrific.

From a domestic point of view, the best atmosphere I ever experienced was down in Cork the year we won the league in 1997. That game basically at that stage had knocked Cork out of the running for winning the league, but Turner's Cross was absolutely rocking that night. The place was elec-tric. And that night we came away winning 1-0 and the match went a long way to us winning the league. Obviously Cup Finals and things like that as well, but domestically, that Cork game sticks out.

Y IS FOR YOUNG...

What is your earliest memory of going to a football match?

My earliest memory was always going to the Brandy-well. I remember my mother taking me across the street

PAUL DOOLIN

SPONSORED BY CONOR DEVLIN, DARA DEVLIN & ODHRAN DEVLIN

A IS FOR ANNOYING...

Which of your former team mates was the worst to sit beside on the bus for long away journeys?

Well, I always sat on my own! The most annoying though... It's hard to pick! We had a very jovial squad! I'll go for John Cunningham though with all his bad jokes! Bugsy!

B IS FOR BEHAVIOUR...

Which team mate was always the most likely to get booked?

Oh, I'll have to be careful what I say here! I think I might have been mentioned once or twice for that one was I by the other lads?! I'll go for Paul Hegarty maybe. Actually, Kevin Brady! I'll say Kevin Brady!

C IS FOR CHAMPION...

I think you've won everything that it's possible to win in Irish football north and south as both a player and a manager, but is there one trophy that stands out to you over the others?

Well, I think with most players when you haven't won anything yet, and you do win something, I think that always stands out. I mean, the first league I won was at Rovers, but I'd have to mention the treble in there as well to be honest, you know. But I think if I had to pick just one, the treble was sort of later in my career, so I think the first one I ever won was special for me. I think the first trophy that you win, either as player, or as a manager is always the one you'd remember fondest I think, you know?

D IS FOR DERRY CITY...

Do you remember the story of how you signing for Derry City came about?

Yes, I do. Yeah. I think at the time Rovers had moved from Milltown to Tolka Park and then I think it was the

33

year after that then that the club sort of struggled and I think Kevin Brady, Mick Neville, myself, and Noel Larkin all moved to Derry as a package I think, if I'm not mistaken. So that's basically how it started. That was the first time. The second time I came back was under Felix Healy.

E IS FOR EUROPE...

Which team was your toughest European opponent? At any club.

Well going back to the days when we played in Europe, it's totally different now. You're drawn now against teams maybe on your own sort of level, whether it be Norway, Sweden, you know, or Iceland or whatever. But going back to us, obviously the Brandywell would stick out when we played Benfica. They had a lot of good players. The Brazilian in the middle of the pitch, Valdo, and the Jonas Thern, who I thought was a really, really good player. So he would have been probably one of the toughest opponents in terms of players that I remember.

Then we had a few decent draws at Portadown as well. That Red Star Belgrade team that won the Champions League when it was the old European Cup before we played him the following year, you know. There

was another load of good players in that team, Robert Prosinečki, Darko Pančev, Vladimir Jugović, you know, a lot of really, really good players. Siniša Mihajlović played as well.

I think the Jonas Thern was a really good player though out of all of them. He ended up playing for Fiorentina, Roma, and Rangers I think.

F IS FOR FAI CUP...

What's more stressful, a cup final as a manager or as a player?

Well, I think when you're a player, it's totally different. I think, you're out there, you can affect things, whereas you can only affect things from the start of the game when you're a manager, you know? So, I'd say probably a manager is probably worse than being a player. When you're a player, you're out there, you're caught up in a game in terms of you're playing whatever position you are, you stick to your job and hopefully the team plan all comes together. But when your manager, you can only get out information. So, it's probably worse when you can't really affect the game on the pitch as such.

G IS FOR GOAL...

What was the best goal you've ever scored?

I scored a few so, I'll have to

think about them to be honest! Actually, I think Derry in the FAI Cup. I remember Bohs away in Dalymount Park. We were behind the semi-final the year we won the treble, and I scored one from the edge of the box, and we ended up winning 3-1. It was a left foot shot, which I'm not really known for. It's not my strongest foot, but it was a low, hard shot, a daisy cutter into the bottom corner.

H IS FOR HAHA...

What was the funniest thing you remember from your time in football?

Well, I think there's a lot of things you find funny over the course of a career in football, but I remember one day I was playing for Rovers in Dalymount Park. I won't name the player, but he realised before the game that he didn't have any cigarettes, so went across the street to the shop and he got hit by a car! I won't name the player! But yeah, he got knocked down before the match! Bad enough going for cigarettes, but not being able to play because you got hit by a car has to be a new one!

I IS FOR INFLUENCE...

Who would you say was been the biggest influence on your career?

I think at the start Billy

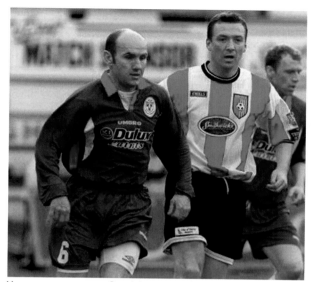

Young gave me my first big break at Bohemians, and I kind of looked up to him at the time and the four years I was there, I was only about 18. He gave me a good start, but I think from the time I got involved with Jim McLaughlin. I went from Rovers to Derry and had him again at Dundalk, he was probably the one manager that have had a longer spell with and gave me a lot of chances, so I'd say Jim.

J IS FOR JOKER...

Who was the biggest practical joker you've met in football?

I'm just trying to think because I've had a few teams as you! Currny was always good for a laugh when I was at Derry. But as I say, I've had a few characters along the

way that were a good laugh, you know.

K IS FOR KIT...

What was your favourite football kit that you've ever played in?

There was a few nice one over the years. I think there was an away one at Derry that was purple and green that was nice. But I usually liked the home jerseys as well.

L IS FOR LIFE AFTER PLAYING...

Did you have a plan for after football? Was management something you always wanted to do?

No, not really. I never actually set out to say I'm definitely going to be a manager. I think when you're playing,

maybe the more you come towards the end, you start being a sort of figure that younger lads look up to and you end up giving a bit of advice and coaching. But I think it's probably a bit different now. Most players back then when they finished playing, they've probably had good careers and then they just moved into it. But I think it's changed now with all the coaching badges. For me, it was just as I got older, I was sort of helping younger players as well along the way, and it was something I enjoyed, so you're hoping you get an opportunity at management, but I never thought 'I'm definitely going to get a manager's job', because when the time came for me, it wasn't as straightforward as maybe people may have thought, because as I said, basically the way it was done back then was if you had a good career, you got a job as a manager. Well, I didn't get one, and I didn't have a bad career, you know? I got a chance then at UCD and it's probably because when you're a player and you're on the pitch, you might talk a bit more as well. So maybe it was just fortunate to get the opportunity at UCD while I was still playing to be player manager. And I always thank them for it because it's not easy when you're looking for a job and

have never had one before. It's a big risk for the club, because I do think nowadays sometimes fellas take jobs and they're not ready for them and can be disastrous for any future they hoped to have in the game, and disastrous for the club as well.

M IS FOR MEMENTO...

What is the one football memento you own that you'll never give away?
Well, I have a lot of mementos, between jerseys and trophies and that, you know. I'd probably say the trophies. Well, not he trophies themselves, but the medals I mean.

N IS FOR NIGHT OUT...

I have a feeling I know the answer to this one, but which team mate was usually the first to initiate a night out?
Currny! Paul Curran! There's a few others I could name as well! Different guys at differ-

ent clubs. Neville Steedman is another one I'd throw in there from Shamrock Rovers! I'm not sure if people would remember him.

O IS FOR OPPOSITION...

Which opposition did you always look forward to playing the most in your career?
No, not particularly. I think, at the time when I was playing there was some that you might have thought 'Well, I have no problem playing them', you know? Like when you'd go to Milltown to play Rovers when I was at Bohs and it was always great down there, beautiful pitch and good support at the games as well. I always looked forward to those games.
Obviously Milltown was gone just after that, but that was probably the main one because Rovers were good then as well. They were starting on their four in a row. So they were probably the games I looked forward to. It was always good to play with Bohs and Rovers, you know. The derby games.

P IS FOR PASSTIME...

Outside of football, what keeps you occupied now in your spare time?
Well, a few different things. A bit of gardening, and the grandsons and the fam-

ily, that's probably what I do now. I enjoy a few more holidays now as well, now I have more free time. And just doing little odd jobs here and there that I should have been doing the last 30-40 years!

Q IS FOR QUIZ...

Which former team mate would you definitely not want in your team if you were doing a quiz?
Well, we didn't really have quizzes and when we were playing, to be honest. But if we did, I definitely wouldn't want Storky on my team!

R IS FOR RESULT...

Which result stands out or meant the most to you in your career?
I think you have to look back to the cup final. Cork City to win the treble either. That was a big result, you know. Yeah, I think probably the result against Cork in the league that gave us a massive step towards winning it would be one, so take your pick! One of those two I'd say.

S IS FOR SETANTA SPORTS CUP...

You've won the Setanta Cup twice as a manager. What are your memories of the competition. Do you think you'd like to see the competition return?

To be honest with you, I remember not being in it! At the time I was at Drogheda we were just starting and had a really young team and it took time. I remember watching Shels and Linfield in the final though and it reminded me of European football. You played your league game on the Friday and then played on a Tuesday and it was brilliant.

When we got into it then with Drogheda it was brilliant. Not because we won it, but because I thought it was a brilliant competition. But obviously as it went on they changed it and then it was on at a different time and that and it kind of killed it, but it was great when it started. And as I said, and I remember Shels being in there, I think Cork were in it, and then obviously winning it and being the first team from this side of the border to win it, and then retain it. I think before that no one would have never thought that Drogheda could have won it, that's being honest. Especially when you see the other clubs that were involved. But yeah, I thought it was great.

T IS FOR TALENT...
Who is the best player you've ever played with?
Oh, there's a few there! Very hard to name just one to be honest! You could name

probably several at Derry, several at Rovers, several at Shels you know. You would have Felix and Liam at Derry, Mick Neville, then the likes of Pat Byrne. I mean, there's been a lot of great players. I played with a few great players up north as well. I was lucky enough to play with a lot of good players, so it's a difficult question. I think Tony Sheridan was another outstanding player at Shels now that I'm thinking through some of the teams. But, yeah, I have to say it's difficult because you have different players that play in different ways with so many good teams. So let's put it this way... too many to mention!

U IS FOR UNPARALLELED...
Who is the best player you've ever played against?
Well, I think you'd have to look to the European games that we had, with all due respect to the league. Although, as I say, there were many great players in the league as well. One of the toughest players I think I've ever had to play against in the league was Tony O'Connor. He played with Bohs and Pats. He was always causing a few problems. But, yeah, as I say, we came up against a lot of good players in Europe

as well, the likes of Branco, the Brazilian player at FC Porto when we played in the Champions League or the European Cup as it was then. But again, to pick one player out of them all, I think you could use my last answer again! Too many to mention!

V IS FOR VANITY...
Which team mate spent the longest in front of the mirror?
Tim Dalton!! Without any doubt, Tim Dalton!! He was using Nivia when no one else knew what it was!! And then his hair routine as well! Not because I've none, but he had one of those perm combs!

W IS FOR WISHES...
Is there anything you'd change about your career if you could do it all again?
No, absolutely not. I think, obviously when you start no one knows what way you're going to go. I was at Bohs playing youth football, and there was about three or four of us that came from Saint John Bosco where we played first, and funny it was it was a decent year in youth football, in the Dublin schoolboy league, and there's a lot of us that ended up playing against each other in the league later in life. But, yeah, I went to Bohs,

and I was fortunate enough that I got a start in the first league game of the season the first year I was there and scored up in Sligo, and as they say, the rest followed. So I couldn't really say I'd like to change any of that.

I've played European football, I've won club football trophies, I have some international caps at Olympic level, I've represented the League XI, you know, I couldn't really say I'd want to change anything.

Did you ever have a chance to go to England that you'd wish you'd taken?

Well, to be honest, I did actually when I was at Derry. I was at Sunderland for a week, and then there was talk of going to Sweden as well, but nothing ever worked out for one reason or another. And yeah, to be honest I would have liked it, but the way I look upon it is, when you set out on your career and you have memories like I have, and any player will tell you, it's not about that. It's not about the money. You can't earn enough money as a player to go out and buy a Champions League medal, or even a League of Ireland medal. You have to earn them. So it feels better to have said that you won all that stuff by working hard, not that you made a load of money,

but won nothing.

X IS FOR EXPERIENCE...

What's the best atmosphere you've ever experienced?

I think you'd obviously have to look at the Benfica game. I mean, there was 74,000 at that match in the Stadium Of Light. Huge atmosphere. It was brilliant. Most of the European games had a great atmosphere. I remember playing in Cyprus for Rovers. That was one of the the the most hostile atmospheres I've ever played in and there might have only been 25,000 at it.

The Brandywell had a great atmosphere too. I remember the FAI Cup semi-final. Bohs at home on a Thursday night. It was a midweek replay I think, but the atmosphere was brilliant and we beat them 1-0. I remember saying to Felix the next day, the atmosphere was unreal. I think going back to them days, and I'm sure it's the same now at the Brandywell. Maybe not as big of crowds, but maybe not far off it, you know. It's always had a good atmosphere to be fair.

Y IS FOR YOUNG...

What is your earliest memory of going to a football match?

Well, I lived on the South side of Dublin, so I remem-

ber going to Milltown a few times. Not all the time. I couldn't say I was a supporter, you know? But I would have gone to a few Rovers games at Milltown because it wasn't a million miles away from us. I remember as well going to Dalymount to watch Bohs and Newcastle in the UEFA Cup in 1977. It was a midweek game. There was a lot of trouble at that game as well I remember, the players had to be taken off. But, yeah, I didn't really go to many games other than a few here and there. I mostly would have just played football with younger kids groups rather than going to games.

Z IS FOR ZONE...

Did you ever have any pre-match rituals or superstitions to get you in the zone?

No, never. I was old school. Get ready, get out and do what you have to do. I didn't do any of that put your right boot on first or anything like that. Different strokes for different folks as they say. I've seen some strange ones though in changing rooms! Like Pascal Vaudequin! He used to eat a spoonful of sugar before every game! He claimed it game him an energy burst! It got him going anyway. Running up and down that touchline when he was at right back!

DERMOT O'NEILL

SPONSORED BY
SEAN CASSIDY

A IS FOR ANNOYING...
Which of your former team mates was the worst to sit beside on the bus for long away journeys?
Well, I never really sat on the team bus because I went by car to away games. Every game was an away game for me living in Dublin! But let me see. Who was the most annoying... I'll say Donal O'Brien!!

B IS FOR BEHAVIOUR...
Which team mate was always the most likely to get booked?
Paul Hegarty! I didn't have

to think about that one!

C IS FOR CITY...
Do you remember the story of how you signing for Derry City came about?
I do, yes. I had asked for a transfer from Bohemians and I expected it to be for nothing, but they put a price on me, which then limited any teams that might be interested. But Roy Coyle rang me up one day and asked me would I be interested in signing for Derry City. So, I met him in Dublin the after the call and I signed there and then. After talking to him once! Yeah, so that's

how it came about. I wasn't happy at Bohemians about the way things were going and I asked for a transfer.

D IS FOR DUBLIN GAA...
You almost played GAA instead of football. What swayed your decision?
Yeah, I played a lot of GAA when I was younger and I played Minors football for Dublin at the time and it was a case of talking to John Giles. He had come in and asked me to play for Shamrock Rovers youth team, and with that there was as little carrot dangled as well that I would be considered to

39

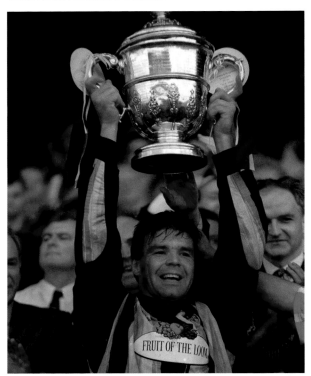

FRUIT OF THE LOOM

play for Ireland in the youth team. There was only one youth team at that at that time, which was an Under 18 team. So, that kind of persuaded me to choose soccer over GAA. Well, it wasn't really that I was persuaded because I loved soccer anyway, you know. But, it was probably the one thing that kind of ticked the box from me and said, well, OK, that's that for the GAA.

The only problem I had going to Rovers was that my older brother Alan was there, and he was a goalkeeper too. So that was my predicament! But I knew I

wouldn't be pushing for first team football at 17 or 18, he was the first team goalkeeper. But it was good to train and play with him because we'd been doing that our whole lives, you know. So yeah, that was why I away from the Gaelic.

E IS FOR EUROPE...

Which team was your toughest European opponent? At any club.

I think Werder Bremen, they played Glenavon when I was there and they beat us 7-0 I think. They were one of the toughest anyway. Toughest

in terms of atmosphere and all that sort of stuff though I would have to go with Rangers. Which was 40 years ago as it turns out, 1984. We played Rangers in Ibrox and Rangers here in Dublin and I think that was my first game in Europe in terms of playing. But between the fighting and the actual game itself, that was probably the most difficult.

F IS FOR FAI CUP...

What are your memories of that 1995 FAI Cup final when you finally got a winners medal?

Yeah, I finally got one! The one thing that kind of struck me about the whole thing was, we had played Athlone the week before and Stuart Gauld had missed a penalty. And for some reason I just knew we were going to get a penalty. And I knew he'd score it. I just had so much confidence in that lad. He was superb. So I remember that. And sleeping with the cup! I slept with the cup that night! But the one thing that sticks in my head was Stuart putting the penalty away.

G IS FOR GOALKEEPER...

Where did you start your youth career? Did you always play as a goalkeeper?

No, up to Under 15s I played centre forward! But my late

father, he played in goal for Shelbourne and for Dublin. And then of course, Alan played in goal as well, but both of us played outfield and then around the same age we both became goalkeepers. I think he went in to goal earlier actually, but I went in at Under 15.

H IS FOR HAHA...

What was the funniest thing you remember from your time in football?

Oh God! You couldn't print it! I couldn't...! Look, I'll tell you one, but I'll not mention any team names or player names or anything! So, we were away playing a team in Europe and our flight home wasn't until the day after the game, so we went into town after the match and there was a bit of a red light district. Anyway, one of one of the boys says to me we'll go in here, so I said well I'm not going in. The rest of the lads were all still due to arrive into the town, so I said I'd wait on them. So anyway, he goes in and he gave me his phone, and his wallet and whatever and went into the room. So I kind of stayed in the waiting area, and there's a girl in the window and I start chatting to her for a while and out the window I see all the lads coming down the street. So I put the girl out and I got in the window!! I took my shirt off and

started dancing in the window of this place! You want to see the lads faces when they walked past!! Even the girl was roaring laughing!! She actually gave me a bottle of Heineken as well!

I IS FOR IT'S TIME...

Did you have a plan for after football? Was management something you ever wanted to do?

No, I didn't. I had no plan at all. When I finished I was playing for Ballymena and we just avoided relegation and it was against Portadown and I told Nigel Best, who was the manager, I said 'that's me done'. It was the travelling killed me really. I'd been up and down that road for years and years. And that was it, I was finished. And then Packie Bonnar rang me one day and said 'we're doing a coaching course for ex-League Of Ireland goalkeepers and we'd like you to take part in it'. And that was really it. It kind of mushroomed then because halfway through that course, Stephen Kenny rang me and he asked me to join his staff at Longford to look after Longford's goalkeepers, and they were in Europe at that point, so I did that and it brought me into coaching. But I never really had a plan that I would go into coaching. That never really crossed my mind. And then

2003, or 2004, the late Sean McCaffrey rang me up and asked if I'd come in to the International setup and coach the Irish U17 goalkeepers, which I'm still doing to this day, I'm coaching the U19 goalkeepers now. But, no, I never set out with a plan to go into coaching.

J IS FOR JOKER...

Who was the biggest practical joker you've met in football?

I would have to say Joe Hanrahan! Joe was always good for a laugh! He used to put on this voice, the man just died there recently, Mícheál Ó Muircheartaigh. He was the GAA commentator with RTÉ for many years, and Joe would do his voice! And actually, if you got his brother in the car as well, he'd do Michael O'Hehir, who was another former RTÉ broadcaster, and the two of them would go to and fro, doing like a comedy skit! Brilliant craic!

K IS FOR KIT...

What was your favourite football kit that you've ever played in?

No. I always liked the colour blue, but other than that, no, not really. It didn't bother me what I looked like! As long as I saved the ball, that's all I cared about!

L IS FOR LEAGUE OF

IRELAND XI...

You played for the League Of Ireland XI a few times. What do you remember of those games, do you think it should come back?

Yes I do. Absolutely. Because the way the league has gone now, obviously it's full time professional and all that, but they still have very little chance of getting into the international team on a long term basis. But that was our chance to represent Ireland. We played competitive football as well as friendlies. We nearly got to the Olympics actually. You see it at the Olympics this year with teams like Argentina and whoever. They're made up of players who wouldn't be consistent players in the full International setup. Ireland could do something similar. I always remember it was a brilliant time. Great managers, great players, and some brilliant trips. I mean, I went to Singapore, the United States, and although I didn't go, but the others went to New Zealand, Trinidad and Tobago. And it wasn't just an in and out job, like United States has 15 days. It was incredible stuff like. Really, really good. And half the Derry team came with us! Mick Neville, Paul Doolin, Paul Curran, Peter Hutton and fellas like that. So I absolutely believe that something

like that should be brought back. Maybe at the end of the season or something like that. Not necessarily for a trip away, but certainly some representative honours for Ireland that they could play even preseason games against the likes of Man City or whoever wins the Premiership over there. They did that most recently I think a few years ago. And I think a combination of the League Of Ireland's best players could give those teams a good game. So, yeah, I believe they should get some sort of recognition. Absolutely.

M IS FOR MEMENTO...

What is the one football memento you own that you'll never give away?

The FAI Cup medal! I mean, I had played in 3 Cup Finals before that I never won. And I don't even have the runners up medals. But that one I do have. That was Derry against Shelbourne.

N IS FOR NIGHT OUT...

Which team mate was usually the first to initiate a night out?

Well, you probably know about Rocky O'Brien. He

would have been the one in Bohemians alright to be the one to bring it up. But there was no need to initiate it! We were all up for it and that was the time that was in it. Like, you played and trained hard, but you had the release then on a Sunday night. You'd get home after a game for about half eight or whatever, and you'd have a quick turnaround and go back out, and you get up for work the next morning and you carry on again. And you'd train Tuesday, Thursday, Saturday and play on Sunday. But it would have been Rocky that would instigate it all.

O IS FOR OPPOSITION...

Which opposition did you always look forward to playing the most in your career?
I loved playing against my. Brother. It didn't do much

for the atmosphere in the house when we were both single. My poor mother and father! Because it was only the two of us, there was no sisters or brothers, just me and Alan. So I really looked forward to those games. And you know, I suppose deep down you wanted him to do well. You wanted a top corner goal that he could have done nothing about. Us winning 1-0 with me playing well and him playing well would have been the best result and we'd both go home happy... ish! But yeah, I always look forward to playing against him. Actually, and not just because you're talking to me now, but when Derry first came into the league, the crowds they brought was amazing. And it's funny, I was at a reunion thing for Bohemians recently for the team that played Rangers in 1984, we were at the Bohs and Rovers game and we

were actually talking about the Derry crowd that used to come. Bus loads and bus loads used to come, and they made a whole day out of it. Them games. They were the best. They were just amazing. The atmosphere that the people created, you know, and to this day they still do. And even when I was playing for them, they still created an amazing atmosphere. But at that particular time when they came back into the league it was huge. We couldn't believe it. And Dalymount is the way it is now, but when we were playing back then the terraces on the far side from the stand was full. Behind the goals were both full. It was just incredible. They were great days. They were great times to play.

P IS FOR PASSTIME...

Outside of football, what keeps you occupied now in your spare time?
Well, I'm still coaching the Irish U19s. But to be honest, I don't really have a pastime. I watch the telly. I watch a bit of football. And the grandkids as well. I have two grandkids, 2 little girls. So they would be my past time really.

Q IS FOR QUIZ...

Which former team mate would you definitely not want in your team if you

were doing a quiz?
Paul Curran! No need to think about that one either!

R IS FOR RESULT...
Which result stands out or meant the most to you in your career?
There's a few. I mean the Cup Final obviously. The game against Rangers here in Dublin, that result. We beat them 3-2, although we lost 4-3 on aggregate, but them two would stick in my mind. To pick one though, I'd say the winning of the cup because that was my first trophy. And I was captain of the team as well, which made it even more special for me, you know? So, yeah, the result in the Cup Final, because I was captain as well.

S IS FOR SAVE...
Is there a save that stands out for you as the best save you've ever made?
Yeah, we played Finn harps at Dalymount, I was playing for Bohemians at the time, and Noel King, who yous all will now, Noel was playing for us, he was with Bohemians at the time, but he was in the box defending a corner, and the corner was put in and he was kind of faced in towards my goal and it deflected off his knee and flew into the top corner and I changed position in a split second and saved it. That one for some reason always sticks in my head. Don't ask me why. Whether it was instinct, or whatever I know, but it just sticks in my head.

T IS FOR TALENT...
Who is the best player you've ever played with?
Stuart Gauld. No question. In terms of defenders, yes, absolutely. I mean you could go along and you could take Jackie Jameson, Liam Coyle, Paul Doolin, I could say loads of players. And they were brilliant, brilliant players. But Stuart Gauld and myself, I don't know what Stuart feels, but I always had this kind of, I don't know, telepathy or something where I knew exactly what he was going to do. He probably knew what I was going to do as well and that made playing behind him an absolute joy.

U IS FOR UNPARALLELED...
Who is the best player you've ever played against?
Liam Coyle. You can ask Liam, he stuck one in against me with a back heel one time and made me look stupid! But that was him. He was just different class.

V IS FOR VANITY...
Which team mate spent the longest in front of the mirror?
Joe Hanrahan! Joe liked looking at himself!

W IS FOR WISHES...
Is there anything you'd change about your career if you could do it all again?
I probably would be more professional. I think in the younger years I wasn't as professional as I should have been. You know, like going to bed early, that sort of stuff, prepare properly.

You know, I could have been better than as a goalkeeper. But, yeah, that would be the only thing. Being more professional.

X IS FOR EXPERIENCE...
What's the best atmosphere you've ever experienced?

That Rangers game. Incredible. Funny enough, the Rangers game in Ibrox, there was the four stands, one each side, but the one that was facing me in the first half had 15 Bohemians supporters in it! And it was a two tier stand. There was nobody allowed there. They were board members or whatever. But I could count them! I could actually count them! But on the other three sides the atmosphere was just incredible.

Another one as well, Liverpool played a game here at the Aviva against an Irish XI for that man, Sean Cox, and Mick McCarthy asked me would I warm up the goalkeepers. That atmosphere when they started singing, You'll Never Walk Alone was incredible. Because I've never seen that live. I've seen it on TV, but I'd never actually experienced it live. That was incredible. The hair stood on the back of the neck sort of job.

Y IS FOR YOUNG...
What is your earliest memory of going to a football match?

My father bringing me to Dalymount Park to watch... I'm going to say, Bohs against Shelbourne I think, and he put me over the turnstiles. That was my earliest memory of going to watch a game.

Earliest memory of playing a game was... We had road leagues in our area growing up. So each road would play against each other. That was my earliest memory of actually playing.

Z IS FOR ZONE...
Did you ever have any pre-match rituals or superstitions to get you in the zone?

No, not really. Bar warm ups. I would always do the same warm up, but no real superstitions. I was never really into it. I know my brother was! If he were an under shirt and they won, he'd wear it until they lost but I didn't really believe in any of that.

THE 🦆PICKLED DUCK CAFÉ
GREENHAW ROAD & STRAND ROAD, DERRY

PETER HUTTON

SPONSORED BY
MATT MORRISON

A IS FOR ANNOYING...
Which of your former team mates was the worst to sit beside on the bus for long away journeys?
There's too many of them!! I'm trying to think because it's almost like a couple of different generations, even from the earlier days when we had completely different types of buses. On the buses in the early days we would have played cards and bet a wee bit or whatever, but the later on generations and nowadays, there is no cards or anything like that. It's a bit more professional.

Times change I suppose. But there's nobody that really stands for me. Maybe wee Eddie McCallion with his choice of choice of films! He always had a dodgy selection of bad films for the boys to watch on the bus!

B IS FOR BEHAVIOUR...
Which of your former team mates was always the most likely to get booked?
I'll go with Sean Hargan! Hargy had a rule for tackles... nothing below the neck!

C IS FOR CITY...
Who would you say is the

best player that Derry City have ever had?
That's a tough one! Again, I'm thinking of different players from different eras. Obviously Liam Coyle would be up there. Then you have more recent players, the likes of Paddy McCourt. Around the time of Coyler as well, I thought Neil McNabb was an exceptional player. He was coming to the end of his career, but he was very, very good for Derry.

You would have played with Adrian Doherty as well didn't you?
Yeah, Adrian was a truly gifted player. It was just unfortunate how things panned

47

out for him, but he was a serious talent. I mean, all the reports say he was ahead of Giggs and the rest, and he was! I've spoken to people who would have been connected with the club at the time, and they were saying as well that he was just unbelievable, even at United. Because as a player, he was predominantly a winger and there wasn't much to him, but he did fill out and that, and he was shaping up to be one of the best. But again, he was brave as a lion, and he'd have run through a brick wall, you know? Funny you mention him because I suppose he would be up there as well, but when he came back to Derry, we didn't see the best of him such, but what a talent he was.

D IS FOR DERRY CITY...
Do you remember the story of how you signing for Derry City came about?

Well, I remember... not the actual signing as such, but how it was initiated! As in, how I made my debut for Derry! I was asked to guest for Derry City in a friendly they had coming up against Spurs, and I'm a Spurs fan! And obviously the Spurs team at that time had the likes of Gascoigne, Lineker, and them. So, I was at Coleraine at the time. I was only 16 or 17, and Derry asked Coleraine would it be OK to guest. Ian McFall was the Coleraine manager at the time, and he just said 'No chance!' Obviously for fear that either I'd get injured, or that Derry would be trying to make an approach for me on the sly or whatever. But I didn't let it settle! So, unannounced to my father, I pretended to be my father and

rang the since deceased, God rest him, Jack Doherty who was the Chairman of Coleraine at the time letting on to be my father! I remember chatting away to him for ages, him thinking he was chatting to my Da, and in the end then just says, 'Look, tell your son it's no problem at all. We couldn't stop him playing against his boyhood club! Go ahead, tell him to play away and I'll get that sorted'. So I put the phone down and rang Jim McLaughlin straight away and he said 'right, be at the Everglades at 3 o'clock' or whatever. And then the following week, same again, I was asked to guest for Derry again, this time against Man United! So, it was a mad couple of weeks, you know! I seen out the season for Coleraine, but then Derry came calling again and I signed this time. I actually think I was Jim McLaughin's last signing.

E IS FOR EUROPE...
What are your memories of the European run that ended in the Parc De Princes?

Just unbelievable! Special memories. But for all the Paris and the Gothenburgs and, you know, obviously those big clubs as such, to me and a lot of the players, it's the Gretna one! The fact that we took so many supporters to Gretna and we weren't even given a chance in the game by the press, but that night was just a really special night. Even the goals that were scored, they were worldies! Every single one of them were really good goals. It was just one of those nights where everything just lined up. Even the fans as well. The staff, the stewards, and the people at the ground all remarked after the game that how they'd had Celtic and Rangers come there there and didn't bring as big of a crowd, but even just the behaviour of the fans as well, they were all in good spirits, and they really they enjoyed themselves and to be part of things on the pitch on a really special night was amazing. I think that one just set the tone for the rest of the European adventure as such.

Did you swap a shirt in Paris?
I didn't, no. I still have the jersey from that European run.

F IS FOR FAI CUP...

What's more stressful, a cup final as a manager or as a player?
100% as a manager! Mostly because as a player all you do is just worry about yourself and making sure you're right and you're prepared for the game as such. A Cup Final for manager is worrying about everybody else! Making sure everything

is lined up, everyone's fit and all the different sort of things that are involved in a Cup Final. Even the accommodation and making sure everything is sort of looked after and that. As a player though, you just have be sort of selfish, but for the sake of the team if you know what I mean. You have to look after yourself, and make you that you're alright a ready to go on the day.

G IS FOR GOAL...

What would you say was the best goal you've ever scored?
I don't remember who it was against, now even to tell you the truth! But I know it was from a corner and I'd backed off around the back post and the ball was headed out and I think I chested it, controlled it and volleyed it back in over all the players and the keeper and in the far top corner. I don't even know where that was! That was probably one of the better goals, but for importance probably the one that secured the league against St Pat's at the Brandywell. Just for the significance of it, and it rounded off what was a fantastic season.

H IS FOR HAHA...

What was the funniest thing you remember from your time in football?
One thing jumps out at me!

Just going back to wee Eddie! I remember one day we were training out at Clooney Park West and we were playing on grass that had just been freshly cut, and all the cuttings were still on the grass in big clumps because it was freshly cut. But it was a kind of mizzley old day so the grass was kind of sticking to your boots and your legs and that. But we were playing this training game anyway and Paddy McCourt was just running riot! Just playing like Paddy plays! Anyway, he's nutmegged Eddie, so Eddie went after him to get him back and as he was getting close to getting him, Pady turned and nutmegged him again! But Eddie then slipped and fell and hit the ground and you hear the anger from him, but when he got up off the grass, his face was just completely green! He was covered in grass! All you could see was the raging blue eyes coming through the green! Everyone was just doubled over laughing, and the more people laughed, the angrier Eddie got, and the angrier he got trying to kick Paddy the more people laughed!!

I IS FOR IRISH INTERNATIONAL SOCCER TOURNAMENT...

What do you remember about the Lansdowne Road tournament and

playing Newcastle and Celtic?

Again, great times. Like, you remember we'd just won league and things were going well. Just one of those things that when we beat Celtic then, we just thought, 'when's this run going to end', sort of thing, you know! We were beaten then by a good Newcastle team, but I remember both nights I slept soundly after the amount of chasing I done! At the time I was center mid with Higgsy. It was tough, but really enjoyable though. The Celtic game was a really, really good game, and they obviously went on and

won the league that year themselves. But it was a good battle, and Ryan Coyle is still living off that goal! But, the Newcastle game as well, I remember Higgsy was exceptional in it. But it was great to pit your wits against teams and players of that sort of calibre.

J IS FOR JOKER...

Who was the biggest practical joker you've met in football?

Hargy! Hargy was always the changing room jester!

K IS FOR KIT...

What has been your fa-

vourite football kit that you've ever played in or owned?

Not really, no. They've all changed. When you look now and you see kits from years ago, they're absolutely massive compared to kits now. I wasn't overly fond of the one I called the Ribena one! The purple one we had! I liked the white away one we had though one year. We wore it in the Sligo final. Didn't help us that day right enough! I didn't mind the yellow away one we had as well. Le Coq Sportif. Their stuff was nice.

L IS FOR LIFE AFTER PLAYING...

Did you always have a plan for after your playing career ended?

Not really, no. I left school halfway through my A-Levels because I got a bad eye injury playing football and it just hampered my A-Levels then as such. But I ended up going back to university when I was coming near the end of my career, when I was about 33, I went back and did a Bachelor's Degree in Social Work, because I knew I wanted to have a career in youth work and that, but that was the first time I ever started thinking about what I'd do after football.

M IS FOR MEMENTO...

What is the one football

memento you own that you'll never give away?

Metals just really. I have jerseys and stuff from important games, but I think just medals. I think my sons have taken any signed shirts I had anyway!

N IS FOR NIGHT OUT...

Which team mate was usually the first to initiate a night out?

There has been a few! Probably Stephen O'Flynn! Or any of the Dublin ones! In the older generation as well Curny would be up there! Paul Curran! But, yeah, more recently, any of the Dubs would have loved a night out!

O IS FOR OPPOSITION...

Which opposition did you always look forward to playing the most in your career?

I always enjoyed playing against the likes of Bohs and Shels because they were always up there or thereabouts. But I always liked to play whoever was up there challenging with us. I always liked the big games. Always enjoyed the battle. I think you got that excitement and that buzz of the crowd and stuff like that more in the bigger games. The bigger the game the better, type of thing. And challenging against the better

players and stuff. But, yeah, whatever clubs we were up against at that particular time, and whoever was up challenging with us. Or if we were in a relegation battle either. Same thing.

P IS FOR PASSTIME...

Outside of football, what keeps you occupied now in your spare time?

It hasn't changed! It's still football! My wife will back me up on that one! She thought he might have seen more of me, but that's not happening! Nothing has changed!

Q IS FOR QUIZ...

Which former team mate would you definitely not want in your team if you were doing a quiz?

Darren Kelly! 100%!

R IS FOR RESULT...

Which result stands out or meant the most to you in your career?

I would say the Pats one in the league that night that won us the league, Pats at home. There was one that year as well down at Dundalk that we were 2-0 down after 10mins, and nothing was going well, then we came back and won 4-2. That night I think was a turning point for the team, as in, we knew then 'we have what it takes to go on to win the league this year'

kind of thing. To come back and do that to a really good Dundalk team, and we annihilated them, especially in the second-half. So I think it just gave everyone that confidence and that boost to think 'right, we're going to make a challenge here'.

S IS FOR SHELS...

You went to Shelbourne, won the league and came back again. How did that come about at the time?

How long have you got!! I was out of contract at Derry and I waited and waited for the club to offer me a contract and it didn't happen. But Shelbourne had offered me a contract to signed early on in the year. Just for a year though, because Dermot Keely wasn't going to be there after the year. If they didn't win the league he was going to stay on. So, with only one contract offer on the table, I eventually agreed to go to Shelbourne and we won the league. I came back to Derry again the following year though. Shels did ask me to stay and go full time. They were moving me full time football, but I wasn't long married, so I didn't want to go full time really at that time. Gavin Dykes took over as Derry manager though and I signed back with Derry and that year we won the FAI Cup. That was the year of the two cup finals.

T IS FOR TEAM MATES...

Who is the best player you've ever played with?

Probably, Coyler and Paddy McCourt would be the two stand outs. And probably one of the most under-rated would be Paul Hegarty.

U IS FOR UNPARALLELED...

Who is the best player you've ever played against?

It would either be Ronaldinho or Boban.

When did you play against Boban?

I played in a team that played the Croatian national team before the 1996 Euros. They came over to Ireland to train and they played against a League Of Ireland select team in Drogheda, so they played their full strength team, so, Boban, Prosinecki, Davor Suker, Alen Boksic, Slaven Bilic... They had a great team that year I actually got Prosinecki's jersey as well, but Boban from AC Milan was absolutely frightening! Ronaldinho was even worse!!

V IS FOR VANITY...

Which team mate spent the longest in front of the mirror?

Where do I start! We had the 'Tan-tastic' boys at one time, Eddie and Paddy McLaughlin, and Darren Kelly! There was a few of them! And then you had your boys with their Gucci bags! Neil McCafferty and them!

Well, Tony O'Doherty said you! And also added that it was payback for Cork?

Ah right! That obviously means it's not me! But, aye, in Cork, we sort of, stayed up later then we should have I think. Myself and Coyler. We roomed together and we... let's just say Tony didn't get much sleep that night!

W IS FOR WISHES...

Is there anything you'd change about your career if you could do it all again?

Nothing really. It would be more in terms of looking after myself because I've played in a more part time set up and stuff, you know? But I suppose I did really, I played until I was 39.

You never had a chance to go to England or anything that you'd wish you'd taken?

I had, but again, sometimes it was out of my control. The closest one was Derby and I think they were going to pay Derry and everything, but for one reason or another the whole thing just fell flat and they just said the deal was off. But, naw, I'm more than happy with the career I had, so, no, not many regrets.

X IS FOR EXPERIENCE...

What's the best atmosphere you've ever experienced as a player?

I always say that the Parc De Princes was something else, but I would say even the Gretna one as well. Just the game that night, the atmosphere and the noise, the supporters were exceptional. But even the Brandywell when it was full with the old shed and stuff like that was hard to beat. Setanta Cup matches as well with the likes of Linfield were great nights.

Y IS FOR YOUNG...

What is your earliest memory of going to a football match?

Going down to watch my father playing in the Summer Cups in Buncrana. When there was Summer Cups!

Z IS FOR ZONE...

Did you ever have any pre-match rituals or superstitions to get you in the zone?

Yeah, I always put everything on the right first and then left second, and then going out the door I'd always splash a bit of water on my face, or squirt a bit of water over my head or whatever. Most of the time the linesman behind me got it in the face though!!

LIAM COYLE

SPONSORED BY
LIAM HEGARTY

A IS FOR ANNOYING...
Which of your former team mates was the worst to sit beside on the bus for long away journeys?

You know something, I usually sat on my own at the front. I sat beside Hargy the odd time as well, but he wasn't too bad. Most annoying though… most of them were annoying, that's why I sat on my own!! I just used to sit at the front and watch videos. There used to be a TV on the bus and somebody would bring a film.

B IS FOR BEHAVIOUR...
Which team mate was always the most likely to get booked?

I'm picking two! Hargy and Higgsy! 100%! One of them them two!

C IS FOR CUP...
You've won several FAI, League Cups, & IFA Cups. Is there one final that stands out over the others?

I would probably say 1995 against Shelburne. Even though I scored the winner in 2002, I think '95 was more special. Especially after los-ing the league at Athlone and then winning the Cup a fortnight after it. I think that was the best final that I played in as well. So I think that one stands out more than the other ones. Even above the treble one as well, because we already won the league that year and we were already on a high. But the fact that we lost the league in Athlone and then to came back and win the cup in '95, I think that sort of took more, you know what I mean?

D IS FOR DERRY CITY...
Who is the best player Derry City have ever had?
Does that include the Irish League days as well? Or is it just since '85?
Any era at all
Easy answer then. Fay Coyle.

E IS FOR EUROPE...
Which team was your toughest European opponent? At any club.
In terms of teams, it'd be Benfica. They got to the European Cup Final that year we played them like! But that was enjoyable playing against them compared to

53

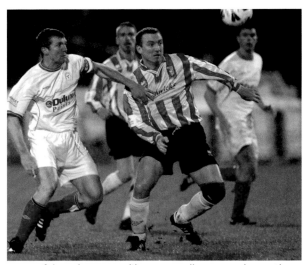

some of the other teams like Maribor and Lokomotiv Sofia and teams like that who were just dogged, you know what I mean? But yeah, Benfica just had more quality, and that was more enjoyable to play in than the other matches.

F IS FOR FRIENDLIES...

You've played some high profile friendlies, Barcelona, Celtic & Newcastle, etc. Is there one team or player that stands out from those?

100% the Celtic game. 100%. Down in Lansdowne because it was a tournament game, I mean alright, it was classed as a friendly, but it was a tournament, you know what I mean? So we wanted to do well in it and show were there for a reason and the fact that we

actually went down there and the fact that we actually beat them as well was great a great occasion. I remember the ground was packed with supporters as well, and mostly Celtic supporters, and even most of them were from Derry! But I actually hated friendly games! I hated them! I hated playing in them! But the fact that that was a preseason game and it was in a tournament made it more enjoyable. The way we went into the game, it wasn't played as your normal friendly where there was no tackles and a slower pace, it was 100% commitment. And that went for both teams. That's what made the result more impressive like, the fact that we did beat them, you know.

G IS FOR GOAL...

What was the best goal you've ever scored?

I'd say the one at Athlone. In that game where we couldn't get it over the line that day. We drew 1-1. So, that goal sticks out.

Another one that sticks out, it was actually my 100th goal for Derry that I scored against Cork in the Brandywell was a really good goal, and the fact it was my 100th, and I was the first player to get a hundred goals for Derry in the League Of Ireland as well.

Then obviously the Cup Final goal against Shamrock Rovers in Tolka Park. They would be the three that are standing just off the top of my head at the minute.

H IS FOR HAHA...

What was the funniest thing you remember happening from your time in football?

There wasn't too much on the pitch, but off the pitch there was was plenty! Well, I remember something that wasn't too funny at the time. At the time it was the most embarrassing thing ever! But we did a modelling thing for Derry in the Richmond Centre one day! Me, Hargy, Eamon Doherty and them. That was the most embarrassing thing I've ever done!! And the thing about it, Felix roped us into doing a Full Monty thing for Children In Need! And that wasn't as bad because we had a few glasses of wine in us on the night! But that time we did the modelling up in the Richmond Centre…! I'll never forget it! It still haunts me to this day! There was some strange things that we had to do for Derry at the time, but that one stands out! But it was funny because we all had a laugh about it! But it's not something I'll ever do again, put it like that!

I IS FOR INTERNATIONAL...

Do you remember how you got your first International call-up?

Well, what happened was, I was called up to what they called a B International. It was for U21 and U23 players that were being considered for the senior team, or senior players who were coming back from injuries and stuff like that. So, I was called up for that against the Republic and the match was in Dalymount on the Wednesday night. But we played Shamrock Rovers on the Sunday and I picked up an injury. I still went to Dublin, but I couldn't play. I got a knock on my ankle and it was swollen up, so I couldn't play in that match. So there was only about half a dozen games to go in the season

and obviously we were going for the treble at that time and I was playing well and scoring goals and Billy Bingham said to me 'look, there's going to be a full international game at the end of the season and I'm going to call you up for it'. This was after the B International game. So I said 'Right, OK', but I forgot all about it by the end of the season! But then, I think it was only a couple of matches left when I got the word from the the club. The club got an official letter from the IFA to say that I've been called up for Northern Ireland and I remember Jim ringing me to tell me that I've been selected. So, that's how it happened. The next hurdle then but was that I didn't drive at the time! So I didn't know how I was going to get to Belfast! Fortunately enough Felix drove me up because he obviously played for Billy Bingham. So, he took me up and got me introduced to everybody and got me settled in. So that's how it happened. It was basically because I didn't get to play in the B International that that I got the chance to play in a full International then!

And were there any more chances after that?

Well, Billy Bingham said to me 'Look, I'd prefer if you move to England or wherever because I will pick you, but it's going to be hard

picking you playing League Of Ireland'. But he said 'If you move, you'll be in every squad'. But unlucky for me like, it was only 3-4 months later that I picked up the injury down in Dundalk. So that put all the stops on the international career, you know.

J IS FOR JOKER...

Who was the biggest practical joker you've met in football?

Out of interest, when you asked the other lads I was playing with, did they say me?

A few of them did, yeah!

Yeah, no wonder! That's all I'll say! I'd say Hargy though! That's probably another one everybody said! Him or Paddy McLaughlin! Because you used to come out at times and your car used to be covered in red sauce and flour and whatever, I mean, you'd know who it was! Either that or your boxers were covered in Deep Heat! So, stuff like that, you know, but Hargy was mainly at the heart of it all!

K IS FOR KNEE...

What can you tell us about the injury that forced retirement, and how did you find the comeback?

Well, what happened was, I went through a couple of operations that time I was out. I went through two operations to take bone out of my knee, and I never played for about a year other than messing out, you know. But I basically just started playing indoor football and then I just felt 'The knee's grand. I'll just start playing D&D football again', and got back into it again at a lower level and within about four or five months, we were playing down in Buncrana in the Buncrana Cup and I was playing for Brandywell Harps and Roy McCreadie had just taken over at Omagh Town just the year before and Roy came to me said 'Look, I'm not expecting you to work as hard as you did before or anything because I don't know if the knee will hold up, but do you fancy coming up to Omagh and giving it a go and see how it goes? You don't have to train or anything, just come up and play the matches'. But I wasn't sure, I hmm'd and haa'd about it and I just thought 'I'll give it a go and see. There's no harm done if it doesn't work out'. But fortunately enough I had a good season. I think I scored about 25 goals that season, and then a few of the teams in the Irish League were circling around me, like Portadown, Glentoran, Glenavon and teams like that. I actually nearly signed for Glentoran and then Derry came in at the last minute the day

I was due to sign for Glentoran and made an offer and that's sort of how I ended up back at Derry again.

L IS FOR LIFE AFTER PLAYING...

Did you have a plan for after football? Was management something you ever wanted to do?

Well, no, I never had a plan or anything. But I never wanted to get into coaching or anything like that. But as you come near the end of your playing career you think 'maybe I'll go to management' because it's all you know, basically. But I'd done my B License at that time, but when it came down to it, I just thought I don't really fancy it. I didn't want to go out and spend another 15 years coaching and managing and doing

stuff like that. I did bits and pieces of it. Once I finished up I stayed behind to help Gavin Dykes when he was manager. You think to yourself then 'I want to do it', and then, 'No I don't'. But then I thought, no. It's not for me. I wasn't cut out for management. And I wasn't cut out for coaching either, so I just said no, I'll step away.

Fortunately for me though the interest came from Radio Foyle when Jobby retired from doing the matches and they were looking for somebody else to do it and they came to me and I enjoyed it. So, that was my interest not to give up on football completely. They gave me an interest to keep going to the Brandywell and keep watching football, you know?

But, no, coaching and management wasn't for me. But

I never had plan about anything in my football career. I just fell into everything that happened to me. So, I think that when I stopped playing that was me done with that side like game.

M IS FOR MEMENTO...
What is the one football memento you own that you'll never give away?
I have a few. Well obviously I've all the metals I won with Derry. But the only Derry jersey I have belonging to me is the Cup Final one from 2002. That's the only jersey I kept. Every other jerseys I've given away for charities and things like that, you know. But I made sure I held on to that one.

I have my international jersey as well. And I have a Barcelona jersey that I swapped, and I have Les Ferdinand's jersey from when we played Newcastle down at Dublin.

But the only one that I have that'll never be given away would be that 2002 jersey.

N IS FOR NIGHT OUT...
I have a feeling I know the answer to this one, but which team mate was usually the first to initiate a night out?
Paul Curran! 100%! That's probably the biggest answer from everyone you've asked! Curnny would be the first one after matches and after training going 'Right, where are we going then?'

O IS FOR OPPOSITION...
Which opposition did you always look forward to playing the most in your career?
I always loved playing against Shamrock Rovers. Because no matter what you think of them, Rovers are the biggest team in the South. You know what I mean? In my time playing it would usually be the two of us going for the league. I always liked playing against the best teams. I always used to hate playing the Longfords and the Drogheads and teams like that. They were just horrible games to play in. But you always knew when you're playing against Rovers and Bohs and St Pats and all, you were getting a good game, you know. So, for me, I always loved playing against Rovers.

And I always say this; I could never have played against Derry. I couldn't have done what Patrick McEleney and Mickey Duffy and boys like that done and come up and play against Derry. I could never have done that. But if I did have to leave Derry, if there was one team I would have had the chance to play for, it would have been Shamrock Rovers. I'd say if they came in for me I probably would have. And I nearly did! When Jim was managing. He was in contact with me, but he actually came to Derry shortly after that, so I never got that chance to go to Rovers.

P IS FOR PASSTIME...
Outside of football, what keeps you occupied now in your spare time?
Very little! Just work, and going to watch my son, Jack. He plays for Ardmore in the North West on a Saturday evening. But very little other than that! We had the Derry City Legends team going for a long time. We had a good 15 years at that, but I think everybody's at that stage now where nothing works anymore! So, that sort of came to a natural end. That was really good. That kept us all going like, you know. Because what happens is, when you stop playing football you sort of lose contact with all the boys you played with, but the legends thing kept us all in touch and we still have nights out and we still get together now. So, that was a good thing. But no, I think just my main thing now is just watching football and watching my own young fella playing.

Q IS FOR QUIZ...
Which former team mate would you definitely not

want in your team if you were doing a quiz?

Darren Kelly, definitely! Darren's not as stupid as he lets on but!

R IS FOR RESULT...

Which result stands out or meant the most to you in your career?

Well, funny enough, the one that always stands out is probably Athlone! Athlone always stands out because, not for good reasons and I don't dwell on it, but it's a result you look back on and think 'I won the league twice, but I should be sitting here with five or six winners medals'. Because that was definitely one that we threw away. That result cost us the double as well that season. So, it's not just the winners, although they're always more enjoyable. It's the ones that you don't win that you always look back on and think about what we should have done, you know.

S IS FOR SIGNING...

You told us there how you signed for Derry the second time, but do you remember the story of how you signing for Derry City came about the second time?

Well, the first time, the story was that I was playing in a 7-a-side tournament out in Maydown, and we were

playing Celtic Swifts in the final and it was a Friday night and I scored eight in the final. I think we won 18-3 or somthing, but I scored in the final. So the next night there was a presentation and all out in the Mullans Club out in Maydown. So we were all out having a drink and stuff like that after the presentation. I'd just turned 20, and I was lying in my bed the next morning and my mother came up the stairs and she said that Jim McLaughlin's down the stairs! And Derry were playing Finn Harps in the Ulster Tyres Cup down in Finn Park because the Brandywell was all getting redeveloped at the Southend Park Stand. So I got up and shook myself and went downstairs and Jim McLaughlin said, 'Right, I what you at the Everglades at 1 o'clock, bring your boots!' Now this is about 11 o'clock! So I didn't know what was going on! But he said 'Just be at the Everglades for 1 o'clock, and I'll see you there.' And he just got up and walked out! So I was like, 'Right. OK' So I went the Everglades that day and the following week I signed for Derry. But I was sign for Kevin Mahon. Kevin had taken over as reserve manager, so McLaughlin made me sign for Derry and then I was put into the reserves straight away. So, that's how I signed for Derry. Because

I was still what would be classed as an amateur back then, and I'd just left Hinn Harps. I actually could have signed back for Harps again, who were offering me a clean fortune for them days. But McLaughlin signed me for Derry and gave me £20 a week! That's what I signed for Derry for! He said to me 'when you prove yourself you'll get more', and he was good to his word.

T IS FOR TALENT...

Who is the best player you've ever played with?

Felix Healy

U IS FOR UNPARALLELED...

Who is the best player you've ever played against?

Best I played against in the League Of Ireland was Paul Doolin.

V IS FOR VANITY...

Which team mate spent the longest in front of the mirror?

Well, in the early days it was John Coady when I first appeared. As it went on then, when we won the league you had all the Spice Boys then! Darren Kelly, Eddie McCallion, Paddy McLaughlin were all into the sunbeds! But no, definitely John Coady! John loved himself, so I think he would just

wise, that were amazing. Probably one of the best games I was ever involved in was when we beat Bohs in the semi-final in 1995 after three games! I think it went to two replays and then in the last one we were behind twice and then came back. That night was one of the best games that was ever involved in. The atmosphere that night was incredible as well.

Y IS FOR YOUNG...

What is your earliest memory of going to a football match?

You know something, I remember I was only about 9 or 10 when I went to watch Coleraine. Derry were out of the league at that time, and Coleraine had a lot of Derry players. And my Da, who played with Coleraine in the 50s, was invited up to a game. There used to be a minibus that used to go up to the Coleraine games. Jackie Cooley used to run all the Derry boys up and my dad was invited up and I remember being about 9 or 10 and sitting on the bus with Felix and Kevin Mahon and Shakes McDowell and Eddie Seydak actually played that match as well, and Eugene McNutt. And I always remember sitting amongst all these football players thinking it was class. Derry were out of the league

come out on top! I'm not going to say Felix because Felix wasn't that bad to be fair. Pizza was another one! Pizza was very Italian looking! He had the long hair gelled back and wore all the best of gear and all! But he wouldn't have been a boy that sat in front of the mirror. Darren was like that but! Big Floyd Gilmour as well! Floyd was the same! All the spice boys!

W IS FOR WISHES...

Is there anything you'd change about your career if you could do it all again?

Obviously injuries are the main thing. They derailed me for a while. But I think any footballer would say the same. If they could play their career without injuries

they'd be flying. I don't think I would change anything about my time at Derry though. I enjoyed 90% of it, you know. Apart from injuries. I think if I hadn't been as injured as much as I was, I think we probably would have won more.

X IS FOR EXPERIENCE...

What's the best atmosphere you've ever experienced?

Probably the two matches where we won the league at the Brandywell. The first one against Cobh especially, and then that Cup Final in 1989 was unbelievable. When we beat Pats as well to 1997, that last match, the atmosphere that night was incredible. So, there's been a few matches, atmosphere-

at the time, so I'd never really seen these players before, so that was my first real experience of seeing senior footballers at that level.

Z IS FOR ZONE...

Did you ever have any pre-match rituals or superstitions to get you in the zone?

No, not really. Well, I did have some things, but it changed every time we were beat! There's times you'd try different things. You'd put your left sock on first and that would work for a while, and then you'd change to your right boot on first or something like that. Or the odd time I would have went and sat on my own for 10 min-

utes, or walked out on to the pitch on my own. It always changed. But every time we were beat I went 'Alright, I'm not doing these any more'! I know other boys had things they would do, but mine changed. Mine changed with the wind! I would stick with something thinking I've finally found it if we won five or six matches in a row, but once we were beat I just didn't bother!

I would have worn my full kit out for warm ups as well. The whole lot. I couldn't go back in and start to get ready at that stage and start putting shin pads on and everything. I'd just wear the whole lout out to the warm up. But, hi, players are simple, you know what I mean?!

What sock you put on first isn't going to affect you really, but it's just a mental thing for some boys and, hi, whatever helps you on a match day that's the main thing.

I remember, as well, after games, I used to be the last out. It used to drive Paula mad! She'd be waiting for me and I used to be the last one out all the time! Because I used to just sit in the changing room after the match for about 10-15 minutes before I got into the shower. I used to sit with a towel over my head for a while just because the adrenaline was still going. But, aye, it ended up then that I was still getting ready when everybody else was away on home!

TONY O'DOWD

A IS FOR ANNOYING...

Which of your former team mates was the worst to sit beside on the bus for long away journeys?

I would probably say Tommy Dunne, because he never stopped talking! He's always talking about tactics and what we're going to do, and you know, how we're going to play and all that and how Felix is getting the tactics wrong! Felix ended up winning the league, so I'm not sure Tommy was the one to listen to!

B IS FOR BEHAVIOUR...

Which of your former team mates was always the most likely to get booked?

Ah that's an easy one! Higgsy! I think it got to the stage that the refs were just giving him a yellow card even before he got on the pitch so they didn't have to bother stopping the game!

C IS FOR CHAMPIONS...

What are your memories of that 1997 league winning season with Derry?

There's kind of two... When we went down to Shel-

bourne it was really like a cup final in Tolka Park, if they'd have won it, they were right back in the race. I'm not sure of the points, they might went level or a point ahead or something, but it was very tight and it was like a cup final atmosphere and I think it was, I'm not sure now, but I think it was the first televised league game on RTE. We went 1-0 down and showed

great character. I think Gary Beckett got the equaliser, but we should have won that game. It wasn't done and dusted then, but you could see after the game, mentally Shels were done and then I think I think they ended up finishing third.

Obviously the other big one is actually winning the Brandywell against Pats 2-0, and the whole night after, which was just fantastic, the pitch

invasion and you know, the whole weekend. We went to the Trinity Hotel as it was called back then and had a fantastic night, celebrating just getting it over the line, you know? It kind of looked like, for a few weeks, that we were going to win it, but you don't dare believe until you actually you get over the line and then it was just relief more than anything, you know, and you can just relax then!

D IS FOR DERRY CITY...

Do you remember the story of how you signing for Derry City came about?

Well, to be honest, I didn't really know how it came about. I was out of favour at St Pat's because I was having a few run-ins with Brian Kerr at the time, so I wasn't playing and so I ended up actu-

ally playing Gaelic football for a team down here called Saint Anne's to get game time and someone saw me playing and Pats fined me two weeks wages on the last day of the season, so I just thought fuck that, I'm out of here. Then all of a sudden I got a phone call from someone at Pats telling me to meet Paul Diamond and Felix up in Dundalk in a hotel, I can't remember the name of it, and it was kind of done and dusted then. I don't know how it came about though. They were obviously looking at me at the time. Dermot O'Neill was obviously playing well at that stage and I think they'd won the Cup Final that year and just missed out on the league. But it was out of the blue for me. A kind of overnight thing.

E IS FOR ERA...

Money and technology included, would you prefer to have played when you did, or in modern football?

Funny enough, it would probably suit me better playing now because I could actually play with my feet as well. I started out as a centre forward for Cherry Orchard. But, I think the quality is not as good now to be honest. I don't know if quality is the right word, it's more, you know, if you look back then, every team had a superstar. You know what I mean? You had Liam Coyle, James Keddy, Pizza, Gary Beckett up front, then at Shels as well you had Stephen Geoghegan, Tony Sheridan, at Pat's you Eddie Gormley, Bohs you had Kevin Hunt. Top of the range players, which I don't really see now. Probably better overall teams now, but for entertainment and as well then, you know, those lads had to put up with a different era for tackling, you know what I mean? You'd literally have to kill someone to get a red card back then! You know, you were able to have the craic with the fans as well. That's when stories and memories were made. You couldn't do it now with camera phones and all, you know, having a few pints with the fans or you know, even the celebrations and the Trinity afterwards when we won the league, you'd be kind of a bit wary of, you know, getting too intoxicated because some fucking eejit would be filming it or something. It's probably going on the bleeding web within two minutes! I think it's harder for lads now, but I wouldn't swap it. Back then I really enjoyed it and I wouldn't swap it.

F IS FOR FUNNY...

What was the funniest thing you remember from your time in football?
There's a few! For me, when I was with Pats at the time we were playing Bohs and we were playing down Harold's Cross and Dave Henderson was playing against us, he was playing in goal for Bohs and someone went down injured around the centre circle. Well, he was a he was a fireman at the time,

so he was trained in first aid and all that. So he was up the halfway lying treating someone, whoever it was either one of their players, or one of our players. So he obviously had to take his gloves off. But I ran up and took his gloves and we hid them! We hid them on our bench and he had to play the rest of the game with no gloves on! You know, there's obviously a few more stories that wouldn't be able to be printed from nights out and that, you know? But, yeah, on the pitch that was just, that was kind of funny!

G IS FOR GOALKEEPER...

Did you always play as a goalkeeper? If so, why?
Well my Da was a goalkeeper, but I started off with a team down here called Cherry Orchard, and I played centre forward. I was actually their top scorer! But we played against the top team in Dublin at that stage, a team called Stella Maris, and

our keeper never turned up! So I said I'd go in goals just for that game. I saved two penalties in the game and had a great game but we still got beaten 6-0! But after the game they asked me would I sign for them as a keeper. They never saw me playing centre forward, just asked me would I sign for them as a keeper! So it kind of went from there!

H IS FOR HERO...

Who was your footballing or sporting hero growing up?
It would have been actually Pat Jennings, who played for Spurs at that stage. But when when I was playing for Stella Maris then as a goalkeeper and one of the lads that was running the club knew Pat Jennings fairly well. He went to his wedding and he got me a signed autograph and a pair of gloves. So that was like unbelievable for a kid back then to get that, you know what I mean!

I IS FOR IRELAND...

Do you still get a chance to get to League Of Ireland games?

Yeah, I'd be up at most Rovers home games, when I'm not working shifts. They're the closest club to me anyway so, I get up as often as I can.

J IS FOR JOKER...

Who was the biggest practical joker you've met in football?

It probably would have been Tommy Dunne and Ritchie Purdy! They were just, like a double act! There was always something going on, you could never take your eyes off them! Luckily for me though, the butt of the joke was normally James Keddy! He was a couple years younger than us at that stage. But when you saw Tommy and Richie together, the whole dressing room would be on alert! But it was great for team morale.

K IS FOR KIT...

What has been your favourite football kit that you've ever played in or owned?

My favourite football kit was the Ireland U21 kit and that was back when they had the Adidas kit. I have a few of the yellow 'keeper kits that I wore,

but my brother played U17s, so he has the green ones and the white away ones, all original. I actually liked the Derry gear the year we had Le Coq Sportif. That was top notch stuff as well. Even the leisure wear they did.

L IS FOR LIFE AFTER PLAYING...

Did you have a plan for after your playing career ended? Was management something you ever wanted to do?

No, not at all. We never really had a fancy for management. But back then you were always part time as well, you know. So you had a job already and you knew what you were doing when you finished. So all the way up through youth level I would have had a job. Not like now where you're kind of a full time

footballer and then at the end football you don't know what to be at. But, I never really had any thoughts of going into coaching, you know. I used to think some of the coaches only did it for themselves you know. You had lads that literally never played the game in some instances telling you what to do. And, you'd know the language they were using wasn't football language, you know what I mean? Everything they were saying to you was a direct quote from, you know, page 29 of the coaching manual! You know what I mean? I didn't want to get into that. To be honest, I didn't have much respect for coaches. I think at times coaches, especially with young kids, are coaching by numbers. But in saying that I do a bit of helping out with a junior team down here, but it's just helping out though, you know, it's not 'coaching' as you'd call it. But, no I've never had any inkling that I wanted to make a career our of it or anything.

M IS FOR MEMENTO...

What is the one football memento you own that you'll never give away?

Probably the league medal. that takes pride of place. There's not many people have them. Well, a few people have loads of them, but I only have one, so I'd never give it away. I've given away U21s jerseys to relatives and that, and my Leeds tracksuit from the time I was there when they won the league. I gave that to a relative that's a mad Leeds fan, but I'd never give away that medal.

N IS FOR NIGHT OUT...

Which team mate was usually the first to initiate a night out?

Probably me! The other three Dublin lads there hardy ever went out, and I was never in! But apart from me, I'd say Curney! Paul Curran. He loved a gargle! But it was different then. I remember we played Cork down there in another kind of top of the table clash, and we went down there overnight to stay, you know? So we'd have the team talk in the hotel the night before. I think it was a 12 o'clock kick off or something like that. So then Felix says 'Right lads, you can have a couple of pints to help you sleep', you know, take the edge off the nerves. But he says 'no more than five'! I tell that to youngsters today and they're like 'is he for real?!'. We probably went to bed hours before the game! And you could guarantee Curney had at least seven! We won the game though!

O IS FOR OPPOSITION...

Which opposition did you always look forward to playing the most in your career?

Well, when I was at Rovers the fixture we all looked out for was the Bohs game. That'd be the big one for us down here, so that's the game I used to love playing in. At Derry as well I used to love playing in Finn Harps games or the Sligo games, because there was a bit needle in them, you know what I mean? So that meant a bit more. When you play Dublin clubs at Derry it's just another game, but when there's a bit of needle in it for derby games it makes them a lot better. And it's the same with Rovers and Bohs. You know, you'd get a big build up to it the week before and media attention, and it was probably nearly always on the telly, you know, so they're the ones you like. You don't want the UCD's away or anything!

P IS FOR PASSTIME...

Outside of football, what keeps you occupied now in your spare time?

And to be honest, I don't really, I'm not a golfer or anything like that. I do help out with the men's Cherry Orchard team and my young fella playing, so that keeps me busy. You're going down there three nights a week and then the games as well, and then out for a few pints as well after. But I could never get into golf or anything like that, you know. Too boring for me! So no real hobbies as such look at just watching junior football. James Keddy is at Wexford now obviously, so going to watch junior teams and just you know, giving him pointers as to which young players I think could make the step up you know.

Q IS FOR QUIZ...

Which former team mate

would you definitely not want in your team if you were doing a quiz?
Richie Purdy! The thickest man alive! Great player, but just no common sense at all! I don't think he's read a book in his life! You know these videos you see on YouTube where they ask Americans to point out London on a map? He wouldn't have a clue! I heard him chatting up a girl once and she had a thick Welsh accent and he said 'Where you from?' and she goes 'I'm from the capital of Wales', and he said 'Oh, I love Edinburgh!' and he was serious! She thought he was having a laugh!

R IS FOR RESULT...

Which result stands out or meant the most to you in your career?
The one in Tolka that I was on about earlier the year we won the league kind of stands out to me. I really enjoyed that kind of game, and the family were there and everyone from Dublin was there and there was a good crowd from Derry as well. That, or the time we beat Celtic 3-2 at Lansdowne. I think they had hoped that Celtic would get through to the final and play Newcastle, so I don't think they were too pleased when we beat Celtic in the semi-final. I don't think that was really in the script for the organisers. And the team we were

playing in Europe, I think was a team from Slovenia, they were all watching that! I'm sure they came away re-thinking their plans as well! Yeah, that was that was enjoyable, because it kind of got a bit of media attention for the league and that sort of thing. And at that stage, certain people would be taking the piss out of the league, and when you go and beat Celtic, they kind of paid a bit more attention to it, you know.

S IS FOR SAVE...

What sticks out for you as the best save you've ever made?
Probably would be a save I made for Pats against Bohs at Dalymount which was a great save. Fenlon was playing for Bohs at that time and he knocked it across and Alan Byrne had a header that was going into the top corner and at that stage he was just back from Leeds and I thought I had a point to prove that I was good enough. I literally got a fingertip to it and tipped it onto the bar and out for a corner. Then there was one playing for Rovers in the Leinster Senior Cup against Bray Wanderers in Bray and there was a shot from about 25 yards, but just before me it took a deflection, so I was already diving the other way, so I just got my leg to it and it kind of just went up

into the air and when it hit the ground someone hit a shot and I saved that as well and knocked it off the goal line with my hand. Probably those two. Blowing my own trumpet!

T IS FOR TALENT...

Who is the best player you've ever played with?
To be honest, it probably boils down to two. One would be Liam Coyle. Unbelievable player. I know people go on about him and all, but Jesus he was some player! And Eddie Gormley would be the other. The two of them for me were just on a different level, you know. To be honest with you, if they were playing now they wouldn't be in the league for long. I know Liam wouldn't have played in the league anyway if it wasn't for injuries. But the two definitely wouldn't be playing in the League Of Ireland for long before going across the water. Eddie Gormley

had it all. Left foot, right foot… He's a left footed player but he used to take penalties with his right foot to confuse the goalkeeper! That's how confident he was. I know people go on about players like Kevin Hunt, but to be honest I'd play against Kevin Hunt every day of the week. He'd get the ball alright, but he only ever played it backwards or sidewards, so that tends to make people look like better players than they are, but the likes of Eddie Gormley, literally anywhere within 45 yards from the goal you wouldn't know what he'd do. It could be a through ball, could be a shot, could be a run, anything. Same as Coyler, I remember I was playing the Brandywell one day, and you know how at the Brandywell the wind comes down the pitch like a hurricane! So I launched the ball up in the air, and it was going about 150 miles an hour! But came over Liam's shoulder, and I'd launched it out of my hand, it wasn't even from the deck, and he took it on his right foot and brought it down all in one movement, and put the centre half on his arse! I was just outrageous to watch Liam play and it was like it was nothing to him, you know! Another time we were playing Home Farm in the Cup that year and he was on the bench because he had

a little niggle. We were 1-0 down, then he came on for about 10 minutes with 20 minutes to go, he came on and scored two goals and then went back off!

U IS FOR UNPARALLELED…

Who is the best player you've ever played against?

Well, I was there at Leeds when Eric Cantona was there, and he was just a different level like. Training-wise I know he looks a bit arrogant, but he used to train his arse off. There's no messing in training with him. That's why I'm convinced that's where Keane got it, because I know Keane really well from the U21s and he was a messer! He wasn't all this, you know, professionalism and all. I'm convinced that when Cantona went to United, Keane saw the way Cantona was and then kind of copped himself on because with Cantona in train-

ing, if he didn't score every shot he would go bananas! And if someone else wasn't trying in training he'd bark at them! His skill was unreal though.

V IS FOR VANITY…

Which team mate spent the longest in front of the mirror?

Pizza had the long locks gelled back at the time. There was three of them though, Pizza, Ryan Semple, and Ryan Coyle with the long hair. And it seemed to me, now I can't say much, but it seemed to me they were going out a lot together, you know? In fairness to Pizza though, he's a good looking chap apart from the broken nose!

W IS FOR WISHES…

Is there anything you'd change about your career if you could do it all again?

Probably, yeah. There was a chance for me to go back

67

up to Derry when Keely was there. I think I was at Rovers and I think I wasn't getting on, and then I did get on. But, he said he'd bring me back up to Derry then at the end of the season, but he got the sack, so that fell through. But, yeah, I would have liked to go back up to be honest. You kind of don't realise what you have until you leave it, you know. But at the time I left Derry I had the chance to go to Rovers and back to Dublin where my family were and at that stage I was the only Dublin lad left at Derry and I think Felix was trying to reduce the wage bill. I was probably just a bit young and naïve, and I probably should never have left Derry when I did.

X IS FOR EXPERIENCE...

What's the best atmosphere you've ever experienced as a player?

It was probably when Derry played over in Slovenia when we played in the European Cup. Even our training session. You'd usually train the night before, but they had the ground packed out with the fans and they were chanting the whole session! We didn't know what they were chanting right enough! But it was something that we'd never seen before. Even in other European games, you didn't get it. And even as we arrived they were outside with the

flags and the drums and all that. We were unlucky in that game. I think we were 1-0 down from the first leg. We had a great chance, but they got a late goal, kind of against the run of play and we were just left thinking 'We should have beaten them. We should have gone through'. You know, it wasn't one of those that was common at the time where you're going to European games saying, 'Geez, we should have been beaten four or five here.' It was genuinely a missed opportunity.

Y IS FOR YOUNG...

What is your earliest memory of going to a football match?

The earliest memory would be a Pats and Rovers game at Richmond Park. My Da would have gone to a good few League Of Ireland games around that time so I remember going to that. That would be the only one I would be able to go to because down here, we play our schoolboy games on a Sunday, so the League Of Ireland usually played on a Sunday as well. It was only if the schoolboy game was called off that you could go and see a live League Of Ireland game. There were very few grounds with floodlights then, so they couldn't have them on a Friday night or anything.

Z IS FOR ZONE...

Did you ever have any pre-match rituals or superstitions to get you in the zone?

Yeah, well, I used to always wear a brown scapular. And the Friday before a game I would always going to visit a couple of graves or whatever to say a few prayers. I wouldn't be mad religious or anything, but just to try and get in the right frame of mind. Get your mind at ease. Just that sometimes in big games if you're a 'keeper, you don't want to let anyone else down because you know generally, it's a team, so there's a lot of responsibility on yourself. You know you don't want your family hearing 'Tony made a mistake and cost us this, that, and whatever'. People come out of the woodwork when you made a mistake, and when you have a good game you never hear from them. But when you have a bad game and you hear from people you haven't heard from in years! But, yeah, you'll probably see it in a few photos from back then I would always have my brown scapular on. I still do. I wouldn't play a game without it. You know, some people say that if you have a superstition you're mentally weak, but for me I just wouldn't feel right playing a game without it.

TOM MOHAN

SPONSORED BY
LIAM O'CAOMHANAIGH

A IS FOR ANNOYING...
Which of your former team mates was the worst to sit beside on the bus for long away journeys?

That's a good question! It would have to be Gary Beckett! I had to sit long enough with him in cars, so on the team bus as well would be too much!!

B IS FOR BEHAVIOUR...
Which of your former team mates was always the most likely to get booked?

Probably Richie Purdy covering for me!! He let nobody past him! What a man to have behind you!

C IS FOR CITY...
Outside of the club, what memories do you have of the city?

Probably, you know, even when I would drive to Derry for non-footballing events the first thing you'd always see is the Brandywell, and I'd known a bit about the history of the club when I was growing up, you know, Derry City were so high profile and getting a lot of coverage and took a lot of fans everywhere they went. I'd have been a young fella growing up in the 80s and Derry City just arrived on the scene and were massive straight away more or less. But, yeah, every time I drive into Derry the first thing I always see is the Brandywell across the water, and the lights from the Brandywell can be seen from a lot of places around the city as well, you know.

D IS FOR DERRY CITY...
Who is the best player Derry City have ever had?

That's an easy one that! Liam Coyle! You won't need me to explain my answer to that question!

E IS FOR EUROPE...
Which team was your toughest European opponent? At any club.

Red Star Belgrade when I was at Portadown. They'd just won the European Cup the year before before, but I was only a sub! I was enjoy-

69

ing it from the bench! But we had a tough one with Derry as well with Lokomotiv Sofia away. We were 1-0 up from the home leg I remember, but we went out there thinking we might have a chance, but Tony O'Dowd got sent off and Anthony Tohill went into goals. We ended up losing 2-0. That was that was a tough one as well, and it was even harder with 10 men and no goalkeeper. But we nearly done it too! If we had have known that Anthony Tohill could kick the ball 80yrds over their defense from his first kick out we might have

used it as a tactic!

F IS FOR FUNNY...
What was the funniest thing you remember from your time in football?
Well, it was actually on the pitch against Dundalk. Dundalk were beating us 2-0, and one of the Dundalk strikers said to Pizza, 'You're missing a good game here!' and laughing as he ran past. Later on in the game though, we were 4-2 up with about 5mins to go and the same player was being substituted, and as he ran past Pizza, Pizza said to him 'Are you not going to stay

and watch the rest of this game?!' That was one that I always found funny!

G IS FOR GOAL...
What was the best goal you've ever scored?
I shouldn't have to think too long anyway! There wasn't that many of them! I think the most important one anyway was the fluke I scored against Home Farm Everton. It was the year we won the league. We were 1-0 down and they were bottom of the table I think at the time, but I just crossed it in aiming for the back post, but I think the wind took it in!! People watching might have thought it was spectacular, but it was a fluke I can assure you!! It mightn't have been the best, but it was probably one of the most important anyway in terms to the title race that season.

H IS FOR HANGING UP THE BOOTS...
Did you always have a plan for after football? Was management something you always wanted to do?
Yeah, well, obviously when I was playing I was doing coaching badges and stuff, and then I was doing some part time work with the FAI as well. It probably fell into place like that, you know, that I would end up in coaching in some capacity. I mean, I had a few of the badges already done while

I was playing, so I think it must have been one of the plans anyway to fall back on after football and just stay in the game.

I IS FOR IRISH INTERNATIONAL SOCCER TOURNAMENT...

What do you remember about the Derry City, Newcastle United, Celtic, & PSV tournament at Lansdowne Road in 1997?

Yeah, I remember my friends give me a hard time for beating Celtic! And I remember Higgsy before the match telling me 'You know, you're allowed to kick these boys too!', so he was all up for a serious challenge! I went to get Paolo

DiCanio's jersey after the game as well and he told me the club wouldn't let them exchange jerseys and I was devastated! So there's a lot of different memories from that one, but it was a great occasion, yeah.

J IS FOR JOKER...

Who was the biggest practical joker you've met in football?

Tommy Dunne! Tommy was always a joker! He was a sharp witted boy!

K IS FOR KIT...

What has been your favourite football kit that you've ever played in or owned?

That's a tough one! I never give it an awful lot of thought! We had a black and green one at Derry that was nice. It has black and dark green stripes with I think a thin bit of white in it as well? I liked that one.

L IS FOR LEAGUE...

What do you remember most about that league winning season in 1997?

Beating Bohs at Dalymount. That was a sort of six pointer at the time, you know. They were in the hunt for the title as well. I think we beat them 2-0 that day, but it was a really, really good performance. And with it being at Dalymount as well it was a real statement like, and it just put them completely out of contention and stretched

our lead as well. Our character and everything was on display that day and it was just one that sticks out that year as a real, kind of, cup final atmosphere.

M IS FOR MEMENTO...

What is the one football memento you own that you'll never give away?

I have a few things that I've kept, but I'd say my league winning medal.

N IS FOR NIGHT OUT...

Which team mate was usually the first to initiate a night out?

It had to be the Derry boys! The likes of Paul Curran and them!

O IS FOR OPPOSITION...

Which opposition did you always look forward to playing the most in your career?

I liked playing Dundalk because I liked playing in Oriel Park. For whatever reason I don't know! I just liked the ground and the pitch and that.

P IS FOR PASSTIME...

Outside of football, what keeps you occupied now in your spare time?

Well, I'm interested in all sports really. I'd go to any sporting event be it horse racing, greyhound racing, gaelic, you know, kind of anything really, but that would generally be it outside of football.

Q IS FOR QUIZ...

Which former team mate would you definitely not want in your team if you were doing a quiz?

That's a good one there now! I'm trying to go through everybody... I'd say Tommy Dunne! Not because of his intelligence, but I just know there's be too much laughing and joking! We'd never get the questions answered!

R IS FOR RESULT...

Which result stands out or meant the most to you in your career?

I kind of remember the good and the bad! To give you a positive one though... Probably that one at Dalymount the year we won the league that I spoke about before. Obviously I remember some of the negative ones as well like the Cup Final we lost to Shelbourne 2-0 at Dalymount, but I prefer the positive ones, for obvious reasons!

S IS FOR SIGNING...

Do you remember the story of how you signing for Derry City came about?

Well, I was approached about getting a call from Felix. I was at Omagh Town at the time. And I remember the minute I heard Derry were interested I couldn't wait to get signing! It was a big moment in my career.

So Felix rang me and we spoke and he said he wanted to sign me and I was thinking 'How soon?!', you know! But I remember as well that when I found out Derry were interested and he was going to ring me, I was due to go on holiday! And there were no mobile phones back then, so the whole time I was away I was panicking that he would be ringing me and I wouldn't be there and he'd think I wasn't interested or something, you know!! But, no, thankfully it all worked out and it was a massive move for me.

T IS FOR TALENT...

Who is the best player you've ever played with?

Liam again! Liam Coyle!

U IS FOR UNPARAL-LELED...

Who is the best player you've ever played against?

I'd have to say Paolo Di-Canio, wouldn't I?!

V IS FOR VANITY...

Which team mate spent the longest in front of the mirror?

There were no mirrors in the changing room back then, so I'm trying to remember which lads complained the most about that! Definitely not Higgsy anway! Beckett and Pizza looked after their hair! Some of the Dubs as well. Tony O'Dowd for sure!

W IS FOR WISHES...

Is there anything you'd change about your career if you could do it all again?

Yeah. I'd retake that penalty in the play-offs for Harps and score it this time instead of letting the 'keeper save it!!

X IS FOR EXPERIENCE...

What's the best atmosphere you've ever experienced as a player?

There's been a few!. You could probably put two down here, because there's two that come to mind, and they were both against Cork!

In fact, was that earlier question the a most memorable goal? I think you could put the most memorable goal as being that last minute winner against Cork in the Cup Quarter Final for Derry. Just amazing to score a goal in that situation. The place went mental, you know! The other one was when we beat Cork in the Cup as well actually with Finn Harps when we weren't expected to. Another one I'm just thinking of as well would be the night we beat Lokomotiv Sofia 1-0 at the Brandywell. That was an unbelievable atmosphere. What a night that was. Because teams in Ireland weren't beating teams in Europe. There wasn't too many results like that! But the place was packed and it was a nice summer's even-

ing and we played really well and it all just came together for us.

Y IS FOR YOUTH...

You're Rep Of Ireland U19s manager now, how is the future of Irish football looking?

Yeah, you know, there's a lot of young players in Ireland that are really good, and you're dealing with a lot of potential. You can never tell who's going to make it and who's not going to make it, but we try and teach traits that players should have to succeed in the game. You know, it's always the lads with good attitudes that go the distance. It's a game of variables. Players that make the wrong choices in life and achieve a lot less than you thought they should, whether it's not making a move at the right time, or not going to a particular club, getting a bad loan move, or making choices outside of football that affect their game. But there is a lot of talented lads coming through. A lot of them got a chance under Stephen Kenny too, so it's good to see them achieving what they should in the game, and I hope they can kick on. We have a fair few lads playing in the Premier League, the likes of Kelleher, Nathan Collins, Evan Ferguson and those lads all getting Pre-

mier League experience. So, we have a good few players coming through that hopefully just get better.

Z IS FOR ZONE...

Did you ever have any pre-match rituals or superstitions to get you in the zone?

Yeah, I would always put on my left boot first! I always said though, if I go out there and don't play well myself, I'll make life hell for my opponent anyway, you know! If you're not getting to do much in an attacking sense, you have to start working on your defensive side as well. It's something I teach the young lads too. Don't just throw the head if things are working out, adapt. You've got to keep that effort and desire and hunger and work hard. They're key ingredients to your game as well. Oxo, Paul McLaughlin, always told me 'You know, if you're honest and you work hard you'll never problem with the fans'. I remember that was my first pre-season friendly. Oxo was great. I played with him at Omagh as well. I think he might have been pushing Felix to get me to Derry a bit too! But I never forgot that message throughout my career you know, if you work hard, and you're honest, the supporters will love you. It's a simple message but a very effective message.

TOMMY DUNNE
SPONSORED BY
J&KCOACHES
miles ahead

A IS FOR ANNOYING...

Which of your former team mates was the worst to sit beside on the bus for long away journeys?

You could take your pick on that one! But do you know who was extremely annoying, and he was in the car when we'd be travelling up to Derry all the time was James Keddy! He's funny! Funny, but annoying! And he'd be mostly talking about himself! He's a really great lad. Hilarious as well, but completely annoying! And I'd say Richie Purdy was a close second! Yeah, so it was James Keddy for me! Honestly, the reason why he was annoying was because all he kept talking about how good he was himself!

B IS FOR BEHAVIOUR...

Which of your former team mates was always the most likely to get booked?

Well, I think that would be Heggsy. Like he was an animal in the middle of the pitch, you know. Him and Pizza, but Heggsy was the sitter. I didn't know until we started to play together that Heggsy was basically felling trees! That was his job, you know, he was a forester. So he used to cut down trees all

day and then chop people's ankles in the evenings! He was extremely aggressive in the middle of the pitch, but that's what made him good, you know, that side to his game. So it was either him, or it could have been Dykesy. It could have been a number of players, but it

was, it was probably Heggsy first, Dykesy and Paul Curran second and then Purdy, then probably myself next cause because none of us in the back four could run, so that's why we gave away yellow cards!

C IS FOR CHAMPI-

75

ONS...

What are your biggest memories of that league winning season in 1997?

I remember we started the season and we were sort of a little bit unknown because Felix had only put the group together that summer. But I remember we played Dundalk up in Dundalk and we were two nil down after about 20 minutes and heads started to drop like it wasn't going our way. One of them was definitely offside I remember. So, we are two nil down in Dundalk and we went on to win 5-2 I think and I said to myself 'We have a team here', you know? And we played brilliantly from then on and we had a great balance. Aside from that game, I think the next thing that I remember about that year was that the team was so balanced. We could defend, we could play, we could score goals, we could mix it if it became a scrap, so we had everything really. And when you think about it, we sort of won the league comfortably in the end. 10 points we won it by in the end up. So I think the main memory for me was that Dundalk game and thinking that we're not bad like, you know, we have a chance.

D IS FOR DERRY CITY...

Do you remember the story of how you signing for Derry City came about?

Yeah, I was with Shelburne at the time and Damien Richardson was the boss, and we sort of, not that we fell out, but there was just obviously a difference of opinion, and so we were talking about maybe me going out on loan because I wanted to play. So I remember Linfield came in for me to go on loan and they seemed to be really keen and Shelbourne were talking to them and

everything, but I couldn't sign for Linfield because of my father and the way I was brought up and that, it would have been sort of like 'what are you doing', you know? But then at the last minute Derry came in for me to go on loan. I don't know how it happened. Felix got in contact. I don't know whether Paul Doolin had mentioned it to him because I played with Paul at

Shels or whatever. So I went on loan until the end of the season, and then I signed a two year contract after that. I did quite well when I went up, and so Felix signed me then the following season. I remember there was a bit of an issue in that Shels were looking for money for me, but the Bosman thing only just came in at that time, and because Derry were in a different jurisdiction, Shels couldn't get any money for me. So I remember that was a bit of an issue. They wanted money, but the Bosman ruling kicked in just at that time and I was a free agent at the end of that year anyway, but that Bosman thing meant I could make the move to Derry. I don't remember the exact rules, but I was under a certain age and I was going to a different jurisdiction or something, but that's how it came about.

E IS FOR EUROPE...

Which team was your toughest European opponent? At any club.

Trying to think now who we played. I remember a Ukrainian team, but we beat them over the two legs, but I'm trying to think who would be the toughest. There was an Icelandic team that we played, Akranes was the name of the team, and we were expected to beat them, but they were tough. They obviously play in the summer league, and we were just coming back off pre-season, going back to the time that we were the winter league. So, we came off pre-season and we played them, this is with Shels at the time, and they were flying and it was a nightmare because they were ready and we went! So that was a tough one.

I'm trying to think who else. We played Panathinaikos in Greece. They were very good. At Dundalk there was a team from Budapest, now I was only I was only on the bench, but watching them they looked really good. But the toughest one for me was probably that Icelandic team.

F IS FOR FINLAND...

How did it come about that you've both played and managed in Finland?

Well, I met my wife when I was away on a trip, and so once we got married we ended up moving to Finland. So, I ended up playing and managing here, and I'm still coaching here at the moment would you believe. So, that's how that came about. It wouldn't have come any other way, I wouldn't think! I'd probably be still involved back home I'd imagine if I hadn't married my wife, you know!

G IS FOR GOAL...

What's been the best goal you've seen scored that you were on the pitch for?

It was Liam Coyle playing against Home Farm Everton in the Cup. Liam was injured and Felix had left him on the bench and we didn't really start the game very well and Home Farm were one up. So Felix brought Liam on. And there was a throw in from the side, and Liam turned Peter Eccles, who was a top centre half in the League of Ireland at the time. Liam actually scored two goals that day that were brilliant, but the first one was the best. He turned Peter Eccles one way, then went back the other way and buried the ball into the far corner. Then the second one that day, which was a brilliant goal as well, I remember playing a ball into him and he turned and hit it up into the top corner to give us the lead, and Felix took him back off again! So he came on, scored two goals, and then was taken back off again! It was Liam all over, you know. Ridiculous skill and his awareness, and that was a brilliant goal.

H IS FOR HAHA...

What was the funniest thing you remember from your time in football?

We had some funny moments! I suppose one Derry related story that spring to mind; we used to travel up for games in the car, and it was myself, Tony O'Dowd, Richie Purdy and James Keddy. But there was this one trip towards the end of the season and we'd already won the league, you know, but we stopped half way up for a sort of pre-match meal, which we didn't usually do, it was just usually something from a shop and back on the road. But this time we sort of thought to ourselves, 'listen, it's the end of the season, so we're going to have something nice to eat.' So we ended up having, for a pre-match meal, a full roast dinner and black forest gateaux after it! So next of all, we came out of the restaurant and Richie Purdy had a brand new shirt on, because in those days you had to show up to matches in a shirt and tie, but we looked down at Richie's shirt and there was black forest gateaux all over it! So we had to say to him 'you can't wear that! We'll get caught', you know, so he had to wear this white Fred Perry polo shirt with a tie on and his jacket over it! That was one of the funniest things I've ever seen! But there was loads of funny times. Too many to mention!

I IS FOR INTERNATIONAL...

What do you remember about getting your U21s international call-ups? Was there ever a chance for the senior squad?

Yeah, with for the U21s I think I was with Dundalk at the time if I'm not mistaken. Maybe even between Dundalk and Shels for the U21s, but yeah, I got a call up and I was delighted. I hadn't got any call ups for the U15s or U19s or anything before that. I was quite small at 16 and 17, and the youth call ups kind of came and came and went and I wasn't mentioned. But with the U21s I was doing full time training, Morrie Price was the U21s coach at that time, and I went into the Home Farm first team and because we were full time playing in the league, myself and Richie Purdy and there was one or two other League of Ireland players, I think Barry O'Connor got into the Under 21 squads as well. I remember that we played some good games at the time. It was the Jack Charlton era and we played in the youth team that qualified for the European Championships the same day Ireland qualified for the World Cup. We were both in Malta, both teams. So they were fantastic trips and the campaign for the U21s was with Denmark, Germany and Spain, so we had some really, really good matches, you know. It was a brilliant time.

The closest I got I suppose

to a senior call up was when an Ireland Select managed by Jack Charlton was playing against Man United in a testimonial at Lansdowne Road. Packie Bonner was playing, Alan Kernaghan, Kenny Cunningham, they were all playing, and I played in that match. So that was the closest I ever got to the senior squad.

J IS FOR JOKER...

Who was the biggest practical joker you've met in football?

Paul Curran was a joker! There was one other when I played with Dundalk and that was Gino Lawless! Oh my God! He used to cut the ends off your socks and rub Deep Heat in your underpants while you were in the shower! I remember going to the PFAI or the Soccer Writers do at the end of the season. Big formal event anyway in a suit, and I took my jacket off and I was at the table with Gino. Anyway, I put my jacket back on after it and there was two desserts in my inside pockets! So, yeah, Gino was unbelievable! Well, Curny was the same! He'd be of similar ilk!

K IS FOR KIT...

What has been your favourite football kit that you've ever played in or owned?

I's between two. I have to say I loved the Candystripes of the Derry jersey that year

we won the league. Obviously, there was the Rovers jersey as well. I used to love the hoops, you know. And if I was to say one more, I was a schoolboy at Home Farm and they used to have blue and white hoops. I liked that jersey as well. So they're probably 3 favourite teams to be honest, and the jerseys matched it. I still have the Derry jersey from the year we won the league upstairs would you believe! The Le Coq Sportif one. That was a lovely jersey.

L IS FOR LIFE AFTER PLAYING...

Did you have a plan for after football? Was management something you ever wanted to do?

No, I didn't have a plan, I think it just sort of happened! I got a bad injury with Rovers, sort of a groin injury and my contract was out, so with the injury I knew it was coming to the end. I remember going to the First Division and played for a couple of months, but it wasn't the same. So Paul Doolin was with U.C.D. at the time managing and he asked me to take the U21s because he was short of a coach to take them, and then when Paul moved to Drogheda, I went with him as his assistant. I was in the middle of doing my licenses then. I'd only got my B license at that stage,

and then I moved to Finland and I played again for a while because the injury had sort of settled down a bit and I played in the Second Division over here for a year and then that team asked me to take the manager's job, so I managed there for three years before I ended up managing the SJK senior team for about 6 months and then we moved back to Ireland, and that's where I hooked up with Paul again, because I went down to Cork with Paul. That's where the Cork and Galway jobs came from just after that. I'd done my A license in Finland, and then I did my Pro License back in Ireland. So that's how it came about. I didn't really plan to go into a club and manage, but I suppose because my Dad had done it., and at that time I would have known the people who were managing. They were all sort of, ex-teammates of mine, so I knew it could be done. So that was the reason why it came about. Me and Paul Doolin would have spoken and talked about football quite a lot when we'd be travelling in the car up and down the road, so we knew we'd get on well and had similar ideas.

M IS FOR MEMENTO...

What is the one football memento you own that you'll never give away?

I suppose my League Winners medal and my caps. I'd never give them away. Because they were special times and special occasions. I was hoping at some stage, and I forgot to do it at the reunion that was on a few years ago, but I was hoping to get my Derry City jersey signed by all the lads and I forgot to bring it with me! But that's maybe another thing I'd hold on to, that league winning jersey. The Le Coq Sportif one.

N IS FOR NIGHT OUT...

Which team mate was usually the first to initiate a night out?

That one's obvious! Tony O'Dowd! Well, if we were in Derry it would have been Paul Curran, but around Dublin O'Dowd loved a night out! He'd probably be the main one! Because he was always out himself anyway, so inviting the rest of the lads was nothing to him! Even now anytime I'm home and we're hooking up for a pint Tony is always on, you know!

O IS FOR OPPOSITION...

Which opposition did you always look forward to playing the most in your career?

I used to always look forward to playing against Bohs, whether it was with Rovers or whether it was with Derry, because at the time with Derry, Bohs were there as well. There was us, Shels and Bohs that were really going for the for the league that year. And I used to always love playing at Dalymount for some reason. The pitch was big and we'd always get great results. So, yeah, I'd probably say Bohs.

P IS FOR PASSTIME...

Outside of football, what keeps you occupied now in your spare time?

Golf. I love playing a bit of golf. Here where I'm living, it's really only five months of the year that you can play, because the snow is down for the other six or seven months. But I like playing golf, yeah.

Q IS FOR QUIZ...

Which former team mate would you definitely not want in your team if you were doing a quiz?

Definitely Ritchie Purdy! He was absolutely useless! I played Trivial Pursuit with him one day! I don't think he got one answer right!

R IS FOR RESULT...

Which result stands out or meant the most to you in your career?

The one that stands out the most I suppose was when we beat the Ukrainian team in Europe. That was a big result. I remember as well being involved with the Dundalk team down in Cork in

1991 and I was involved in the Dundalk team that beat Cork 1-0 to win the league. I suppose from a coach side of thing, the result when I was with Cork beating Shelbourne on the last day to win the First Division, that was a big result. But I suppose with the Derry team, it was the semi-final of the cup in Dalymount when we beat Bohs. That was a brilliant result. It was always going to be tough as I've said, but we played brilliant and we won the match to get us to the Cup Final.

S IS FOR SHELBOURNE...

What are your memories of those two FAI Cup Finals between Derry and Shelbourne? You played for both teams, but were on the losing side both times.

Yeah, I was on the losing side three times! Well, Shels against Derry when I was with Shels and Derry won, and then Derry against Shels when I was with Derry and Shels won! I lost both of them! And then Dundalk when we were beaten by Shels! I was involved in that one, but I didn't play. But I played the other two! Yeah, obviously not a nice one for me, but the worst one for me was, when I was playing for Shels I gave away a penalty! Liam came across me, Liam was cute as fuck, you know! He just came across

me and took a dive! It was a definite dive, all day long! Until this day we still argue about it! But, yeah, I was really disappointed at all of them, because the FAI Cup was something I wanted to win because my Dad had won one and I was hoping to win one as well, but didn't for whatever reason. And the last one when I played for Derry, I thought I'd get another chance, but it never materialised.

T IS FOR TEAM MATES...

Who is the best player you've ever played with?

There's two players that I'd probably say in terms of the club side of things in the League of Ireland, it was it was Liam Coyle and Terry Eviston. On international duty, Roy Keane was in our team, so we obviously went through the youth setup together, but as a team mate in an international team., he probably would be the one you'd pick.

U IS FOR UNPARALLELED...

Who is the best player you've ever played against?

We used to play a lot of a lot of pre-season friendlies and stuff like that, and Liverpool and all these teams would come over. So I suppose that time we played Man United with Ireland, David Beckham came on in the game, and I was direct against him mark-

ing him and I don't need to tell you that he was good! In the League of Ireland terms, there were wingers like Johnny Kenny that were really hard to play against. He played with Sligo and Finn Harps. He was quick, but he was he was so strong as well. You could kick lumps out of him and it just didn't have any effect on him, you know! We played against Portugal in an international as well and the likes of Figo were playing, but I wasn't really up against him directly.

V IS FOR VANITY...

Which team mate spent the longest in front of the mirror?

I played with a fella at Dundalk called Ricky McEvoy. He ended up playing in the north with Bangor and Glentoran I think. He was with Dundalk when he was there and he just, I wouldn't say loved himself, but he wasn't far off it, you know?! Always in the mirror checking himself!

W IS FOR WISHES...

Is there anything you'd change about your career if you could do it all again?

How long have you got for that one!! I'd change a lot of things. I suppose the preparation and training and the biggest thing I found that was the problem when we were in the League of Ireland at the time was our training facilities were a joke. No matter which club I was at, it was always an issue for training facilities and it really didn't allow us to prepare properly and do things properly. But from my own point of view and I probably would have changed some of the things that the things that I know now. I would have worked a bit harder maybe. Of course we were good pros and dedicated to the clubs and that, but there were times on a Friday night when we used to go out for a night out and you're playing on the Sunday and all that. You didn't

look after yourself as well as you could have. Well, in saying that I have to say I enjoyed all that as well at the time. It was only later on in my career that I would have to stop those nights out. You'd pick up injuries a bit easier. You just think 'I could have looked after myself a bit more'. I really do feel that we had a really good era of teams and players, but we just didn't have the right facilities to be able to go on and do what we needed to do, or maybe what we were fully capable of. It was like what the players have now. You can see the difference

in them. If we'd had those kinds of facilities we could have achieved much more.

X IS FOR EXPERIENCE...

What's the best atmosphere you've ever experienced as a player?

Some of those European nights had a great atmosphere. But I think the Cup Finals were just electric. Even though I lost, they were amazing occasions to be a part of!

Y IS FOR YOUNG...

What's your earliest memory of going to a football match?

I would have gone to watch my father's games. He was manager of UCD at the time and I used to always go to the games with him. I used to always love going to Belfield especially because there was plenty of space in the grounds around it to bring a ball and go and play football when the match was on!

Z IS FOR ZONE...

Did you ever have any pre-match rituals or superstitions to get you in the zone?

No, I never did you know. Nothing like that. I know some guys have all sorts of things they do. I suppose at some points I did try things like right sock and boot on first and things like that, but I didn't have any hard rules or anything!

GAVIN DYKES

SPONSORED BY
FRANK HOUSTON

A IS FOR ANNOYING...
Which of your former team mates was the worst to sit beside on the bus for long away journeys?

I'm trying to think who I used to site beside. I'd say Higgsy would probably be the most annoying because he never shut up! That's what makes him good at his job though!

B IS FOR BEHAVIOUR...
Which of your former team mates was always the most likely to get booked?

There's a few of us in that as well! I suppose, in terms of getting into trouble, it would have been Paul Hegarty again! Well, it was either me or him!

C IS FOR CHAMPIONS...
What are your biggest memories of that league winning season in 1997?

It was just such a special time. It really, really was. I think we were great throughout. It was a special bunch of people, and the night we won it in the Brandywell is something I'll never forget, you know. Because there was always a big crowd. And the travelling support as well was amaz-ing. The amount of people that travelled up and down to the country for us was unbelievable. But we had a great bunch of lads, we really, really had. We worked really hard for each other. But, yeah, the main memory would be that night in the Brandywell when we won it.

D IS FOR DERRY CITY...
Do you remember the story of how you signing for Derry City came about?

I do. I decided that I was leaving Sligo and Felix Healy make contact with me. I was either going to go to Shamrock Rovers, Linfield came in for me as well, or Derry. And to be honest, the only thing that put me off going to Derry at the time was because we had beaten them in the Cup Final only a couple of years before that, and I just thought I wouldn't fit in and the fans wouldn't like me because of that. But I met Felix and I was really impressed and I met Paul Diamond as well. I was really impressed with his plans, and he was very truthful with me. He told me 'Look, I just want to come in and boss it and be yourself. I don't need you to do things you won't be able to do', in other words, don't try passing the ball out from the back, because I wasn't able to go and do it. He just said he wants someone in the dressing room to come in and lead and, yeah, we hit it off straight away and as I say, it was a great group of lads, and once I met them I was very happy to go there.

E IS FOR EUROPE...

Which team was your toughest European opponent? At any club.

At any club? We played Club Brugge at Sligo and they had a fella called Eijkelkamp was his name. Big centre forward, he was 6 foot 7! He was only after a signing for them for 5 million. There was a guy as well played for them, Daniel Amokachi, that went on to play for Everton. When they took Eijkelkamp off, Amokachi came on instead of him! So, yeah, we got a good run around that night! So they were probably the hardest, Club Brugge.

F IS FOR FUNNY...

What was the funniest thing you remember from your time in football?

There's a couple of funny ones! I won't name the player, but I had a player once that had a groin injury, and we had a physio at the time that was… Let's just say, not

very highly qualified, right? So this player was nursing this injury a bit but thought he was alright to play, so he went to the physio before the game and the physio applied an awful lot of Deep Heat in the wrong area! After 10 minutes the player had to come off! He just couldn't continue! And it wasn't because of the groin injury!

G IS FOR GOAL...

What's been the best goal you've seen scored that you were on the pitch for?

There was two of them. Liam Coyle scored one against Home Farm was an FAI Cup game the same year we won the league, and he came on as a sub and scored two in the space of 10 minutes, one with his right foot into the top corner, and the other one with his left foot into the bottom corner! He was the most talented person I ever met in football. He was gifted, you know, and he made it look so easy. But, yeah, those two were definitely the best goals I've ever seen scored.

H IS FOR HANGING UP THE BOOTS...

What was your deciding factor in retiring as a player?

I think the major reason was just age! I was lucky enough that I got out at the end of it, at probably the right time.

I ruptured a disc in my back and I got back playing after that at junior level, but never at a level that I wanted. But I had a good career, was very happy with it.

I IS FOR IRISH INTERNATIONAL SOCCER TOURNAMENT...

What do you remember about the Derry City, Newcastle United, Celtic, & PSV tournament at Lansdowne Road in 1997?

That was another funny one! Because we went there and nobody gave us a chance! We didn't give ourselves a chance never mind anybody else! And I remember we went up the day before and we played head tennis and had a bit of craic in the hotel. It was like a pre-season thing for us, so the other teams thought we were mad! No preparation for the opponents, nothing! And I'll never forget the Celtic player's faces the following day when we beat them! But then the problem we had was, we all played hard and none of us could move that night and we had to go back in and play Newcastle United the next day! That was really unfortunate. A great game though. But it was like a friendly to us before we got to the ground, but the thing with me is that I don't do friendlies! They're all serious games for me! That was one of the reasons I remember Felix saying to me when I signed, like I said earlier, when it comes to push and shove he needed people to get it over the line, and me and Higgsy were real brawlers, you know. But we had huge talent beside us. Curry was as good a centre half as you'll get, and Pizza was brilliant in the middle of the park, but Higgsy was superb that weekend. He was out on his own! And the funny thing about him, because I remember well, we used to arrive in the Brandywell early, and he'd go down and get a burger and chips and a coke! And I'd be doing lookout to see if Felix was coming! But he'd go out and end up Man of the Match!

He was great, and it's great to see him back at Derry. He just brings that fight with him, you know.

J IS FOR JOKER...

Who was the biggest practical joker you've met in football?

James Keddy was good craic. There was always something going on with him! And he was sort of Felix's pet as well, so he would get away with murder! But, yeah, he was up to up to no good all the time!

K IS FOR KIT...

What has been your favourite football kit that you've ever played in or owned?

I think the one that we won

the league in. The real Candystripes one. It was absolutely lovely. And there was a blue and white version of that as well for away games, like an Argentina kit that was really, really nice as well. And Philip Johnston used to look after them well. The one thing I will always say, and I played for a lot of clubs, but there was never a kit man like Philip. He had everything to a T. He's a great character as well, you know, and he probably doesn't get the recognition he deserves. He was a huge part of when we won the league. He was there and he got everything spot on, and he was so unassuming, you know.

L IS FOR LIFE AFTER PLAYING...

Did you always have a plan for after football? Was management something you always wanted to do?

No. I had no interest in management at all. I fell into it. I never applied for a manager's job at all. I fell into them. I didn't want to do it at Harps only Charlie McGeever left and I was stuck with it! I didn't want to do it at Derry only Dermot Keely left and I was stuck with it! And both times everybody was saying 'look, do it until we get out of it', and that was me for a while then!

I enjoyed being around the players and enjoyed the coaching side of it, but no, management wasn't for me. But I enjoy coaching and I enjoyed that part of the job. I enjoyed the underage coaching more than the senior squads. I really enjoyed that. I've done a lot of that at Sligo. But the management side brings too many problems. Too many headaches. I don't think people realise what's involved in it until you do it. I listen to people who are abusing managers from the stands, but you have no idea what's going on. There could be anything going on that morning before the game. And as human beings, footballers are hard to manage!

M IS FOR MEMENTO...

What is the one football memento you own that you'll never give away?
I suppose I have two of them. I have the FAI Cup winners medal that unfortunately Derry City suffered from! I won it as captain of my home town club, so it's very special. And my league winners medal with Derry. I left Sligo under controversy. I left under the new Bosman ruling at the time and I got an awful lot of stick for it. A lot of people questioned was it a good move for me, and was a good move for Derry and everything else. But I went up there and the first season went really, really well. So, yeah, the two medals are probably most

important.

N IS FOR NIGHT OUT...

Which team mate was usually the first to initiate a night out?
Curny! Without a shadow of a doubt! Curny was planning nights out at half time if we were winning! If we losing, he'd still be planning a night out! That's all he wanted! That was his motivation!

O IS FOR OPPOSITION...

Which opposition did you always look forward to playing the most in your career?
For me personally, Shamrock Rovers was always the big one at the time. There was a huge rivallry between Sligo Rovers and Shamrock Rovers. You always felt that, even though they were in

Dublin, it felt like it was a local derby, so really enjoyed it. I used to enjoy trips to Derry funny enough until I went back as Harps player. I found it kind of difficult to be honest with you, I really did. Because I found the Derry people were so welcoming. It's such a such a smashing place and smashing club. I love going back there.

P IS FOR PASSTIME...

Outside of football, what keeps you occupied now in your spare time?
I enjoy a game of golf. Badly! I do a bit of walking. Things like that, yeah. I'm not too pushed on other stuff, you know.

Q IS FOR QUIZ...

Which former team mate

would you definitely not want in your team if you were doing a quiz?

Gary Beckett! Because even if the answer was right, he'd argue!

R IS FOR RESULT...

Which result stands out or meant the most to you in your career?

A few of them I suppose. I mean, the Cup final win against Derry was huge for me on a personal level. I remember another one as well, the year we won the league, there was a game live on TV. We drew with Shels and I think it ended up 1-1, but I remember I gave away a penalty early on they missed the penalty kick and it was such a relief. But I remember, we knew that if we didn't lose that day we would sort of win the league. It was Gary Beckett that scored for us. That one always sticks out in my head. It was a real turning point for us in the league that year.

S IS FOR SLIGO ROVERS...

You won the FAI Cup with Sligo in 1994 from the First Division, beating Derry City in the final! What are your memories of that game?

I remember it was raining and I was delighted to see the rain! It was it was my job that day to look after Liam Coyle. I suppose I got him on a very bad day for him. He didn't play well at all that day and I played very well, I suppose, because when you keep Liam Coyle quiet, you have to be doing something right! But, look, we rode our luck a few times. I remember, Lord of Mercy on big Crack McKeever, he missed a few chances. Our goalkeeper played well and then going on the balance of play, we got a goal from a set play. And I remember the noise and the colour afterwards, you know, it was so special and like I said, I was captain of my home town club, and my father was chairman of the club, so it was a very, very special day for me as a person and for my family.

Yous won it from the First Division as well didn't yous?

Yeah. We were. We won somewhat of a treble that year. We won the First Division, the FAI Cup and there was a shield as well at that time. So we we'd won the three. But again, we had a very young team. A great bunch of lads. Declan Boyle played alongside me and later played at Derry with me as well. I remember standing in the dressing room looking at the Derry squad and thinking, 'Oh my God, they're all superstars!' Dermot O'Neill in goals, Paul Curran, they had so many good players. Joe Lawless up front with Liam Coyle. They had an unbelievable side.

T IS FOR TALENT...

Who is the best player you've ever played with?

Liam Coyle. Without a shadow of a doubt. He's the best footballer I've ever seen on a pitch and I've been lucky enough that I've played with some great, great players, but nothing would ever touch him.

U IS FOR UNPARALLELED...

Who is the best player you've ever played against?

I've played against a few. I played against DiCanio in that game against Celtic. He was really good. I suppose locally, Stephen Geoghegan was always a good player as well. I mean people talk about modern formations, but Stephen Geoghegan played up the front for Shels for years by himself and scored a lot of goals. He was a really, really good player as well.

V IS FOR VANITY...

Which team mate spent the longest in front of the mirror?

There's a lot there as well! Pizza used to spend a long time in front of the mirror! He definitely did. He'll not thank me for saying that, but it's a fact!

W IS FOR WISHES...

Is there anything you'd change about your career if you could do it all again?

Yeah, well, I probably left Derry too early to be honest with you. I was offered a deal to stay and should have stayed, but I went to Harps instead and I remember I was thinking just that it might get me closer to home. But I should have stayed because I felt that I was still at that level. I went to Harps and had a great season. Got to a Cup Final and everything else and finished third. Their highest ever league finish. But I think there was there was more potential at Derry. I suppose the one regret I would have at Derry was that we won the league and then for one reason or another we nearly got relegated the following season! But I think there was enough in that team that we could have went on to achieve more. I really do, you know.

X IS FOR EXPERIENCE...

What's the best atmosphere you've ever experienced as a player?

I played in Lansdowne Road a couple of times, and it might be a strange one, but the one with the best atmosphere was the day we lost the Cup Final! The same double year when Shels beat us. It was a strange atmosphere because we were sort of Lord have mercy on Tony O'Dowd's brother. He had just passed away and it was very difficult to play football on that occasion. But yeah, I'll never forget it. There was a huge crowd in Dalymount that day and we started well and then we started making a couple of mistakes. But I remember after the game it wasn't like we lost a match. It was like, we still were celebrating the league, if that makes sense. Because we didn't celebrate the league because of the Cup Final coming up. So, yeah, it was great.

Y IS FOR YOUNG...

What's your earliest memory of going to a football match?

I remember my father taking me to the Showgrounds, and I suppose I remember going down and watching Sligo as a kid when they played Shamrock Rovers in 1977 I think it was. And that's the memory that had me hooked on football. Just the noise and everything about it was great.

Z IS FOR ZONE...

Did you ever have any pre-match rituals or superstitions to get you in the zone?

Didn't eat a lot. I used to have a bar of chocolate just. I used to buy a lotto ticket for my wife every game believe it or not. We never won though! And I didn't eat an awful lot. I watch people know eating a load of pasta, but I could never eat. And I had to be first in the dressing room! Mad things like that! I had to be first because I was always find out who was referee was first and have a chat with him! I'd be first in and eat nothing and Higgsy would be down eating a burger and chips! The mentality of footballers, you know!

JAMES KEDDY

SPONSORED BY
KEVIN MCDAID

A IS FOR ANNOYING...
Which of your former team mates was the worst to sit beside on the bus for long away journeys?
Tommy Dunne! He never stopped talking! We used to share a lift up from Dublin. Myself Tommy, Tony O'Dowd and Richie Purdy, but definitely Tommy was the worst!

B IS FOR BEHAVIOUR...
Which of your former team mates was always the most likely to get booked?
Heggsy! There was a few to be fair to him, me included, but I'll go for Paul Hegarty!

C IS FOR CHAMPI-ONS...
What are your biggest memories of that league winning season in 1997?
My biggest memory would be the game that we played against Dundalk. We were two nil down and came back to win 4-2. That was a big game. And I think we could sense it that night that we were going to do something that season, you know. And that was early on. I think it was the middle of the season, but you could kind of sense it after the game that there was a

fair bit of belief that we had something special that year and we could go on to do well in the league if we kept going.

D IS FOR DERRY CITY...
Do you remember the story of how you signing for Derry City came about?
I do! Well, I don't know how it originated. I think Paul Doolin or Tommy Dunne

might have recommended me to Felix, I don't know. But Felix rang me for a chat and when I heard that Derry were interested I kind of had my mind made up. But I did have a choice to make because there was a couple of clubs in Dublin that were sort of half interested and were making enquiries, Shalebourne and Shamrock Rovers, but when Felix showed an interest I think I

89

signed straight away when I met him. I met him in Dublin. Derry were playing Shamrock Rovers and I was playing for UCD at the time and we'd arranged to meet in a hotel in Ballsbridge and I think I signed straight away there and then.

E IS FOR EUROPE...

Which team was your toughest European opponent? At any club.

We played against Rosenburg when I was at Shelbourne in 2001 I think it was and they were very tough at the time. They made it on to the group stages, but they'd been in the groups a few times before that as well in the Champions League. Very, very good players. Very technical and athletic, and very difficult to play against.

F IS FOR FUNNY...

What was the funniest thing you remember from your time in football?

I might have to think about that one!

Well, you were involved in Tommy Dunne's funniest story when you all went for a roast dinner and Richie Purdy dropped Black Forrest Gateaux on himself!

Haha!! Yeah, and I'll tell you, the story was, I think Richie had to come on that day as well because I think Declan Boyle got injured or some-

thing! We kind of knew we weren't on, so we went for a full dinner, and we were all fine on the bench, but Richie was called to go on really early in the game! And he was after eating steak and soup and Black Forest Gateaux! Declan got injured after about 10mins and I was beside Richie when he got the call and and he's looking at me and I just said to him 'Good luck with that Richie!' because, you know, there were less subs in them days, so it was very rare that you'd get brought on. Especially as a full back! But, yeah, Richie was very funny! He went up there another time and you were meant to wear a suit, shirt and club tie to the game, but for what-

ever reason he showed up with an aertex on him, like just a sports top and a really flashy multi-coloured tie and an Umbro jumper! Felix asked him what happened and he said 'I have a bit of a flu, Felix, that's why I wore this', you know! Like that made any sense! But, yeah, Richie was hilarious in fairness to him! He was a great player. He probably didn't get the credit he deserved at the time, but he was exceptional player. I remember as well after the Cup Final that we lost after Tony O'Dowd's brother passed away. We were having a bit of a night out that evening, but Richie's wife was there, and she must have been the full 9 months like! Any day now sort of thing for the baby, and he had a few drinks in him and his missus was giving him the look like 'I'm going to batter the head off you!' She wouldn't be one that was afraid to say it to him either! But he had the tie around his head at this stage! The dinner was only about to start as well!!

G IS FOR GOAL...

What's been the best goal you've seen scored that you were on the pitch for?
I've seen Liam Coyle score some great goals. The day he came on against Home Farm he got a great goal there! He came off the bench, scored two great goals that day and then he went back off! The first goal was exceptional. Actually, another one as just come to mind that I seen him score. I was playing for Shelbourne at the time and we hadn't been beaten in so long. Dermot Keely was the manager and he just said before the

game 'Lads, I've never won up here, so just be careful of Coyler and we should do alright'. And it wasn't even that long into the game when Coyler chipped Steve Williams from about thirty yards! It was an exceptional goal. They beat us 1-0! But, yeah, Liam was just Liam. He was different class.

H IS FOR HANGING UP THE BOOTS...

Did you always have a plan for after football? Was management something you always wanted to do?
It wasn't a plan or anything, but I always kind of fancied myself to have a go at managing because I love football, and I've played under some really, really good managers and I was probably a very quiet fella in the dressing room, but I was a good listener, and I took different stuff in from different managers. I was lucky that nearly all my former managers were ex-internationals

as well. They were a really good pedigree. Felix was probably my best manager that I played with for different reasons though, but I think I took a bit from everyone else as well, and I always said I'd fancy having a go at it because I love football and it would have been a regret not having a go at it. So, at least I can say I had a bash at it. I mean it's up and down at times, but we're going OK at the minute at Wexford. It's a small budget we have, so it's very hard as well. Like, I mean, three players up in Derry would cover my entire wage bill, so that's the difference. But at the same time, you just don't know. Being the underdog, especially in big Cup games can have it's advantages too.

I IS FOR IRISH INTERNA-TIONAL SOCCER TOUR-NAMENT...

What do you remember about the Derry City, Newcastle United, Celtic, & PSV tournament at Lansdowne Road in 1997?
Yeah, well, it was different for me. I got injured in the Celtic game early on. I did my hamstring. But the lads were fantastic. It was a great thing to be involved in at the time but yeah, it was a different time for me. It's mostly my own fault as well. I didn't look after myself that summer as best as I could and I got injured in the first

game.

J IS FOR JOKER...

Who was the biggest practical joker you've met in football?

Tommy and Richie never stopped! I travelled with them all the time, and the two of them was always a good laugh. They were always up to something. Richie probably more than Tommy, but I could say either of them in fairness.

K IS FOR KIT...

What has been your favourite football kit that you've ever played in or owned?

I always liked that gear that we had at Derry the season we won the league. The Le Coq Sportiff jersey. And there was a yellow away shirt as well that was really nice that season. Even their tracksuits were really good as well I remember.

L IS FOR LEAGUE...

You've won the league three times with three clubs, is there one that stands out more than the others?

Yeah, the one at Derry, definitely. It was my first time with a Premier Division club. My first year with Derry as well. We had a fantastic team and everything went well, so it's the one I'm most fond of. I'll always remember that night at the Brandywell. I scored the first goal and Pizza got the second and just, I wouldn't say relief or anything, but just glad that the hard work paid off and we were kind of underestimated by people in Dublin that season. But I think we had the belief internally that we were going to win the league. We were just quietly confident. I think when you look back at the players that we had like Beckett, Tom Mohan Heggsy, Pizza, myself, you know, that's even just across that midfield! We had an exceptional midfield!

Up front then Liam Coyle as a bit special and then you had a few headbangers at the back, you know! Tony was very good in goal as well, so yeah, that team was great to play in and as I say, amazing to win the league in my first season.

M IS FOR MEMENTO...

What is the one football memento you own that you'll never give away?

I don't really have anything at all. My Dad has my league medals. I have them in my head that I won them and that's enough for me. But the medals and that I gave to my Dad. He was kind of more proud that I won the league than I was, you know. They're going to mean more to him I think. I'd say if someone took them off me I wouldn't really mind, but if someone took them off my Dad he'd go mad!

N IS FOR NIGHT OUT...

Which team mate was usually the first to initiate a night out?

Tony O'Dowd I'd say! Tony loves a night out!

O IS FOR OPPOSITION...

Which opposition did you always look forward to playing the most in your career?

I always liked playing against Cork. Yeah, I didn't mind playing down there.

came in late for me after I'd signed with Felix were saying 'you're making a big mistake' and all this. But it justified the move going up and being successful, you know. I was really glad to prove all the doubters wrong.

S IS FOR SETANTA SPORTS CUP...
You won the Setanta Cup twice with Drogheda. Would you like to see the competition return?
Yeah, I think there's a place for it. I think the league in the North is a bit better as well now. More full time teams as well. So I think it would be good if it was organised properly.

T IS FOR TEAM MATES...
Who is the best player you've ever played with?
Liam Coyle! By a country mile. He was just different class, you know. Different than the rest us!

U IS FOR UNPARALLELED...
Who is the best player you've ever played against?
There was a little fella, I can't remember his name, for Rosenburg. He was a little small number eight that played with them that year. I think it was Sorensen. I have his jersey at home actually, I swapped with him, but I think he signed for Dortmund the year after that

I didn't like them because they hated Dubs! They absolutely detested Dublin lads! We would get dogs abuse! So, yeah, I enjoyed going down there.

P IS FOR PASSTIME...
Outside of football, what keeps you occupied now in your spare time?
The dog! I love the little dog I have. A little cockapoo. He keeps me busy! A few walks on the beach does the both of us the world of good!

Q IS FOR QUIZ...
Which former team mate would you definitely not want in your team if you were doing a quiz?

I'd say Richie Purdy wouldn't be much use!

R IS FOR RESULT...
Which result stands out or meant the most to you in your career?
That's a tough one. I think the night we won that league. That was fantastic. As I say, it was my first league as well. First Premier Division anyway. I was after winning the First Division with UCD the year before, and to win the Premier the year after was amazing. And it justified going up to Derry as well. People were saying 'he won't be able for it' and all that. I remember some of the other clubs when they

93

V IS FOR VANITY...

Which team mate spent the longest in front of the mirror?

That's probably Tommy Dunne! Tommy thought he was gorgeous, but he was in bits like!

W IS FOR WISHES...

Is there anything you'd change about your career if you could do it all again?

Yeah, probably that season when I was getting ready for my second year at Derry, I should have looked after myself a bit better. Because I was playing well. I had a really good season the year before, and I think if I'd have looked after myself a bit better I could have done a lot more, and maybe could have gotten a chance to get away to England or somewhere as well. That's a big regret, you know. That second year at Derry we could have

pushed on and improved, me especially I think. I trained the previous summer with a fella one to one during the close season. He was a friend of my dad's and I used to do a lot of off-road mountain biking as well, but I didn't do the same kind of programme the following year and it was a big lesson for me. You can't be working hard all season in training and then just stop working and rest for a few weeks. So, yeah, when I look back that's a bad mistake by myself.

X IS FOR EXPERIENCE...

What's the best atmosphere you've ever experienced as a player?

I've played against Liverpool in Lansdowne Road. I think there was about 30,000 at it. It was a centenary year or something, but there was a fantastic atmosphere at it.

Y IS FOR YOUNG...

What's your earliest memory of going to a football match?

I used to go along with my Dad. He had a team in Dundrum at the time and he always used to bring me down as a kid. Myself and my older brother. So, yeah, just being in the dressing room and getting to see all the lads getting the kit on and going out to play football was magical when you're that age. Getting to be among footballers and getting used to that environment.

Z IS FOR ZONE...

Did you ever have any pre-match rituals or superstitions to get you in the zone?

No, not really. Felix used to try and keep me awake before every match! I was always very relaxed before a game! So no, I was never worried about games and never really got nervous or anything! I kind of find it difficult looking at lads getting nervous because, I mean, and Felix used to say it himself, win lose or draw we're all going to be here after the game! So I never really believed in any of that. But you'd see fellas banging heads with their hands and banging balls against walls and all that I used to think God love that fella because I'd never experienced that! I was always fairly easy going, but that's me!

GARY BECKETT

A IS FOR ANNOYING...

Which of your former team mates was the worst to sit beside on the bus for long away journeys?

I didn't get on the bus until Monaghan! I've thirteen years of team mates to go through here in my head! Let me seem the league winning team, or maybe the 2005 or 2006 squad. The two times that we should have won the frigging league! I'll go Eddie McCallion actually! Just to annoy him!

B IS FOR BEHAVIOUR...

Which of your former team mates was always the most likely to get booked?

Sean Hargan! Easy one there. Hargy loves a tackle!

C IS FOR CHAMPI-ONS...

What are your biggest memories of that league winning season in 1997?

Well, I've seen some of the games over again now a couple of times, because I think there's a couple of videos and things on Facebook and Twitter and stuff like that. But I think the biggest memory would have been the actual clinching of it. Actually, no, now I think back, the biggest memory would have actually been the game before that. I don't think we knew for sure, but we knew something was happening judging by the crowd that Finn Harps had just beaten Shelbourne. So if

we had have won that night against Shamrock Rovers, it was all over. It was 1-1 in the 89th minute and Pizza had a chance with the last kick of the game. There was a great move and he got a great connection and just put it wide. And if that had been scored, that would have been it all over that night with the last kick, and the atmosphere that night was probably, and it may sound strange to say it, but the atmosphere was a wee bit better than the night when we actually won it! Because of the murmurations of the crowd about the score elsewhere and stuff like that with people talking about the Shelbourne score. Both us and the crowd realised

95

that we just need one goal now to win the league. And I'm not joking. If you ever see it, it just goes past that post by inches! And that was to clinch the league there and then that night! I just remember that night standing out that season as well, but obviously the night we beat Pats 2-0 to actually win it was really special too.

D IS FOR DERRY CITY...

Do you remember the story of how you signing for Derry City came about?

Yeah, I signed for Derry in Coleraine's manager's office! We where playing in the Irish News Cup. I was a Coleraine player. I remember being on the bench and the lights went out in the second leg in Coleraine Showgrounds, and Felix walked over in the dark while we were all waiting and told me I'm signing for Derry after the game, and I went 'Right. OK!' And it was as easy as that! They paid £17,000 for me, but yeah, that was it!

E IS FOR EUROPE...

Which team was your toughest European opponent? At any club.

I'll not pick the obvious one because it would be too easy. I'll go Nicosia, because out there the heat was unbelievable. We were only allowed out for 40 minutes during the day because

it was that warm! And we were playing that night, so we didn't want to drain our energy and stuff like that. Coyler was up front that night and in Europe he was on his own. I had to play on the right side of a midfield five. It was 4-5-1 that night, and their friggin left back never stopped! He was overlapping time after time, after time, after time! And then Coyler went off and I had to go up front on my own and play against two full backs and two centre halfs! In that heat! I remember I scored as well and I the first player in 40 years to score away from home in Europe for Derry. But I remember that night that friggin left full back! Jesus Christ, he was like Usain Bolt! That would have been one of the toughest nights so, I'm going to say Nicosia, because even though we were beat 2-1, we should have been beat 5! And then they beat us 3-0 comfort-

ably at home.

F IS FOR FAI CUP...

You played in the game voted the best ever FAI Cup Final, the 4-3 win in 2006, what are your memories of it?

Yeah, and it shouldn't have been voted the best ever, because it was the worst day for the weather! It was awful. It was very hard to play on, very hard to get the ball, but I'd say just the ecstatic nature of the way we won it probably just about toppled the weather. But basically that day was just an unbelievable, weird game. It was more mistakes than anything, all because it was blowing 90mph gales, and the rain was beating down! But it was my testimonial year and I ended with a winners medal, so I didn't care in the end up!

G IS FOR GOAL...

What was the best goal

you've ever scored?

I scored one away to Shamrock Rovers. It was a half volley into the top corner. It was 1996 or '97 I think. And then I sat up on the hoardings by myself, waiting for somebody to come, and then when they came, just a big leap in the air. You'll see it if you go through old footage or whatever and you'll understand why that was one of my best goals.

H IS FOR HAHA...

What was the funniest thing you remember from your time in football?

I can't think! There's a few funny ones. I'm sure the boys have told all the Stephen Kenny stories! Where he bumped his head and all that, and the time he went mad saying 'Do yous think I don't know yous are putting stuff in the middle of the floor!'

Actually, one of the funniest that always sticks out for me was when Derry were playing Finn Harps and Paul Hegarty become the Finn Harps manager. Anyway, Hargy got in a bad mood and he was taking a throw in, but as he threw the ball in he went and knee'd and kicked your boy from Harps on the follow through off his throw in! I've no idea how the ref didn't see it! But I remember Paul Hegarty going absolutely mad, roaring and shouting at Hargy and the ref, and Hargy turning round and shouting 'You didn't mind me doing it when you were with Derry!' I thought that was funny. It's just the way Hargy did it. It was so obvious but the ref just never picked up on it! And Higgsy going mad when four or five months before that, they were both the same team! Higgsy probably taught him how to do it!

I IS FOR IRISH INTERNATIONAL SOCCER TOURNAMENT...

What do you remember about the Derry City, Newcastle United, Celtic, & PSV tournament at Lansdowne Road in 1997?

Yeah, I scored the 1st goal of the tournament against Celtic. I just remember, it was new, it was fantastic and for us to turn around and beat Celtic was unbelievable and to score the first goal as well made it really, really special. So yeah, definitely happy memories of that game, but I didn't enjoy the Newcastle game as much. We never got the ball! We weren't professional footballers. They were so used to and playing two games in two days. They were always going to use their full squad, whereas we if we wanted to compete, we couldn't. We had to start with basically our best 11 twice. I remember being knackered after the Celtic game too. But, yeah, it was a very enjoyable, very good tournament. I remember Ryan Semple said to me, 'Geez, you played well today Bing, but I think Coyler stole your the show at the end there with he winner!' after Ryan Coyle scored. So, I thought, 'Yeah, possibly'. The next day, the papers read... I'll tell you now what it's said. It's framed up on the wall here in the house... It says, 'GAZZA'S ON THE RAZZA' in big black letters! 'Beckett's Goal Terrific For City' and then the first two lines are, 'Gary Beckett upstages Paolo DiCanio'! And I remember, I went straight up to Ryan Semple's room with that newspaper and said 'What were you saying about that yesterday? Somebody stealing my thunder?'! and he just laughed!

J IS FOR JOKER...

Who was the biggest practical joker you've met in football?

Hargy liked messing about! He caught a couple of people! Well, he had to be good at something I suppose!!

K IS FOR KIT...

What has been your favourite football kit that you've ever played in or owned?

There was a couple of crackers, but I'd go for the home league winning jersey. Basically because of what we did in it. There was a nice yellow one that year as well. And remember we had a good Argentina one too, you know, the blue and white striped one. Actually, you know what? I'm going to go with the Argentina type one because my supporters club have went with that jersey as well.

L IS FOR LIFE AFTER PLAYING...

Did you have a plan for after football? Was management something you ever wanted to do?

Yeah, well, I went into the Post Office when I was still playing football, and basically when I was getting near the end of my playing career, my aim was to get a full time job and thankfully I got one at 28 in the Post Office. And it's a decent job. So management and stuff like that never really crossed my mind because I don't think it's safe. I needed something with stability. I had three kids at the time and ended up with four, and I needed something stable. I actually remember Stephen Kenny came to me when I was about 31 I think it was, and he says 'Is there any chance you would leave the Post Office and we'll cover what needs to be covered for you money wise', but I couldn't commit. Mostly because it was probably only going to be a two year contract at 31, and what do I do after those 2 years, you know what I mean? I'd find it tough getting back in to the Post Office again. So I couldn't even take that at that time and thankfully he was OK about it. But, yeah, just to get a job, basically was the plan. Football-wise at the end, it was always my plan to come back and play for my home town team to finish my career. I started Enniskillen Town United, and I finished at Enniskillen Town United. So, football-wise, that was always the plan. And professional-wise it was just to get a stable job and I thankfully achieved both.

M IS FOR MEMENTO...

What is the one football memento you own that you'll never give away?

My league winning jersey is framed here in the house. Yeah, it's not going any-where. I have seven winners medals as well and they are not framed, but they are with the other trophies that I have with Derry and my home team in Enniskillen.

N IS FOR NIGHT OUT...

Which team mate was usually the first to initiate a night out?

Paul Curran! Without a shadow of a doubt!

O IS FOR OPPOSITION...

Which opposition did you always look forward to playing the most in your career?

Finn Harps. I always looked forward to the derby games when I was at Derry.

P IS FOR PASSTIME...

Outside of football, what keeps you occupied now in your spare time?

Not much really! The children are nearly all grown up. I used to play a bit of golf. I still play a lot with the Derry City Legends whenever I can. I used to be into cycling, but since the big 5-0 came and went, all those things became far too hard! So I was to say anything I'd probably say a bit of golf though.

Q IS FOR QUIZ...
Which former team mate would you definitely not want in your team if you were doing a quiz?
Darren Kelly! I probably should have said Eddie! Just to even it up a bit because the two boys used to slag about being in each other's class at school. I don't even think they were! But I'll go Darren Kelly for that one. I'll actually tell you a funny one! We were playing Shamrock Rovers at the RDS in Dublin and Darren was asking about what's usually held there and they were saying about the horses and someone told Darren that you have to get an injection to make sure that if you fall in any horse shit on the field that nothing happens, right? So he believed them and he got up on the physio's table and pulled his shorts down a bit at the back and Kevin Mahon got a biro and hit him in the arse with it! So Darren shouts 'Is that it done?' So Kevin says, aye that's you, and Darren went on out and done the warm up. Anyway, we get back in to the changing rooms and Darren says,

'Kevin, I'm starting to feel that injection now you know!' So Darren Kelly deserves to be said for that one!

R IS FOR RESULT...
Which result stands out or meant the most to you in your career?
That 1-1 away to Shelbourne in 1997. It was a chance for the fat lady sang to sing, so to speak. And she did! The one all draw did it because if they had won on that day, it could have been a wee bit more squeaky bum time, but I remember seeing a sign after the game 'Fat Lady Sings Today'. Plus, I scored the goal as well. I acyually think it was the first League Of Ireland goal to be shown live on TV as well.

S IS FOR SETANTA SPORTS CUP...
Do you remember the story of how you signing for Derry City came about?
They've tried everything for that and can't make it work. I think the League of Ireland would want it more than the north. Simply because it's a stronger league as you can see from the European results most years. But I don't think the Irish League would budge on it. They won't even change to summer football to help the teams in the league do better in Europe, which will allow them to get good money,

let's be honest if they get through a round or two. But I enjoyed it when I was playing in it. Would I like to see it back? Only if it worked. I remember the Linfield games in general though. I know we did get drawn against each other a lot, but they were very atmospheric and I remember the first one that came along, I did an interview for the magazine, Big Issue. And it wasn't a football magazine, so it just showed you how big the occasion was and how people were into it and looking forward to it. As for now, would it have the same impact as it did before? Again, I don't know. I can't see why not considering that the League of Ireland have dropped the League Cup, which is an absolute disgrace as well.

T IS FOR TALENT...
Who is the best player you've ever played with?
Liam Coyle!

U IS FOR UNPARALLELED...
Who is the best player you've ever played against?
I can't turn around and say Ronaldinho and Iniesta and all that! I'll have to stick the league! I'd be interested to read who the other lads said, because I'm thinking hard here on who would stand out.
Who were the two boys that

played for Cork in 2005 at the back? They were good pair... There was an English fella, Alan Bennett, and Dan Murray as well.

Another boy that comes to mind, there was a guy, Shaun Maher. He was tough. He was at Drogheda and went on to play with Bohs. Dan Murray and Alan Bennett were a good partnership. They were they were difficult down there, but at home we had their number. So, I'm going to go with Shaun Maher.

V IS FOR VANITY...

Which team mate spent the longest in front of the mirror?

Darren Kelly probably. In fact, I'll go him or Killian Brennan.

W IS FOR WISHES...

Is there anything you'd change about your career if you could do it all again?

Not really. I would say I would like another go at a couple of games that we got stupid results in in 2005 and 2006. You know, 2006, if we win the league we win the treble! 2005, if we win in Cork, we win the league. You'd like to change them things, but, no, if I could relive the 13 years that I played up there again, I'd start tomorrow.

X IS FOR EXPERIENCE...

What's the best atmosphere you've ever experienced as a player?

The PSG game away was quite unique with their two sets of supporters shouting back at each other. The Celtic Tournament was big. The Barcelona game was a serious atmosphere as well. I'll go with the night we clinched the league though in 1997.

Y IS FOR YOUNG...

What's your earliest memory of going to a football match?

Probably when my father would have brought me to watch his games. He was the manager of Enniskillen Town Reserves. They were my home team, so my earliest memory was always going to watch his team play

and then never I stopped. At the age of whatever, probably five or six. And then I never stopped going to football after that. Even now.

Z IS FOR ZONE...

Did you ever have any prematch rituals or superstitions to get you in the zone?

No, I just always had to wear underwear! I used to have a big panic that I had no underwear with me! I think it just happened just once and it was not a nice experience! It was actually was the time that I was having trouble with the osteitis pubis, which is like a groin injury, and I had to go to stay in Dublin and visit the doctor the next day and I had no spare underwear. I thought it was just a kind of like check-up or consultation, but no! He wanted to inject me! So he asked me to pull my trousers down and I had no underwear on! And the injections were just into the upper thigh, so underwear would have been fine like, I wouldn't have had to take them off anyway, but I ended up having to pull the boyos over to the left and pull them over to the right so they weren't in his way and it was not nice! So, it definitely just proves my point that you should never go to football without extra underwear!!

SEAN HARGAN

SPONSORED BY
FRANCIE MCCAULEY

A IS FOR ANNOYING...
Which of your former team mates was the worst to sit beside on the bus for long away journeys?
Probably Eddie McCallion! Wee Granda!!

B IS FOR BEHAVIOUR...
Which of your former team mates was always the most likely to get booked?
Apart from myself!! Higgsy would have got the odd booking, so I'll say Paul Hegarty.

C IS FOR CHAMPIONS...
What do you remember most about the league winning season in 1997?
Just that it was an unbelievable season mostly! We won the league with such a small squad and probably very little budget. Just the whole atmosphere around the ground with the fans and stuff thinking that it was going to be like that all the time, and we never won another one after it! That was my first year at the club too! It was just unexpected like! And back then we were travelling up and down for games in a Ford Galaxy, which would be unheard of now! And Kevin Mahon driving! Felix used to drive his own car! It's mad now when you think of it and look at teams now and think we won the league and everything seems so amateurish now, but at the time it was normal!

D IS FOR DERRY CITY...
Do you remember the story of how you signing for Derry City came about?
Aye, there was a boy Doc Doherty from Top Of The Hill, and he took me and another boy over when I think Roy Coyle might have been there, but I never stayed, I actually left. But then Bugsy got me involved again and brought me in and I played a few games for the reserves and done well, and then I remember there was a Norwegian Under 21 team that came over to play and I played in that game and then Felix drafted me in to the first team the week after

that. So, I was kind of lucky that everything fell into place for me, you know? Everything just kind of landed at a good time for me, and then that season I was playing up front because Liam broke his elbow, so I was up front and did well. I scored a hat-trick away to Galway and then scored 2 the week after against Cork as well. I don't think I finished top scorer, I think Pizza might have had more that season from midfield, but that was the best thing about that league winning side, there was goals from everywhere, Curny was scoring from centre half, Higgsy and Pizza in midfield, and Coyler and Beckett up front, James Keddy... everyone was kind of just chipping in with goals. But, yeah, I was lucky with the timing, but I knew Liam would be coming back and obviously he was the main man no matter what, and I was only a youngster, so I had to prove myself. I'm lucky too that because I was I wee bit versatile, I could play left or right wing as well. Felix actually played me on the right wing in the cup final in 1997, and I remember I should have scored after about four minutes too, but that's another story! You always remember the stuff you didn't win!

E IS FOR EUROPE...

What are your memories of

the European run that ended in the Parc De Princes?
Oh, just the craic we had and the camaraderie between the boys on the team. It was just an amazing journey we were all on and obviously the results as well. I mean, drawing with Paris St Germain in the Brandywell and to beat Gothenburg away and at home and then the Gretna game was unbelievable as well. And in all three games as well we were kind of brushed off and people thought we had no chance. Even in Gothenburg, there was no press there apart from Richie and Artie! The goal was only captured by somebody on a camera phone or a camcorder or something! It wouldn't have been seen only for that like! Which is crazy considering the amount of press at games now and even the clubs themselves video the games too. But there was just a great buzz about the whole thing for the fans and

everyone still talks about it. It was just great memories for us as well. But, aye, I think it was unexpected to get the results that we did. In fairness though, when we were watching DVDs of them and doing pre-match analysis and stuff, I don't know if Stephen Kenny was playing videos of another team or something, but I remember thinking they're not that great like! He probably picked all the worst matched they'd played in! But it did work and it gave us a bit of confidence that we could actually do it. But, yeah, the European thing was unreal that season but to loss the league at the end of it was just heart breaking.
Did you swap a shirt with anyone in Paris?
I don't think so, no. I've got the Gothenburg one in the house, but I can't remember what happened the PSG one to tell you the truth!

F IS FOR FAI CUP...

You were involved in four FAI Cups. Is there one that stands out over the others?

Aye, the one Stephen Kenny left me out of the squad in! Would have been my last game for Derry! But I'm not one for holding grudges!! Na, obviously the one down in Tolka Park when Liam scored, and the one we won with Stephen Kenny when he came back from Dunfermline. The two we won are the ones I would have most memories about, but aye, I can't forgive Kenzo for leaving me out of the squad on for my last game down at the RDS!

G IS FOR GOAL...

What was the best goal you've ever scored?

Obviously the one in Sweden will be the one people remember, But would probably say... I scored a goal against Finn Harps in the snow at the Brandywell. I hit that one well I remember. That was probably my best one. though. Someone actually showed it to me recently. The match probably should never have went ahead. The pitch was pure white! They just went round the 18 yard box and stuff with a shovel, but they were covered again in minutes! But I just remember Liam ran inside with it and somehow it just broke to me outside the box and I just smashed it and it went in top corner, so

it was a good goal, and obviously against Finn Harps it made it much better!

H IS FOR HAHA...

What was the funniest thing you remember from your time in football?

There's plenty of Stephen Kenny stories! Like the time me and Sammy Morrow were going to a reserve match down in Drogheda or somewhere and we went down on the bus, but Kenny said he would bring us back in the car. But his back wiper was on the whole way! All the way from Drogheda back to Derry! And it wasn't raining! It wasn't even damp! Me and Sammy were looking at each other thinking 'Does he not know?!' He was a brilliant manager, but some of the stuff could be strange! It would leave you scratching your head! I remember as well one time we were playing Finn Harps, and we were doing the pre-match in either Jacksons or Kees. I think it was Kees, but were in there and he was doing a team talk, but the wall came out in a sort of curve, and he was in a whole rant and he turned around fast and walked clean into the wall! Nearly knocked himself out and then Higgsy has to take over! Me and Clive Delaney were sitting right at the front and I nearly fell off the chair!

I IS FOR IRISH INTERNATIONAL SOCCER TOURNAMENT...

What do you remember about the Derry City, Newcastle United, Celtic, & PSV tournament at Lansdowne Road in 1997?

I always remember the match when we were in the tunnel getting ready to go out and Gavin Dykes was roaring and shouting "Let's get stuck into them!" and all sorts of stuff, and your man Jackson that played with Celtic at the time was looking at him like 'this boy here's mental!' Obviously we went out then and beat Celtic and they'd a great squad back then.

I remember then, after the match, we were looking to celebrate, but we played Newcastle the next day in the final! I think Shearer never played, he was injured, but they were a great side as well. We still got a couple of beer after the Celtic match, even though we had a game the next day, but I'm not going to go into it too much because the boy that was along with me in the bar ended up being man of the match the next day! But it was an unreal tournament. I think we ruined it a bit for the organisers too. I think they wanted a Celtic vs Newcastle final, but it was great to play in those games and to get the win over Celt-

103

ic as well.

J IS FOR JOKER...

Who was the biggest practical joker you've met in football?

I would have been up to no good myself most likely! Probably Baz though. Barry Molloy enjoyed a bit of craic in that team back in 2006, he would have been a messer as well! Mark Farren enjoyed a laugh and a prank, even though it was quiet and stuff he enjoyed pulling a few pranks as well.

K IS FOR KIT...

What has been your favourite football kit that you've ever played in or owned?

Probably the Le Coq Sportif one the year we had that. The shirt and the tracksuits and just the gear in general was all nice stuff.

L IS FOR LIFE AFTER PLAYING...

Did you have a plan for after football? Was management something you ever wanted to do?

Yeah, I was doing coaching badges and I was doing fitness stuff, and I kind of thought that would be a good path to go down after the playing career and that's what I've ended up doing, and I'm still at it now. But, I've never really thought about doing anything with the coaching badges. Definitely not management anyway.

There's not enough jobs for the price you have to pay for the UEFA Pro License. You'd need to be managing a top team in Belfast or somewhere to be able to really make the cost of it all worthwhile. Even saying that there's only maybe 3 or 4 jobs that would hire you full time. There's probably more than that now right enough, but back when we were playing there wasn't enough management jobs that were full time enough to make it worth your while. And you would have to give up your full time job to even manage part time, but then there's very little job security in management as well, you could end up giving up a full time job outside of football and ending up with nothing.

M IS FOR MEMENTO...

What is the one football memento you own that you'll never give away?

I've got a few things that I still have. I've got my boots from Gothenburg. I've got my boarding ticket from Sweden. I've got my 3 hat trick balls in the attic. I have my jersey from the match in Sweden as well, so all that kind of stuff, but I have that still on the boots and the boarding pass. I only found that a few weeks ago when I was in the attic for something, it has Gothenburg and my name on it and the date, so that's good to keep. It's mostly just stuff for maybe further down the years for family to look at.

N IS FOR NIGHT OUT...

Which team mate was usually the first to initiate a night out?

Paul Curran!!

O IS FOR OPPOSITION...

Which opposition did you always look forward to playing the most in your career?

I used to love the games with Shels and that whenever Shels were the team to beat. They're back now where they were whenever we were playing, but we used to have great battles back in the day, Derry v Shels. I alwas used to love playing them and the atmosphere at the games, and the whole day around the match, and just kicking the legs out of the two wingers that they had!!

P IS FOR PASSTIME...

Outside of football, what keeps you occupied now in your spare time?

Just family mostly, and cycling. Mountain biking and road cycling.

Q IS FOR QUIZ...

Which former team mate would you definitely not want in your team if you were doing a quiz?

Gary Beckett!!

R IS FOR RESULT...

Which result stands out or meant the most to you in your career?

There's been there's been a few. I was lucky enough that I was involved in a few good teams and we won a few trophies. Sometimes you think about the results when you lost more than the ones that you won, but games like the night we beat Shels in the League Cup with nine men. That was an unreal result. I mind as well scoring the winner away to Cork when we were going for

the league and we won 1-0. And I think I scored a couple away to Finn Harps too to get the winner. It was always good to score against them. And then the Sligo match too in the Irish News Cup Final when we were 4-1 down and came back to win. Higsy scored a wonder goal that night to get the 5th goal. The night at Dundalk when we were 2-0 down at half time and came back to win 4-2. I remember there was a whole fight at half time in the changing rooms! But, yeah, there's been a few that were important and I'd remember well.

S IS FOR SETANTA SPORTS CUP...

What are you memories of the old Setanta Cup tournament? Would you like to see it return?

I don't have a lot of memories of it, to tell you the truth. I remember I got sent off up at Glentoran! But that was Paddy McCourt's fault that wasn't mine! Paddy tried to skin a few boys and wouldn't pass it and then he lost it and didn't get back quick enough, so I ran back and emptied some boy and got sent off and then we lost! But, I don't know if it would be worth bringing back. There's that many matches now. Same as the Irish News Cup Final. It's probably good if you've got a big squad and you want to give a few boys a run out, but I'd say managers now would rather concentrate on the games they have in the cup, league, and Europe.

T IS FOR TALENT...

Who is the best player you've ever played with?

Liam Coyle. Liam's the best I've ever played with. Paddy McCourt would be in there second for his ability as well, but Liam for his skill and his longevity with the injuries he had. He was just unreal.

U IS FOR UNPARALLELED...

Who is the best player you've ever played against?

I don't know. We played against that Barcelona team and things like that, but they were all friendly games, same as the Newcastle match and the Celtic match.

In terms of individual players though I always remember David Ginola. Ginola played for us though, so it's not exactly an opposition player, but he didn't really play for Derry at the same time! I wouldn't have liked him to be playing against me anyway! He played in that select team that we had that played Mick McCarthy's select for the match for Omagh. Ginola was unreal.

V IS FOR VANITY...

Which team mate spent the longest in front of the mirror?

Darren Kelly!!

W IS FOR WISHES...

Is there anything you'd change about your career if you could do it all again?

Probably not. I'd probably just not play as much when I was injured. Now players look after themselves and look after their body better and stuff, whereas back then there wasn't as much of that. We were taking painkillers and getting three matches out of them when we should have been resting. I remember even cutting the cast off my wrist after a week when I broke my wrist. Things like that all come back to haunt you in later life, but at the time you feel grand. But, no, apart from that, nothing really. Just going easier on myself and my body over the years. You look at players now and they can play well into their thirties if they keep themselves right, but back in our day it was just wanting to get out and play no matter what was wrong with you!

X IS FOR EXPERIENCE...

What's the best atmosphere you've ever experienced as a player?

Probably 1997 when we won the league in the Brandywell against St Pats. The atmosphere that night was amazing. I think we still had three games to go after that as well, but after that game we had it won at a canter. I think we had nine points to spare of something, so it was basically over. It was unreal that night though. I remember the whole buzz about the place. Obviously I remember all the Euro-pean nights as well when the Brandywell was sold out and the place was bouncing for the likes of PSG, and I remember people torturing you for tickets and all! The Cup Finals were all great too in fairness. Even the League Cup Finals in the Brandywell, the atmospheres were unreal. But, yeah, I'll say that league game against St Pats in '97. The league was the big one.

Y IS FOR YOUTH...

Where did you start your youth career and did you always play in the same position?

I remember going to see Derry with boys from Top Of The Hill when I was about 10 or 11, walking from Top Of The Hill over to the Brandywell and getting in. They had a place up in the corner. It used to be where the old Hole In The Wall Gang used to stand. The old shed was over there then. But that would always be my first memories of going to see Derry anyway.

Z IS FOR ZONE...

Did you ever have any pre-match rituals or superstitions to get you in the zone?

No, not really, no. I always had to tape my fingers up because I broke my fingers playing. But it wasn't really a superstition or anything. But apart from that, no, nothing really.

THE A-Z OF... EDDIE McCALLION

SPONSORED BY

THE PICKLED DUCK CAFÉ

A IS FOR ANNOYING...

Which of your former team mates was the worst to sit beside on the bus for long away journeys?

That's a tough one! There's been that many journeys! I'd say Hargy said me did he?

He did, yeah!

Aye, I thought he would, cause he was the first person I thought of as well!! Hargy wouldn't leave you alone!

B IS FOR BEHAVIOUR...

Which of your former team mates was always the most likely to get booked?

Probably the same boy again! Hargy!

C IS FOR CAREER...

You played 537 games for Derry City, which is the second highest. Did you ever think when you started you'd reach that record?

No, you don't really sort of tend to think too much about that kind of thing. I think once you get to 100 it's a big occasion, but once you've been there for a long time you sort of stop counting and it's only when you stop playing that you realise how many games it actually was and you kind of look around for other players that have done it and realise how hard it is to get to those sort of numbers for one team. I don't think there's been very many that have played over 500 games, so it's not some-

thing I was thinking about at the time, but it's definitely a good achievement.

D IS FOR DERRY CITY...

Do you remember the story of how you signing for Derry City came about?

I think I had just come back from holidays and Felix rang the house and just asked if I wanted to come in and I walked over from the house and I was probably there about 10 minutes and he offered me a five year deal and I agreed to sign and that was that!

E IS FOR EUROPE...

What are your memories of the European run that ended in the Parc De Princes?

I think the main memory was the feel good factor within the town around that time. There was just such a buzz about the place. The first game, I think people didn't expect us to win, so when we won out there and then back at the Brandywell, that give us an opportunity to sort of show that we were capable of beating these teams. Even the second game then against Gretna was the same thing. I think they were on a great run of form in the league at the time and they were unbeaten in so many games and that and people were thinking that they were going to beat us, certainly in Scotland anyway and once they went one up early on I think those same people were thinking that's it, this'll be 3 or 4. But we won that game comfortably enough in the end up and the atmosphere was unbelievable. Even the PSG game at home, everyone thought the same, we were written off and then we went out and drew with them, and we created chances against them as well with Killian Brennan hitting the bar and then Kevin McHugh was brought down for what should have been a penalty, so I think that kept the whole buzz about the town going. People were thinking, you know, we could get a wee late goal in the away game and win

this! But we held out as long as we could and I think the goals we conceded were probably down to our own fault being set pieces and that. But, yeah, just the fans and the whole feel good factor of it all around that time, you know? Like, I'm from the town and I'm a fan as well and I think any fan would have loved to have been playing in those games just to experience what it was like.

Did you swap a shirt out in Paris?
That was the only shirt I ever swapped I think was out in Paris. I kept the other jerseys.

Whose shirt did you get?
It was a boy Pierre-Alain Frau that was on the left wing that I was marking. It would never have occurred to me to swap a shirt before in my career, but I just thought after that game, because of the prestige of Paris St Ger-

main and that, that it would be a good thing to have.

F IS FOR FAI CUP...

You won the cup 3 times, 2 with Derry and one with Glenavon, is there one that stands out over the others?
Yeah, probably the first one, because me and my brother Thomas were both involved. I think we were one of the first sets of brothers to win it. So with it being my first win and with that, kind of, record or stat I suppose, it was a great day for the family. I remember there was so much went on in that match as well! We had a we had a streaker on! We, had a fire broke out as well! And I remember Ned (David Kelly) flying in for the game and arriving late at the very last minute and was just about on time to be able to play. There was just so much going on in that final. And we weren't fancied at all that

day to win the game. And I remember big Joe Harkin hardly kicked a ball up until then with injuries that season and he played that game. So there was so much going on before it and during it that I think we could easily have been put off our game, but we went on to win it.

G IS FOR GLENAVON...

What was your deciding factor in leaving Derry City in 2008?

Probably just not knowing come the end of the season would I still be there. There were a lot of fans and others saying they didn't want me to leave, but nothing was sorted for me to stay and I still wanted to play. But I got a phone call from Gary Hamilton saying he was keen on signing me and he didn't think age was an issue and even though it was more or less the only offer on the table, I couldn't have hoped for better. I couldn't speak highly enough about the club and how we were treated, and we had Ciaran Martyn there and Mark Farren and there was a lot of boys I'd have known, so I fitted in no bother at all. But, yeah, the club were first class and treated the players well.

H IS FOR HAHA...

What was the funniest thing you remember from your time in football?

I always remember a game at the Brandywell, and this was back when there wasn't a packed stand every week, and you were so close to the stands, but I remember one of the fans shouted 'Hi Hargy! Use your other left foot!' But, yeah, I remember that really well! I was laughing for ages trying to play a match! I think now if someone was to shout something you probably wouldn't hear it, but back then you heard most of it!

I IS FOR IINFLUENCE...

Who would you say was been the biggest influence on your career?

Probably my father really. He wouldn't have said much, but he took us almost everywhere, my brothers as well. But I remember going up and down to Belfast when we were younger and taking you everywhere. But keeping our feet firmly on the ground as well as being a calming influence.

J IS FOR JOKER...

Who was the biggest practical joker you've met in football?

Hargy would definitely be up there, but Mark Farren was a joker as well! Just because of the way he was he was just someone you wouldn't think of that would be up to something! You could always tell when he just had that wee look on his face! People looking in probably wouldn't be thinking that about him because of the way he was, but Mark would have had the tendencies to be a joker! And he enjoyed it as well!

K IS FOR KIT...

What has been your favourite football kit that you've ever played in or owned?

I think it was the Argentina sort of one. The blue and

white away kit. I think we were in the First Division at the time. But, yeah, the Argentina rig was definitely the one I enjoyed wearing.

L IS FOR LIFE AFTER PLAYING...

Did you have a plan for after football? Was management something you ever wanted to do?

No, nothing at all! I don't think too many people tend to look beyond their playing years really. But I was lucky enough that I always worked anyway while I was playing. I would do Football In The Community with Derry City and then working within the Gasyard and then the Derry City Council, so I was lucky that way because as I say, I didn't really have a plan other than that and once you get to a certain age, what do you do?

M IS FOR MEMENTO...

What is the one football memento you own that you'll never give away?

Well... I don't have anything up in the house, or sort of on display or anything. Everything I have will be in a box. It's just medals and jerseys and things like that. It's all there in a box as far as I know. But probably for the girls that I wouldn't want to give anything away, because it's sort of meant for them as well, you know? I have given

some of my jerseys away already though in saying that. I think the only ones I have in the house now are the European games. I don't think I can see myself giving away the European jerseys.

N IS FOR NIGHT OUT...

Which team mate was usually the first to initiate a night out?

That's a hard one because of the different teams I would have played in over the years, but there's still a few I could mention! Well, you have Flynner anyway, Stephen O'Flynn! He enjoyed a night out. And that would have been around the time of the European run when we had a group of young sort of players at the time. But them boys enjoyed a night out. Flynner would be the ringleader though!

O IS FOR OPPOSITION...

Which opposition did you always look forward to playing the most in your career?

Any of the Dublin teams really. The likes of Rovers and Shels. They were always the big games because there was always at least one of the Dublin teams that would be challenging at the top. The likes of Pats as well. Not taking away the likes of playing Cork too. I think at that sort of stage there was a lot of teams you just enjoyed playing.

P IS FOR PASSTIME...

Outside of football, what keeps you occupied now in your spare time?

Running just. I tend to run a bit now. I just got into kind of long distance running when I was finishing up with Glenavon and then got involved with taking people out in groups too. But I think you need some sort of focus whenever you finish playing

in terms of keeping fitness up. You look at a lot of ex-players and when the finish playing they just stop and you see them and, just physically, that their body is still expecting exercise of some sort. Even ex-Premiership players and all. Even mentally as well I think it helps to be doing something.

Q IS FOR QUIZ...

Which former team mate would you definitely not want in your team if you were doing a quiz?

Darren Kelly! He would probably say me as well! Me and Darren were at school together, Primary School and Secondary School, so we know each other quite well, so I'd have to say Darren because I know how smart he really is away from football!

R IS FOR RESULT...

Which result stands out or meant the most to you in

your career?

Probably winning the First Division. Getting Derry promoted back up to the Premier Division at the first attempt. That night down in Monaghan would stand out the most in that. I know we had to lose by 3 or 4 to not win the league, so mathematically we hadn't done it yet, but just the significance of that game and not being able to afford to slip up, that was a big thing.

S IS FOR SETANTA SPORTS CUP...

What are you memories of the old Setanta Cup tournament? Would you like to see it return?

Yeah, definitely. You'd love to see it back, but I know it's sort of harder because the two leagues play at different times of year, and then what suits one league and what suits another. I think if the Irish league went with summer football you might more have an opportunity for it. And I think the fans would enjoy seeing it back as well, you know, especially when you remember the first game we played at Windsor Park and the crowd and the atmosphere. I remember how motivated we were that night as players. I know, we didn't win the game that night, but we should have won the game. And then to lose the final on penalties as well was sort of,

you know, hard to take.

T IS FOR TALENT...

Who is the best player you've ever played with?

It's hard because I've played with so many! You have the likes of Coyler, Pizza, Paddy McCourt, even the likes of Stuarty Gauld as well, and what they've achieved in their careers in the League of Ireland and with other teams as well.

U IS FOR UNPARALLELED...

Who is the best player you've ever played against?

You can mention that many within that Barcelona team! Overmars, Ronaldinho, you know? So that match kind of stands out, and the players that they had like was unreal. For them to bring their first team there to the Brandywell just shows you the character of the club and the big regard that they had for John Hume for making the game happen.

V IS FOR VANITY...

Which team mate spent the longest in front of the mirror?

That's a good one! We had a fella from Liverpool that thought he looked like Beckham! Jamie Hughes!

W IS FOR WISHES...

Is there anything you'd change about your career if

you could do it all again?

Yeah, not to be injured! I picked up a lot of stupid injuries when I was younger and when you look back now you think what might have been if you were injury free, you know? So, I think that would have been the biggest sort of thing that happened that I'd change, just injuries when I was younger.

Did you ever get the chance to go back to England when you were younger?

Well, I went to Newcastle when I finished with Blackburn and did pre-season with them, but then, as I say, injuries got in the way and they basically said medical-wise that they wouldn't recommend full time football at that stage, so that's a hard thing take when you're that young. But in saying that, I enjoyed the career that I had and I couldn't complain like.

X IS FOR EXPERIENCE...

What's the best atmosphere you've ever experienced as a player?

The PSG away game was some experience, and then the Gretna away game too at Fir Park was amazing as well. In the Brandywell, you had the PSG game and the Gothenburg game as well. Linfield at home and away. And the night that Mark scored the hat-trick. I was suspended for that one but I got to watch it from the stands and the atmosphere was electric. But any of them big occasions really the people of Derry always come out and they're always very vocal and get behind the team.

Y IS FOR YOUTH...

Where did you start your youth career and did you always play in the same position?

I started off with Brandy-well Harps, and then after Brandywell Harps I moved then to Oxford. After Oxford then I got he move to Blackburn Rovers. I started off in midfield though with Brandywell Harps, but they put me back into defense and I played center half for a while, but then kind of filled in and right back and left back every so often and that's kind of where I stayed then with Oxford.

And how did the move to Blackburn come about when you were with Oxford?

I was playing for N.Ireland underage and we played Rep Of Ireland down in Dublin and Pat Devlin recommended me to a Blackburn. I was actually over at Norwich training before that Christmas but I come back and then after that I went over to Blackburn and on the last day they offered me a contract to sign.

Z IS FOR ZONE...

Did you ever have any pre-match rituals or superstitions to get you in the zone?

No, not really. You're always sort of focused within the game and sort of making sure that whoever you're playing against doesn't really get the better you. I was always more focused on the job at hand than any pre-match stuff. I'd rather put my focus into the match just.

RUSSELL PAYNE

SPONSORED BY
DERRY CITY
DEVELOPMENT COMMITTEE

A IS FOR ANNOYING...
Which of your former team mates was the worst to sit beside on the bus for long away journeys?
That's a great question! Well, I know Sean Hargan wouldn't shut up!

B IS FOR BEHAVIOUR...
Which of your former team mates was always the most likely to get booked?
I could say Sean Hargan again, well, he was close, but I'd go with Eddie McCallion!

C IS FOR CUP...
Your last game for Derry was a League Cup Final second leg in 2002. We lost on penalties that evening. What do you remember about that

game?
Yeah, that was a tough one! I remember I was really disappointed because I had a really great record on penalty kicks and I don't think I saved any. Maybe I saved one? I didn't save enough anyway, I know that! But I just remember that was such a talented team and we should have left that season with the trophy, you know? That's what I remember most. We had a talented group. Good people, good players, we had all the pieces, you know, but it just wasn't to be unfortunately.
You won Goalkeeper of the Year that year as well.
I did, yeah. That was one of the most enjoyable years

of my whole career. I really loved that Derry team. That was such an amazing Derry team. I really loved that group of guys.

D IS FOR DERRY CITY...
Do you remember the story of how you signing for Derry City came about?
I do, yeah, it was through Joe Bradley. Joe Bradley connected me with the club. I was playing at the time in America for a club that Joe Bradley was the General Manager of, and it was off-season so I needed to go on loan to play somewhere. To be honest, here's the longer story, I was actually with the New York / New Jersey Metro Stars in the MLS. So I

left Joe Bradley's club, I went to the Metro Stars in Major League Soccer, and then when that season ended in Major League Soccer my loan time with them was up. So, I still had a connection with the Bradleys to go back to, and when I went back I spoke to Joe and said, 'Hey, I need a place to go for the for the winter', and they suggested Derry. I didn't know anything about the city or the club, but it sounded like a great opportunity. And, so, that's how it happened. And I was on a plane with two bags and landed in Dublin airport, hopped on a bus to downtown Dublin, hopped on a bus from downtown Dublin to Derry. It was like a 3 ½ hour or 4 hour bus ride! It was miserable! I mean it was cold, it was wet, the bus stunk, the bus station smelled like piss, but I got to the bus station in Derry and Joe Bradley's brother picked me up. I'm sorry, I can't recall his name, but he picked me up. It was probably 4 or 5pm in the afternoon, so it was late and we went straight to the house and they made me a meal and then straight out to training! I went to training at like 6 o'clock that night and I couldn't believe it because, like, in most circumstances you don't travel on a plane overnight and then all day on a bus and then get off and go and train! So figured,

'Alright, I guess this is Ireland! I guess this is how we do it!' I actually remember having a really good training session as well! And I remember that on the training pitch next to the Brandywell there was no lights! There was like two lights out! I couldn't see anything, and they wanted to see if I was any good! I was just was like, 'Where the hell am I? And where the hell is the ball that I'm supposed to stop!' But, yeah, it ended up working out. It was great that a week later I made my debut and played against Manchester United actually. Yeah, my first game with Derry was against Manchester United! It was a friendly game with the likes of Denis Irwin playing and a few others. What a game to start with!

E IS FOR ELVERSBERG...

How did your move then to Germany come about with Elversberg?

Yeah, so the move to Germany came about because I had already been in Germany on trial with a club there, and I had an American teammate that was still there, and he called me asking about, 'Hey, what's your status with Derry now that the season is over?' And that's how the move hap-

pened, because to be honest, it was just a hell of a lot more money, you know. I was enjoying my time with Derry, but you know, as a professional I needed to earn bigger, higher wages and it was a chance to go to a new place and just earn more of a living. Truth be told, I really didn't want to go. I was kind of sad to go, you know what I mean? But at the same time, I kind of had to ask myself 'What's the end game here', you know? So I made that move and it was tough. It was really tough. I had just met my now wife, and so part of my move was based on if she was going to come with me. She did end up coming to Germany with me and then we got married two years later and came back to Ireland. That's how I ended up with Shamrock Rovers.

F IS FOR FOOTBALL FRIENDS...

Are there any of your former team mates that you keep in touch with?

Joe Harkin. Although I haven't talked to him now in… man, it's been over a year now, but Joe Harkin was my best mate from when I was at Derry. I need to reach out to him again, but he and I kept in contact pretty much, every year up until recently when I moved to Chicago. I moved to Chicago three years ago, and it's been a little more distant. But, yeah, he's still my best mate from my Derry time.

G IS FOR GAME...

Which game or result stands out or meant the most to you in your career?

Yeah, when we beat Bohs at Dalymount Park. I think we beat them 3-2 and I saved two penalties against Glen Crowe and then after the game the team were congratulating me and Kevin Mahon, who's a man of few words, I could see him coming over to say something, but he just came over and he just said to me 'Brilliant' and that was it! But I knew he was proud of me. When you're young footballer and you have a manager like Kevin who doesn't say a lot, a pretty tough character

it means a lot, you know. And I remember the players carried me off the field! Because, at that time Bohs had just gone full time with a bunch of the best players in Ireland and a few other guys had just come back from England to sign, so they were a big deal, and a very good team. Bohs and Shelbourne I think were maybe the only full time teams at that time. But, yeah, we went down there and it was a back and forth game of goals and we ended up beating them 3-2 and I remember we had a great travelling crowd that night as well.

But, actually, there's another one. That Bohs was one was one where my performance stood out. But the one that cemented Derry into my heart forever was the one right after 9/11. That's the one I love to talk about. So, right after 9/11 happened, we had a game that Thursday against Rovers in the Brandywell. So, I think it was maybe four or five days after 9/11 occurred, and I was I was still hurting, you know? I could barely train. I remember when 9/11 happened I was at training and I left early really upset. I had to get in touch with loved ones in New York. It was hard. It was hard for a few days to even think about football, you know? But we had a game and sports events weren't

really going on in America at that time. Things were suspended for a few weeks. So it was tough for me to play that game. But the boys all wore black arm bands. Myself and Derek Phillips both had family in America, and the team wore black armbands, and that meant a lot to me and him. I remember I played against one of my best friends, he's still one of my best friends, a guy called Steven Grant who played for Rovers back then, and I made a great save against him late on and we won the game, maybe 1-0 I think. But the Derry fans were cheering and shouting, and there was American flags waving and after the game. It's making me tear up thinking about it! But after the game the way they just stayed and cheered and supported me and Derek was just amazing! Like, I'll be forever in love with that place, because of things like that!

H IS FOR HAHA...

What was the funniest thing you remember from your time in football?

I can't think of anything right now, but something might come to me....

There must be a Roddy Collins story from your time at Rovers?

Oh man, yeah! So, I don't know how funny this is, but I remember he wanted to take my head off one

115

time after a game because I talked back to him on the field after we lost the game! And hey, it was stupid and it was just an emotional reaction, you know. But then we had to go into the locker room, and I'm sitting there and everybody was quiet. He hadn't walked in yet, and the boys were all looking at me like 'You're about to get it!'

I'll tell you, there was another funny one. At Rovers, we actually trained sometimes at the prison! They had football pitches we used to use right beside it. And I don't know why we used them because it wasn't like some kind of prisoner outreach programme where we met the prisoners or anything! So, anyway, we're sitting there training and all of a sudden out of one of the tiny little windows in one of the cells, one of the prisoners shouts, 'Hey, You alright Roddy?!' And he turns in the middle of the field and shouts back to him! 'Alright buddy?!' and he knew his name!! He knew the guy's name!! You know, I mean like, what are the odds?! And Roddy even knew why the guy was in there! I honestly think he could have had something to do with it! But yeah, we were falling about laughing! That was the funniest thing I've ever seen!

I IS FOR IRELAND...

Do you still keep an eye on results of your former teams in the League Of Ireland?
Yeah, of course. I keep an eye on how Derry's doing and how Rovers are doing all the time. It's great to see both teams still doing so well.

J IS FOR JOKER...

Who was the biggest practical joker you've met in football?
I would say the guy who had the best sense of humour honestly was probably Liam Coyle. He was hilarious! He had a seriousness to him around football, but he also had a funny side to him, a casual side and joking side that was so funny. He cracked me up!

K IS FOR KIT...

What has been your favourite football kit that you've ever played in or owned?
In my overall career? I don't know how well this will go down, but Shamrock Rovers gave me an all white kit one year and I still have it! I loved it, yeah. It was really cool. The white socks, white shorts and a white top.

L IS FOR LIFE AFTER PLAYING...

Did you have a plan for after football? Was management something you always wanted to do?
You know, my initial plan after football was that I

was going to go to medical school and then I realised that it really wasn't in my in my heart to go. I studied for it and I got my college degree in biology pre-Med, so I had the qualifications to go to medical school and become a doctor, but it just wasn't in me. My brother is a doctor and he said, 'Hey, man, I love being a doctor, and I can tell you can do it too, but you probably aren't in love with it', and he goes 'What you do love is football, I can tell. So if you want my advice, go after what you love'. So I got into coaching and it's been wonderful ever since. I've been so lucky. I actually leave to go over to Paris now this Sunday to coach in the Olympics. I'm coaching with the U.S. Olympic team.

Yeah? How did that come about?
Yeah, so I coached a University team in America, and so they're West Point. West Point is the university for the U.S. Army. And so I coached there for 10 years and then I moved to Northwestern University, I don't know if you've heard of it, but it's a big famous school in Chicago, IL. So, I'm the head coach here at Northwestern for their men' soccer team. But I've actually been coaching with the U.S. senior team as a goalkeeping coach as well. So, off and on since 2016 I've coached the with the men's senior team

for US soccer. I've done two U20 World Cups as an assistant coach as well, and now I'm doing the U.S. Olympic team. So I've always been involved with international football as well as the University here which is kind of my day-to-day.

M IS FOR MEMENTO...

What is the one football memento you own that you'll never give away?

Good question. I actually don't think there is one. I'm not as sentimental about items like that, you know. I think I would give anything away in football it made my son smile or a young footballer smile. I still have my goalkeeper of the year trophy from the league that year I was with Derry. It's at home in my parents' house. But, yeah, if I really had to part ways with it, I would. But if I was to pick one thing, I'd probably say maybe that. It was pretty cool to get that.

N IS FOR NIGHT OUT...

Which team mate was usually the first to initiate a night out?

Probably Eddie McCallion! I would say he was a good guy for night out. But let me think about the rest of the group for a second... You know, Pizza wasn't bad at that either. He would organise a good night out. I wouldn't say he necessarily was the biggest partier, but he was good for organizing something at the last minute!

O IS FOR OPPOSITION...

Which opposition did you always look forward to playing the most in your career?

Yeah, I would say probably Bohs. I loved those Bohs games. They were already really intense. Whether I was at Derry or Rovers. Shels as well back when they were really good, but I don't know if I enjoyed playing them as

much. It's just that I knew it was going to be tough playing them back in those days.

P IS FOR PASSTIME...

Outside of football, what keeps you occupied now in your spare time?

Oh man, honestly, I'm the typical soccer coach! I don't have spare time! I just coach all the time! But if I'm not coaching, I'm spending time with my kids. I've got two children. I've got a 14 year old and a 10 year old and I've been married for almost 20 years now. And honestly, when I get free time it's spent with my family.

Q IS FOR QUIZ...

Which former team mate would you definitely not want in your team if you were doing a quiz?

I would say maybe Gary Beckett! Gary wasn't the sharpest tool in the shed! He's going to kill me for saying that!

R IS FOR ROVERS...

How did come about that you came back to play in Ireland with Shamrock Rovers?

You know, I wanted to keep playing, but I knew I was nearing the end of my career. So Stephen Grant was with Rovers at the time. He's a good friend of mine, like I told you about earlier, and Liam Buckley was the manager at Rovers back then, and Stephen was in contact to say that Liam was interested in me. He's been telling him that I was available, and that's really how it worked out. But then, they were in administration back then, so they couldn't sign me. So I had to wait for a little while and Roddy Collins took over, so I wasn't sure if the new manager wanted me, but they ended up getting the money right at the club and Roddy got in touch and he signed me.

S IS FOR SAVE...

What sticks out for you as the best save you've ever made?

I'd probably say the save I made against Rovers in that game right after 9/11. I made a save that was going into the top corner at the Brandywell. Either that one or the penalty saves against Glen Crowe at Dalymount. Either one of those.

T IS FOR TEAM MATES...

Who is the best player you've ever played with?

In my whole career? Probably Lothar Matthäus at New York with the Metro Stars

U IS FOR UNPARALLELED...

Who is the best player you've ever played against?

Hristo Stoichkov. When I was with Colorado Rapids we played against Chicago Fire and Stoichkov was up front. I want to say him, because when we played against

Manchester United, they didn't have all their best players out. And then we played Real Madrid at the Brandywell too, but again they had a bunch of their second team guys. So, yeah, I'd say Stoichkov.

V IS FOR VANITY...

Which team mate spent the longest in front of the mirror?

Man, I'm killing Eddie McCallion right now!! But honestly, Eddie I loved the tanning beds!

W IS FOR WISHES...

Is there anything you'd change about your career if you could do it all again?

Oh man, that's a good question! I think everything worked out the way it should have worked out. I have some great memories made from my time in Ireland. I made a lot of friends, I met my wife, you know. And if I was to change anything prior to that period, who knows what would happen? And meeting my wife and going through the time in Ireland with her and in Germany with her and then going back to the U.S. after, you know, I couldn't be happier with where I am right now, so I'm really happy with how everything went in my career. It was just meant to be that way.

X IS FOR EXPERIENCE...

What's the best atmosphere you've ever experienced as a player?

Probably Giants Stadium when I was playing with the Metro Stars. That was that was pretty amazing. In Germany I never played in front of more than 10,000 – 12,000 fans, but MLS was at times close to 25,000 - 30,000 fans.

Y IS FOR YOUNG...

Where did you start your youth career? And were you always a goalkeeper?

No, I didn't start playing in goals until I was about 12 years old! I started my youth career in Maryland right outside of Washington D.C., and then hopped in goals when I was about 12 years old.

Z IS FOR ZONE...

Did you ever have any pre-match rituals or superstitions to get you in the zone?

Back then I did! I actually did have some when I was at Derry. I always had to sit on the right side of the bus, I would put everything on right to left, and I always had to listen to the same song on headphones, which was Outkast's 'Bombs over Baghdad', and I would always drink just half of a Red Bull. I was always afraid if I drank the whole thing I'd fail a caffeine drug test or something!

KEVIN DEERY

SPONSORED BY
BRANDYWELL PRIDE S.C.

A IS FOR ANNOYING...
Which of your former team mates was the worst to sit beside on the bus for long away journeys?
I think I got asked something similar a few years ago, but the older and wiser you get, you try to be more diplomatic with your answers! We'll go for Jamie Hughes back in the day just because we didn't have a whole lot in common!

B IS FOR BEHAVIOUR...
Which of your former team mates was always the most likely to get booked?
Sean Hargan, I'd say. Probably a popular choice is he?!

C IS FOR CUP...

You played in 4 FAI Cup Finals. Is there one that stands out over the others?
Yeah, I played in 4. I won three and lost one. But I'd say the most recent one 2012. For me, it was a big achievement because I had major surgery in my knee and I only managed to get myself back fit about three or four weeks prior to the final, and I was able to get through the game and help the team win the Cup. So it was a great moment for myself, but also for the club to win against a very good Pats team.
I remember in 2006 as well against St Pats it was a great game, but I was played out of position on the right wing to do a job, so that one was

a great game and a great result as well, but wasn't as enjoyable for me, but listen, they're all brilliant memories, all four finals. I thought we were unlucky in the one I lost though when Bohs beat us on penalties in the RDS, but three out of four isn't bad!

D IS FOR DERRY CITY...
Do you remember the story of how you signing for Derry City came about?
It was actually Oxo that made it all happen. I was like playing in Creggan or something and Oxo just approached me and said to come down some night and train with the reserves. So I went down and played a few games with them and I was

only down there for quite a short time and then obviously Kevin Mahon seen me and promoted me up the first team quite quickly. So I wasn't long in the reserves. I think I went down there when I was around 16 or 17 and then all of a sudden I was in the first team and played a few games at right back. And to be honest, I don't mind playing out of position sometimes, especially when you're young because you're learning game from different aspects.

E IS FOR EUROPE...

What are your biggest memories of the European run that ended in the Parc De Princes?

I think everyone has the memories obviously of Fir Park, when we went behind in the game and then we came back really strong and obviously I scored two goals, so that's probably my most fond memory of it all. I think that's what I'm known for now! Doesn't matter how many games you played for Derry before or after that, or how many goals you score or cups you win, it's the two goals you scored against Gretna people always talk to me about!

F IS FOR FRIENDLIES...

You've played some high profile teams in friendlies, Barcelona, etc. Is there one

game or player that stands out from those?

Yeah, the Barcelona one was amazing. It wasn't a great time for the club. Dermot Keely was the manager at the time and it wasn't going well for him. We had a lot in the squad, but I was only on the bench and came on for 20 minutes, so definitely that Barcelona game, and they had some unbelievable players that turned out for them as well.

G IS FOR GOAL...

What was the best goal you've ever scored?

For me anyway I think the one away to Waterford. I remember it came across my body and I hit it from about 45 yards out and cut across it and it went in the top corner. But thankfully I did get quite a few good ones, so probably the occasion of it and all, and with the fans there and the atmosphere, I'd have to mention the ones

against Gretna as well. I'd say the fans would choose them ones! But I have fond memories of lobbing the 'keeper in Tolka Park and then getting taken out at half time, so there's quite a few good memories! But, yeah, they're all good goals when you score them, you enjoy them all, but mine were usually known for being from the outside the box.

H IS FOR HAHA...

What was the funniest thing you remember from your time in football?

I think just that group we had in 2006! There was always a laugh happening! It was just the environment and the whole culture and all. I think people saw a glimpse of it in the DKTV stuff! We just had loads of banter that whole season. When you're playing well it reflets on the mood, and that whole year was special. We were unlucky that year not to win the treble to be honest. But the European run and everything brought so many funny moments. Just obviously great memories.

There's wee stand out stories as well, like Stephen Kenny slipping and falling in Turners Cross and we all had to come to his aid, let's say! But, I think my funniest memories are that group we had in 2006.

I IS FOR IT'S TIME...
How difficult was the decision to end your playing career when you did? What was the deciding factor?

It was really hard for me. Obviously it didn't go the way I wanted at the end. I had micro fractures done on my knee, which is sort of clutching straws as well now when you look back on it. I had already had six surgeries in my left knee, and that one was just one

too many I think in a bid to get back playing again. But then Roddy Collins came in and as I say, it didn't end great for me, which is disappointing after 12 or 13 years at the one club. If a different manager had have come in, then maybe I could have got back playing another few games, but I'm not looking for excuses or anything though. I have no regrets. I was a one club man and then I just thought about coaching and other bits and pieces, but I was realising that it was too painful afterwards! So, no, it was difficult the way it ended for me personally but that's football. It's only a game of football at the end of the day and it does consume your life, but you always have your family so, it's brilliant memories for me, but difficult the way it ended.

J IS FOR JOKER...

Who was the biggest practical joker you've met in football?

Probably had to be Hargy, to be honest! I always enjoyed Hargy's humour. He had a great wit about him, and he's always up to no good! Mark Farren was a wee prankster as well, God rest him, but Hargy would be the main one! And he used to find it so funny as well when it probably wasn't really that funny! Some of the funniest bits were Hargy cracking himself up!

K IS FOR KIT...
What has been your favourite football kit that you've ever played in or owned?

The one I really liked was the yellow one that we had. The year doesn't come to mind, but I remember we promoted a lot of young players that year so it might have been in the First Division that year. The red and white ones can be fairly similar, so I'd say most of your answers will be the away ones!

L IS FOR LEAGUE...
What do you remember most about that league winning season in 1997?

Yeah, football is for me. It's something I'm really passionate about and I knew I wanted to stay in the game, but I didn't really have a plan. Obviously when you into coaching and manage-

ment, there's a lot more politics than just showing up and giving it your best like when you're a player. But, yeah, I love football, and I love watching hungry, young players striving to improve themselves and giving them their chance and watching them with that desire to go out and win. And we try to create that environment where we're at now, but we allow for mistakes and all that, so it's brilliant watching improving young players competing and coaching them on.

M IS FOR MEMENTO...

What is the one football memento you own that you'll never give away?
Well, my Ma has them all! All the winners medals there's five League Cups, three FAI Cups and the First Division winners medal. She has my European shirt from Paris in 2006 framed as well along with my boots. It's not a medal, but it's something to mark a massive achievement. A friend of mine has, I think it was actually the Gretna jersey, framed as well. So there's a few things I still have!

N IS FOR NIGHT OUT...

Which team mate was usually the first to initiate a night out?
Take your pick! Can I just list everyone?! Killian Brennan,

Brian Cash, Paddy McCourt, Stephen O'Flynn, Ruaidhri Higgins... Kevin Deery! Just that core group, just pick one from that and the rest will follow!

O IS FOR OPPOSITION...

Which opposition did you always look forward to playing the most in your career?
I think once Shamrock Rovers went to Tallaght they had a brilliant record down there and they started challenging for leagues under Michael O'Neill. I could have signed for Shamrock Rovers, as I'm sure everyone knows, but I chose to stay with Derry. But, yeah, Rovers at Tallaght were the games I always looked forward to.

P IS FOR PASSTIME...

Outside of football, what keeps you occupied now in your spare time?
Working mostly! I've gone into a bit of family support

work and I'm hoping to pursue a career in that. It's mostly about helping people and it's something I enjoy and I'm trying to make a career on it. So, that's what I do away from football now.

Q IS FOR QUIZ...

Which former team mate would you definitely not want in your team if you were doing a quiz?
Brian Cash! Actually, I take that back! Put me down for Darren Kelly! I'll bet you Darren even names himself when you interview him! Him and Eddie used to share a joke that they were in the smart class at school together! Neither the two of them would be in my quiz team anyway!

R IS FOR RESULT...

Which result stands out or meant the most to you in your career?
I would say probably that game I spoke about in the Aviva, because of the cir-

cumstances I found myself in getting back from injury. It was a big push for me and something that I targeted and achieved. People were writing us off all year and I think we finished 3rd or 4th or something, but I think for me personally, it was a great result to come back from where I was coming from with the injury.

S IS FOR SETANTA SPORTS CUP...

As manager of an Irish League club, would you like to see the competition return? What are your memories of playing in it?

I would like to see like a couple of cross-border things. I know we're only in the championship so we'd be unlikely to play in it, but some sort of thing involving the Premier Division teams from both leagues, just to test the top four again. Because I think there's a demand from fans as well. They enjoy them games so I definitely think there should be somebody investing in it. The top four in each country but. I think if you asked Institute to go to Turners Cross to play a game, I don't think that would work!! Our resources being in the Championship wouldn't be there for taking the whole team away and hotels and everything! But something like the top four in the Irish

League Premier Division and League Of Ireland Premier Division.

We always enjoyed the games as players anyway, and I know the fans enjoyed them, but people have to conduct themselves properly. It's alright having rivalries and everything, but you have to handle yourself properly when these games are presented and you'd have to assure everyone that they're going to pass without all the nonsense.

T IS FOR TEAM MATES...

Who is the best player you've ever played with?

It's a difficult one like because you had so many different types. Like, you have Mark Farren as an unbelievable goal scorer, but even when you look right through that team, you had big Fordey in nets and what a career he had. What a career James McClean had

too. You had Paddy McCourt who could win you a game from nowhere. You had Liam Coyle as well.

I'd be torn between... for what he did for Derry I'd probably say Liam. Liam's probably the best in terms of what he gave to Derry City, but then obviously, the career that Fordey, James and Paddy had, but then Mark as well like. It's tough to pick just one. I think I've kind of answered that one anyway without giving you an answer!!

U IS FOR UNPARAL-LELED...

Who is the best player you've ever played against?

Difficult one. Really difficult question actually. I'll tell you who I really didn't like playing against, and I don't mind going on record on it, was Colin Healy when he was playing for Cork. I always felt as if I held my own though in

123

most games against all the good players throughout my career, but I always had a really difficult game when I was going up against Colin Healy. Just his strength. You couldn't get the ball off him. So I would say him.

V IS FOR VANITY...

Which team mate spent the longest in front of the mirror?

Definitely Darren Kelly! Wee Eddie was always spending a lot of time in front of the mirror, but he was putting his contacts in! So, Darren and Eddie, but Eddie for different reasons.

W IS FOR WISHES...

Is there anything you'd change about your career if you could do it all again?

No, not with Derry City, definitely not. Obviously I have the regret of going down to Turners Cross on the last game of the season and not being able to get a point

to win the league! That's a regret that's going to live with you! So that's the only one for me really. I've shared that scenario with some of the teams I've coached that that regret is still there that we didn't win that league. And on the management side, the three times I've managed Institute we've got into the playoffs twice and obviously this year was the same again, and I share that story of just missing out with them. But definitely the regret is not getting it over the line to win the league.

X IS FOR EXPERIENCE...

What's the best atmosphere you've ever experienced as a player?

I would say probably the Parc De Princes. It would be a different ball game going there now to play them! Obviously there was a few empty seats, but the noise of the ultras from PSG and then our own fans sitting

up in the top tier was incredible. It was definitely a memorable one!

Y IS FOR YOUNG...

What's your earliest memory of going to a football match?

The one for me that stands out was that time David Ginola came to the Brandywell. I remember everybody rammed into the place and the performance he put on that night definitely lives in my memory. I think we were all in awe at how good he was. But I think just going to the Brandywell in general, or getting to go over to Old Trafford for games as well.

Z IS FOR ZONE...

Did you ever have any pre-match rituals or superstitions to get you in the zone?

Not really. I don't think so. Some of the other boys might be able to tell you if they noticed me doing anything, but I don't have any that stand out in my mind. We were big into, back then, we'd have to get the sugar grip, it was like tight bandages around the shin pads. But I think that was a common thing rather than a superstition or anything. I think for me it was more, sort of, just get yourself in the zone in your head, because my mindset was just about going out to win. That's all I ever tried to do!

DAVID FORDE

SPONSORED BY
DERRY NICE THINGS
derrynicethings.com

A IS FOR ANNOYING...

Which of your former team mates was the worst to sit beside on the bus for long away journeys?

Clive Delaney! He took up about 4 seats!

B IS FOR BEHAVIOUR...

Which of your former team mates was always the most likely to get booked?

Barry Molly! If not me as well!

C IS FOR CUP...

You played in the game voted the best ever FAI Cup Final, the 4-3 win in 2006, what are your memories of it?

I remember that it shouldn't have been played! That's

the main memory! It was blowing a gale that day! But it was a great game and a great spectacle for the fans, and as you say, it was voted the best final, so people seemed to have enjoyed it!

D IS FOR DERRY CITY...

Do you remember the story of how you signing for Derry City came about?

I do, yeah. I was just moving back from England to Galway and had been out of football a while. I was playing with West Ham and then had spells at Oldham and then Barrow and I got released and I remember I was actually going to just leave football behind me and go back to NUIG in Galway to

study as a mature student when I got a call from Derry City. I'd been on loan before so I knew the setup and I thought, sure why not and it worked out for the best thankfully.

E IS FOR EUROPE...

What are your memories of the European run that ended in the Parc De Princes?

Yeah, I remember the games leading up to it were amazing! The result out in Gothenburg, and atmosphere in Gretna, and the atmosphere in the Brandywell as well when we brought these teams back. The game at home to Paris St Germain was amazing and we were very unlucky to be fair to us.

125

Even in Paris I thought we played really well. I have a vivid memory of just walking out through the tunnel and looking up to my left and the Derry fans were all penned in to one corner and the noise levels were unreal from them! And that was just the warm-up!

F IS FOR FUNNY...

What was the funniest thing you remember from your time in football?

There's been a few moments I could mention. Especially with that Derry City team when I was there. I can't think of one specific that stands out as the funniest though, but I'm glad to have had too many laughs to pick just one!

G IS FOR GOALKEEPER...

Did you always play as a goalkeeper? If so, why?

I was always a goalkeeper, yeah. I loved it. My brother was a goalkeeper as well. I just loved it when I was young jumping about the place and diving and then when I got to playing with teams I loved facing a striker one on one and trying to stop him. I was a Liverpool fan as well, so I loved Bruce Grobbelaar growing up.

H IS FOR HERO...

You might have just answered it there, but who was your footballing or sporting hero growing up?

Yeah, Bruce was one. I always loved watching David James as well as a Liverpool fan. Outside of football, the likes of Michael Jordan and Joe Montana were legends of their sports, too many Galway hurlers to mention were heroes as well. I had a few to be fair!

I IS FOR INTERNATIONAL...

What do you remember about getting your first International call-up?

Yeah, I was playing with Millwall and there was a game that Alan Kelly came over to watch. I think I had kept something like 15 or 16 clean sheets in a row at that stage in the Championship and it obviously drew a bit of attention. You always grow up hoping to play for Ireland, but I never thought it was a possibility really. I got a call then from the Ireland camp and I went into a few training sessions and found myself in the office with Alan Kelly, Giovanni Trapattoni and Marco Tardelli and it started to get a bit real then!

J IS FOR JOKER...

Who was the biggest practical joker you've met in football?

Let me see, Kevin Deery enjoyed a joke, Paddy McCourt was always messing around, you couldn't take your eye off Stephen O'Flynn... to be honest, that whole team! We had a great group and everyone got on very well, so we were always laughing a joking.

K IS FOR KENNY...

Some guys have good Stephen Kenny stories, have you got any funny ones?

Yeah, there's a few! I'll try to think of one maybe you haven't heard... Have you heard the one about the back window in the car? We were standing over outside the Long Tower Youth Club just before training one morning and Stephen drove in and stopped to chat, but he pressed the wrong button for the window and put the back one down instead by accident. So instead of putting the front window down, he reached under his seat and moved the drivers seat all the way back and reclined it so he could talk out the back window!! He just kept talking and acted like it was a normal thing to do as well! The boys didn't want to laugh, so stood chatting to him and then he pulled the seat forward again and drove off to park, still reclined! The boys were left looking at each other and eventually had a laugh about it!!

L IS FOR LIFE AFTER PLAYING...

Did you have a plan for after your playing career ended? Was management something you ever wanted to do?

I was never into coaching or anything. I did a bit of it alright, and people would always tell me I had the right attitude for management and that, but I was always a bit softer than all that. I was more into the mind and sports psychology and that, so I studied that and I'm glad to be still involved in that field now.

M IS FOR MEMENTO...

What is the one football memento you own that you'll never give away?

There is something that comes to mind, but I'll have to tell you a story about, because it's not really a football memento. I had left Derry a few years, but I came back for Paddy McCourt's wedding one time with my wife. Anyway, after the wedding we spent a bit of time around the town just and I called in to Badger's to visit Badger. So we were chatting away and it was great to see him after so long and we had a bite to eat and he said to me, hold on there, I have something of yours. So he disappeared off upstairs and came back down with a box and said 'that's yours, you left it behind. Open it'. It was a small enough box, but it had my child's first tooth in it. It just meant a lot to me that he'd looked after it for years where maybe anyone else would have thrown it away. But football related items, I have all my shirts that I played in, I have my medals, my caps and things like that, but would I give them away? I don't know, maybe. I mean, my kids will have them some day if that counts.

N IS FOR NIGHT OUT...

Which team mate was usually the first to initiate a

night out?
Stephen O'Flynn loved a night out! I'd have to say Stephen for that one!

O IS FOR OPPOSITION...

Which opposition did you always look forward to playing the most in your career?
I always liked the big games, so the tougher oppositions. I liked as well if an opposition had a good striker. I liked to test myself against them and try to keep them out.

P IS FOR PASSTIME...

Outside of football, what keeps you occupied now in your spare time?
Travel mostly. I travel to places and learn new mindfulness techniques and things like that. I've been to South America, India, Scan-

dinavia, and a few others.

Q IS FOR QUIZ...

Which former team mate would you definitely not want in your team if you were doing a quiz?
Darren Kelly! Unless it was about heading the ball!

R IS FOR RESULT...

Which result stands out or meant the most to you in your career?
Probably that FAI Cup win in 2006. I'd grown up watching League Of Ireland football and the FAI Cup was always a big deal, so then to be playing in the final and winning it, under the conditions that we did as I mentioned before, it was a special result for me. Especially as I kind of knew it was to be my last game in the League Of Ireland without having made

any announcements or anything, but I knew I was speaking to Cardiff since the end of the league season.

S IS FOR SAVE...

What sticks out for you as the best save you've ever made?
That's a good question! I've never really been asked that before. I remember one from Thomas Müller one time. It was an away match and he cut inside on the edge of the D and shaped to shoot, but the natural shot from that angle would have been to strike to his right hand side, my left, which I was ready for, but he went opposite and hit it to the near post, his left, my right, which might have wrong footed me, but I made it across and got finger tips to it. At the time you just think it's another save, but it's only after when people talked to me about how good that save was and you hear pundits on about it and everything that I seen it back and I was impressed myself!!

T IS FOR TALENT...

Who is the best player you've ever played with?
To be honest, I know I've played with some great players, but to me Paddy McCourt was next level. What he could do with a ball was scary! I mean he had a great career and made it to Scotland and England and

that, but it's just such a pity that he didn't go on to more, because to me he could and should have played at a much higher level.

U IS FOR UNPARAL-LELED...

Who is the best player you've ever played against?
Maybe Cristiano Ronaldo. Ireland vs Portugal. It was in New York in the Giant's Stadium during one of those pre-season type tours.

V IS FOR VANITY...

Which team mate spent the longest in front of the mirror?
I'll pick out a Galway man and say Alan Murphy for that one!

W IS FOR WISHES...

Is there anything you'd change about your career if you could do it all again?
That's a tough one, maybe I don't think I'd change anything in terms of where I played or that because I enjoyed every one of them, but if I could change one thing it would be to get more help in terms of mindfulness and mental health and that. I think every young player should be helped out with that because as I was saying, I nearly quit football completely. My head was just gone that I wasn't good enough or whatever, but thankfully I didn't give up on my dreams and it just shows what you can achieve when you get your head right. Even after playing as well as a lot of footballers will tell you, you need a bit

of support.

X IS FOR EXPERIENCE...

What's the best atmosphere you've ever experienced as a player?
There's been a few. There was a few with Derry City, the European games in Gretna and Paris. I'd say the 2010 Playoffs Final with Millwall at Wembley would be well up there though. Most home games at The Den are loud, but this one was unreal.

Y IS FOR YOUNG...

What is your earliest memory of going to a football match?
We would always go to Terryland Park on a Sunday, me and my brothers and dad. It's now Eamon Deacy Park. It was the old days of League of Ireland football as well, so it was a shed basically, but to us it was like walking into Wembley Stadium! The league has changed now of course and facilities are much better around the grounds, but they were the days! Stand wherever you can see!

Z IS FOR ZONE...

Did you ever have any pre-match rituals or superstitions to get you in the zone?
Too many! To name one... I always have same breakfast. Three toast, two with marmalade, scrambled eggs, etc.

LOCAL, NATIONAL & INTERNATIONAL
REMOVALS & STORAGE

HOME & OFFICE
Door-To-Door
Moving Service

PACKING SERVICE
As well as box
and tape sales

SECURE STORAGE
Long & Short Term
Storage Solutions

INTERNATIONAL
Ireland, N.Ireland,
UK, & Europe

Foyle International Removals & Storage Ltd
Unit 19A Campsie Real Estate
BT47 3XX

T: 02871813623 | M: 07720075629 / 07711213750
W: www.foyledeliveryservice.com

THE A-Z OF... GARETH MCGLYNN

SPONSORED BY
FOYLE REMOVALS & STORAGE

A IS FOR ANNOYING...

Which of your former team mates was the worst to sit beside on the bus for long away journeys?

Let me see… that would probably be… Big Fordey! David Forde!

B IS FOR BOHEMIANS...

How did your year at Bohemians come about in 2010 with Ruaidhri and Stephen Gray?

Yeah, so basically, obviously the whole thing happened with Derry in 2010 and it was unfortunate, but they hadn't paid us in ages. They went the 1st Division and everyone was released, and then I knew that Stephen Grey was speaking to Bohemians, he was the first one to go there. So, he made the move, then Ruaidhri Higgins made the move. We were chatting to Bohs at the same time, but I held out for a while to see my options and that, and then I heard that Rafael Cretaro had signed with them, and they were building an impressive side, so I made the move then and I moved into the same house. The three of us lived in the same house, me, Higgins and Raff. But it was a good experience at the time. I mean, I went there to win the league obviously, and we lost it on the third last game of the season. We had Galway away and they had a lot of injuries, so it was like playing against an U18s team and we were beat 3-2. I know people talk about that Cork game down in Cork and how close we were, but for me that was probably my worst experience ever because all we had to do to secure the league was beat Dundalk at home and an U18 Galway team away and we couldn't get it done.

C IS FOR CAUTION...

Which team mate was al-

131

ways the most likely to get booked?

Eamon Doherty! Him and Hargy or Eddie would have been the three!

D IS FOR DERRY CITY...

Do you remember the story of how you signing for Derry City came about?

Yeah, so it was basically a Cup Final in the Brandywell. It was Tri-Star vs Trojans and Oxo McLaughlin came down to watch it. I was with Tristar at the time. Trojans beat us, like, 5-1 and our heads were down, but then Oxo come in to our changing room after the full time whistle and invited me and two others to train with the reserves and that's how it all kind of started. And then the actual signing and getting into the first team all happened when Badger came down and watched a reserves game down in the Complex and then he invited me up into the first team then. But signing for Derry originally was through Oxo.

E IS FOR EUROPE...

What are your memories of the European run that ended in the Parc De Princes?

The biggest memory has got to be Gothenburg away. I think just the size of Gothenburg as a club and I'd never been to Sweden before going there for the game. I just think that was the biggest result of that

run, winning 1-0 away to Gothenburg I think was just unbelievable. Like, Gretna, in all honesty, you know, they weren't a great side. I mean, we obviously played well and they played poorly and we got an unbelievable result. But I think the Gothenburg one surprised us all and gave us that confidence, you know, to think 'Jeez, it's no odds who we draw now, they were the toughest possible draw and we beat them twice'. I didn't get to play in the Parc De Princes, I was on the bench, but that was a great experience even just being part of the squad that day.

F IS FOR FUNNY...

What was the funniest thing you remember from your time in football?

There's a lot of funny things going through my head, but I'm trying to keep it PC!! There's loads of Stephen

Kenny moments! You've probably got a few of them already? The back window wiper, the time down in Cork that he fell in the showers at half time and couldn't come out for the second half... there's loads! But the funniest one I think was him trying to do a team talk in the dark down at Finn Harps. Whatever happened anyway the light bulb didn't come on, so he powered through it and did an entire team talk in the pitch black!!

G IS FOR GOAL...

What was the best goal you've ever scored?

Probably one of my first goals at the Brandywell, I chipped the keeper, the Shamrock Rovers keeper from just inside my own half. I was only 17 at the time and it kind of set me up for the fans to start warming to me as a youngster coming through. It was the most enjoyable goal anyway, but it was still a good finish. The best goals can be different. The most important goal can be different as well. But I enjoyed that one.

H IS FOR HERO...

You might have just answered it there, but who was your footballing or sporting hero growing up?

Believe it or not, it would have been Gerrard or Jamie Redknapp. And then I think everyone in the world enjoyed watching Ronaldo. The original one! Ronaldo the phenomenal! The one and only!

I IS FOR LEAGUE OF IRELAND XI...

What do you remember about your game with the League Of Ireland XI?

Yeah, I played for the League Of Ireland XI against Celtic at the Aviva. It was unbelievable! Apart from getting injured when Wanyama did my knee and put me out for six weeks! Paddy McCourt was playing in that team, and I remember him taking it past me in the middle of the park. But, I mean, the Aviva itself was phenomenal. It was brand new. And it's funny obviously getting injured after about 40 minutes, I got then to see the medical facilities in around the back of the stadium and it just blew me away! It was almost like walking into a private hospital it was that brand new and the equipment they had!

J IS FOR JOKER...

Who was the biggest practical joker you've met in football?

Let me see... Darren Mc-Cready! Darren McCready had a bit of a dry wit humour which was very funny!

K IS FOR KIT...

What has been your favourite football kit that you've ever played in or owned?

I would have to be the Liverpool Candy one I had when I was younger!

L IS FOR LIFE AFTER PLAYING...

Did you have a plan for after your playing career ended? Was management something you ever wanted to do?

Never! I've got more brains than getting into that world! You see it all the time with managers getting sacked and left with nothing. It's a crazy, crazy, world the football management game. And people don't understand the amount of hours and stress and pressure that these boys are under. I mean, you just couldn't pay me enough now! I always wanted to get back involved in football in some way. And I will someday. But It'll not be at management level! But in terms of away from football, basically I always had a degree, but I never really had a career. I only found a career from it when I went to Perth in Australia and I was able then to fall into recruitment which is what I'm doing now.

M IS FOR MEMENTO...

What is the one football memento you own that you'll never give away?

I'm not sure you know. Nothing physical anyway. I have bits and pieces, but nothing that's over the mantlepiece or anything! Probably just memories. They're always going to be with me I suppose. Memories of the great days we had and the great teams we had.

N IS FOR NIGHT OUT...

Which team mate was usually the first to initiate a night out?

Would have to be... Barry Molloy I would say!

O IS FOR OPPOSITION...

Which opposition did you always look forward to playing the most in your career?

Finn Harps! I loved the derby days!

P IS FOR PASSTIME...

Outside of football, what keeps you occupied now in your spare time?

My own business that I have, and kids! That's basically my life in a nutshell as well as football!

Q IS FOR QUIZ...
Which former team mate would you definitely not want in your team if you were doing a quiz?
Eddie McCallion is one of these simplest people I've ever met!

R IS FOR RESULT...
Which result stands out or meant the most to you in your career?
For Derry, I would say... I'm trying to think which was the most important result for us... Ones stand out to me for all the wrong reasons! I thought the defeat to Bohs in 2009 in the Cup, I always find that hard to forget, down at the RDS, which I thought was a great setting for the final. We obviously got beat on penalties but it was a great match, and a great spectacle. Two of the best teams, around at the time. I mean, I can't remember a time when the two teams were as strong in the league, you know?

S IS FOR STATES...
How did you come to play football in Australia and America?
Basically went to Australia after 2011 or 2012 season. But I just wanted to travel. I wanted to play in a different country, and wanted to experience a different culture and I was just travelling at the time and got work playing football. But I'll tell you what, I played with some great players out there! Jason Gavin ex-League of Ireland, Andy Todd ex-Premier League player, I had a great time out there playing. And New York was just class! And a decent standard as well! I know we've had a few American players in the league and have done really well, and a lot of League Of Ireland players have ended up over there as well, so it's a similar standard in the leagues I was in.

T IS FOR TALENT...
Who is the best player you've ever played with?
Liam Coyle

U IS FOR UNPARALLELED...
Who is the best player

you've ever played against?
Ronaldinho or Xavi at the Brandywell

V IS FOR VANITY...
Which team mate spent the longest in front of the mirror?
Eddie McCallion!

W IS FOR WISHES...
Is there anything you'd change about your career if you could do it all again?
I don't think so you know. Na, I wouldn't change a thing!

X IS FOR EXPERIENCE...
What's the best atmosphere you've ever experienced as a player?
I think you'll find it hard pressed to beat the atmosphere at that Gretna away game in Fir Park

Y IS FOR YOUTH...
Where did you start your youth career and did you always play in the same position?
I started at Tri-Star, but I think I've played everywhere bar nets!

Z IS FOR ZONE...
Did you ever have any pre-match rituals or superstitions to get you in the zone?
I try to always put my right foot on the pitch first, but it's not a hard rule. I'm not a superstitious person at all really.

CLIVE DELANEY

SPONSORED BY

A IS FOR AUSTRALIA...

You live in Australia now, how did you come to the decision to move there?

I travelled to Sydney for a holiday in 2008 as my brother and a few of my friends were living there. And then as my time at Derry City came to an end in 2009, I was looking to get back into work and Sydney was a great option.

B IS FOR BUS...

Which former team mate was the worst to sit beside on the bus for long away journeys?

I needed two seats for leg room so didn't sit beside anyone! I dodged that one!

C IS FOR CUP...

What do you remember about the FAI Cup Final win in 2006? You scored in that game as well.

I remember the wind. Crazy conditions and it led to an entertaining game. I was happy to contribute and the lads deserved the trophy after a long season. The feeling of happiness, support, and celebrations after the game stand out for me too. From the pitch, to the stands, back in the hotel, on the bus back to the city, in the Guildhall, on the stage outside the Guildhall, it went on for days! But they were good times!

D IS FOR DERRY...

Outside of the club, what memories do you have of the city?

I loved the city and the pride the people have for their city. That pride is something that stuck out to me. I lived in Derry for four years, met my wife in Derry, travel to Derry every time we visit from ireland and it remains a part of my children's DNA.

E IS FOR ERA...

Money included, would you prefer to have played when you did, or in modern football?

I would have to say 'when I did'. There are so many reasons why, though I'll keep it simple and say I feel blessed to meet the people I met through football at the time.

F IS FOR FUNNY...

What was the funniest thing you remember from your time in football?

The dressing room environment is the funniest place on the planet. Some of the characters and stories from my playing days still make me laugh out loud today!

G IS FOR GOAL...

What was the best goal you've ever scored?

The two goals that live in my memory are one for Ireland in the European championships (U18) in Sweden and the one for Derry in FAI cup final. Neither were great goals, but they were both unforgettable for me.

H IS FOR HOT HEAD...

Which team mate was always the most likely to get booked?

Probably me! At Derry, I would say Kevin Deery played on the edge. Not dirty, though an incredible competitor and I loved him as a player.

I IS FOR INFLUENCE...

Who would you say was been the biggest influ-

ence on your career?

My parents applied for a soccer scholarship in UCD to get the ball rolling, kept me honest, came to most domestic games, travelled around Europe, and looking back they can take all the credit for the career I had.

J IS FOR JOKER...

Who was the biggest practical joker you've met in football?

Sean Hargan! He's the first one to look at if there's a wind up. He's most likely to be pulling the strings with Kevin McHugh not far behind!

K IS FOR KIT...

What has been your favourite football kit that you've ever played in or owned?

The 1998 Brazil national kit was my favourite kit to own. I'm not Brazilian! or anything though!!

L IS FOR LIFE AFTER PLAYING...

Did you have a plan for after your playing career ended? Was management something you ever wanted to do?

Yeah, I always planned to go back into a profession away from football. I would say I was a leader in the dressing room when I was playing, though football management is a different beast and I knew it wasn't for me. I respect anyone who takes on that challenge, it's a way of life, not a job!

M IS FOR MEMENTO...

What is the one football memento you own that you'll never give away?

There's a few things I wouldn't give away, though if I have to name one, it's my first underage Reo Of Ireland cap. Still takes pride of place in my family home.

N IS FOR NIGHT OUT...

Which team mate was usually the first to initiate a night out?

How long have you got? I'm not one for naming names... Brian Cash!!

O IS FOR OPPOSITION...

Which opposition did you always look forward to playing the most in your career?

I loved playing Bohs and Shels when they were top teams. I was motivated by the challenge of the bigger games and the better players.

P IS FOR PASSTIME...

Outside of football, what keeps you occupied now in your spare time?

I still enjoy playing 5 a side and get to the gym a lot. Outside of that, my kids keep me on my toes!!

Q IS FOR QUIZ...

Which former team mate would you definitely not want in your team if you were doing a quiz?

Darren Kelly. Not a man for a quiz night.

R IS FOR RESULTS...

Do you still keep an eye out for the Derry City and League Of Ireland results?

Yes I do keep an eye on Derry City as the living legend Ruadhri Higgins is in charge. What a man and what a manager in the making.

S IS FOR SIGNING...

Do you remember the story of how you signing for Derry City came about? Both times!

The opportunity to first sign for Derry City came in 2003 when St Pats went into administration. Gavin Dykes was in charge at Derry and the discussions leading into signing of the contract were hilarious, like the man himself, and I ended up signing. Second time around I was doing pre season at Bray Wanderers when Stephen Kenny rejoined Derry. I got a call to see if I was interested in moving back up and I was up there in a heartbeat. The lads had just gone back

from a training camp and I was miles off the fitness levels and it took me a few weeks to catch up.

T IS FOR TALENT...

Who is the best player you've ever played with?

I played for four clubs in Ireland, went through the Ireland international underage system, and had a spell at west ham, played here in Australia, and for jaw dropping talent it was Paddy McCourt. Without a second thought.

U IS FOR UNPARALLELED...

Who is the best player you've ever played against?

Again, Paddy McCourt. I still have nightmares of when Shamrock Rovers came to the Brandwell with Paddy in

their team in 2005. He was frightening. I vividly remember trying to smash him and he nutmegged me. He toyed with us that night. He signed for us two months later and we had words (true story!)

V IS FOR VANITY...

Which team mate spent the longest in front of the mirror?
I would have to throw Ciaran Martyn under the bus on that one!

W IS FOR WEST HAM...

You made the move from UCD to West Ham at the age of 23. What do you remember about that transfer?
I remember it well as I was on the end of season night out with the UCD lads and I got a call from a guy saying he was from West Ham.

I thought it was the lads winding me up and I told him I wasn't interested! I then got a call later in the night from a former team mate who was a football agent. It moved pretty quickly from there. I worked for PwC Ireland at the time and they were great in allowing me to take a sebatical and sign the contract with West Ham. The experience itself was incredible from a football perspective though I would be lying if I didn't say I was extremely homesick. But everything happens for a reason and I wouldn't change any of it.

X IS FOR EXPERIENCE...

What's the best atmosphere you've ever experienced as a player?
We played Linfield in Windsor park and there was something different about the atmosphere there. The 'best' atmosphere was probably when we beat Lindfield 3-0 in the brandywell in 2008 the night Mark Farren scored the het-trick.

Y IS FOR YOUNG...

What is your earliest memory of going to a football match?
Ireland v Bulgaria in dalymount park in 1987

Z IS FOR ZONE...

Did you ever have any pre-match rituals or superstitions to get you in the zone?
The main ritual was a food ritual and I was very militant on what, when, how much. i wouldn't say I was superstitious though I generally like routine and I followed match day preparation religiously.

 **BARRY MOLLOY**

SPONSORED BY
BRANDYWELL PRIDE S.C.

A IS FOR ANNOYING...

Which former team mate was the worst to sit beside on the bus for long away journeys?

Easy! Eddie McCallion! Absolute nightmare! You'd just never get a minute to yourself! He just wouldn't shut up a whole journey! Just talking shite the whole time!

B IS FOR BEHAVIOUR...

Which former team mate was always the most likely to get booked?

I was going to say Deerso for his mouth! Kevin Deery or Rory Patterson either actually, but I'll stick with Deerso! For his tackles as

well actually!

C IS FOR CRUSADERS...

What made you come to the decision to leave Derry after nearly 10 years?

I just wanted a new fresh challenge. I think I just got to the stage at Derry where I thought I wasn't contributing as much as I wanted to and I thought a new challenge might have done me the world of good. And in fairness for the first few months it did and I felt it was a good decision. Stephen Baxter really sold it to me and I thought it was a good step. Stephen O'Flynn signed the same day as well so there was boys that

I knew there, but I actually didn't realise he was signing as well until about a few hours beforehand, but we basically signed around the same time.

D IS FOR DERRY CITY...

Do you remember the story of how you signing for Derry City came about?

Yeah, I went to Drogheda on loan for three months while I was still at Derby County, and then I came back to Derby hoping to try and break through over here but that didn't happen for one reason or another and then I found myself looking for a club and Drogheda offered me a contract. They wanted me to go back again and sign, and they offered me a decent contract to be fair to them, and I loved my time there when I was there like, so it was an easy decision to go back to the League Of Ireland. But, yeah, I was playing for Drogheda and we were playing Longford in the semi-final of the cup. And I just heard that Stephen Kenny, who had just taken over at Derry, was interested in looking at me and then it just went from there really. I mean, it was my home town club like, so it didn't take much convincing. But in terms of how I got the news, I didn't really know anything about it. I just remember there was something in the Derry Journal about Steven watching me and I was potentially coming to Derry and I didn't know all that myself yet!

E IS FOR EUROPE...

What are your memories of the European run that ended in the Parc De Princes?

Just that it was unbelievable, really! I know, obviously, everyone looks back and thinks of Paris and that you know, but the first game over in Gothenburg when we won 1-0, that was that was amazing for me because it was a bit of the unknown for myself and obviously the younger lads

as well and we went over there and we were brilliant on the day to be fair, and we were deserved winners and it was just, sort of, the first time I'd played at that sort of level of level in Europe and it was just an amazing feeling when Hargy scored and then when we beat them. So I really enjoyed that one. Even the one at the Brandywell as well when we beat them 1-0 again. They were both brilliant, because as I say like, we were written off big time, everyone was expecting us to get rolled over but we went there with a game plan and Stephen's tactics were spot on and the team he picked was brilliant. He really did his homework on them and on the day then we were deserved winners.

Did you swap a shirt?

Against Gothenburg? No, Philip Johnston would have killed us!! I swapped one in Paris though. There was a guy that played in the middle of the park Fabrice

Pancrate. Absolute unit of a man! But, yeah, after the game my first thought was disappointment, and then seeing the Derry fans still singing after we'd lost was amazing, and then I thought, 'right, I'd better get myself a jersey here!', know, something to have as a keepsake, you know?

F IS FOR FAI CUP...

You've played in four FAI Cup Finals. Is there one that stands out over the others?

Yeah, 2012! Obviously it's amazing though when you win the first one and the whole occasion, the day, the weather and stuff when we won in 2006, but 2012 for me was the best one. Again, we were underdogs and it's just an amazing playing at the Aviva and I had the two kids with me as well, so that'll always be the stand out one for me. Then when Rory scored the winner it was unbelievable, just, unbelievable! No better man either to be fair to him. It was brilliant, and as I say, we were underdogs. St Pat's were probably a better team on paper, like, but again on the on the day I think we deserved it.

G IS FOR GOAL...
What was the best goal you've ever scored?
At the senior level? I'd have to go for probably the goal against Cork.

Is that the one you hit from 35 yards?
That's the one! It was further than that I think!! Na, I remember I was just coming back from injury and I was a bit of a frustrating time for myself, and that was probably the one that sticks out. It kind of put me on the map at Derry as well, because before that I was getting a bit of grief and that about 'why did the club sign me?' and stuff like that, but after that match then I sort of never

looked back.

H IS FOR HAHA...
What was the funniest thing you remember from your time in football?
Jeez, you could write a book on funny stories alone! I think I told this story before somewhere, but we used to always go down the night before and stay in Dublin for our way games when Stephen Kenny came back the second time and we were away and we had a meeting the day before the game in the hotel and Mark Farren got a hold of Eddie McCallion's work laptop and got his password, so he got on the internet and Googled a load of different pictures of topless men and that kind of thing and stuff, and set it as his background and screensaver! Wee Eddie wasn't the best at computers and that, so he couldn't get it off for ages! All the lads are in the

room watching him getting redder and redder and I just always remember Tam McManus literally nearly falling off his chair laughing! He just couldn't control himself!

I IS FOR INFLUENCE...
Who would you say was been the biggest influence on your career?
Well, I'm lucky to have had many, many good influences! When I was younger my mum was always pushing me to do well and stuff like that, and my managers when I was growing up Charlie Doherty, Charlie Wang, Raymond Carton as well at Trojans. They were unbelievable for me, like. But then you have people like Stephen Kenny obviously as well who was brilliant when I was at Derry. So many good people to be fair that have been really good influences, but I'd have to go back to the early days when I was playing for Brandywell Harps and Trojans and my mum obviously, so they'd be the biggest ones.

J IS FOR JOKER...
Who was the biggest practical joker you've met in football?
I'd say everyone you've interviewed has probably said the same name!... Hargy! Just a messer! I remember I didn't really know Hargy when I signed for Derry, and

141

I thought he was a bit of a loose cannon, but them I got to know him and he's just one of the funniest people you'll ever know! He's such a good lad, but he was always, always winding people up and that and just always up for the craic!

K IS FOR KIT...

What has been your favourite football kit that you've ever played in or owned?

I always liked the black Derry kits as one I've played in. Owned then… I had the full yellow Liverpool away kit when I was younger! The Reebok one back when Michael Owen and that was playing. I used to love that one. It was amazing.

L IS FOR LIFE AFTER PLAYING...

Did you have a plan for after your playing career ended? Was management something you ever wanted to do?

No, no plan at all! It was always about trying to just enjoy football at the time and I probably should have got ready for life after football a bit quicker. But no, coaching and all never really appealed to me. I mean, I'm coaching my wee boy's team and that, but I had no interest in getting involved in senior football coaching. I had a few sort of stints here

and there trying it, but it didn't really appeal to me, to be honest.

M IS FOR MEMENTO...

What is the one football memento you own that you'll never give away?

I'm not really a big one for keeping stuff like that, but probably… I've got my first FAI Cup Final jersey from when we won in 2006. I have it framed with the medal and all in it. I'd never give that away like. That was a nice one and I always have that framed. To be fair, it's still in Derry to be honest. I haven't even brought it over yet, but that's the one that I would always keep. I was really proud of that one.

N IS FOR NIGHT OUT...

Which team mate was usually the first to initiate a night out?

Well, you're going back ten years at Derry like, so there's a lot of names that could pop up! There's a good few to be fair! Flynner was always good, Stephen O'Flynn, big Stewart Greacen loved a night out, big Gerard Doherty too. Different boys, different eras. But there was loads of lads who enjoyed a pint, so you were never short of a friend if you wanted to head out!

O IS FOR OPPOSITION...

Which opposition did you always look forward to playing the most in your career?

I always really enjoyed playing down at Inchicore against St Pats. Just the ground and everything. I remember playing there even when I was at Drogheda and even then I really enjoyed.

It's just a nice wee ground, it's tight, the pitch was usually good, and they were always a good side as well But, yeah, I always really enjoyed playing down there and we played against some cracking St Pats teams too over the years, but I always really enjoyed it down there.

P IS FOR PASSTIME...
Outside of football, what keeps you occupied now in your spare time?
Just going to the gym, really. Going to the gym and then just coaching my wee lad's U15s team. That and then going to the pub every now and then and having a few pints. But yeah, the young lad is playing for the local team. I actually play for their veteran team as well, but I've been coaching the young lads now for the last five years taking them up from U10s like, so that keeps me pretty busy as well.

Q IS FOR QUIZ...
Which former team mate would you definitely not want in your team if you were doing a quiz?
Darren Kelly! I'll tell you a good one! Gary Beckett brought two copies of an 11 plus exam on to the bus one day for Darren Kelly and Eddie McCallion to see who was the worst! Neither of them did very well! I think it was probably a draw! But Big

DK would definitely be the choice for that one!

R IS FOR RESULT...
Which result stands out or meant the most to you in your career?
There's loads I'm thinking of, you know what I mean? Games that you're hanging on and you're up against it and stuff. I always really enjoyed them games where you were 1-0 up and really up against it and defending your lives and that. Probably games like that that I enjoyed the most, but in terms of a single match, the ones come to mind are the cup finals and that, you know? The 2012 cup final where we went 3-2, and then the 2006 one where it was 4-3, both in extra time. Them ones where you're cramping up and you're giving everything but they were brilliant moments like, so probably them two.

S IS FOR SETANTA SPORTS CUP...
You played in the Setanta Cup before, what are your memories of it, and would you like to see it return?
Brilliant! Absolutely loved it to be honest! Again, it was going into the unknown for a lot of lads that played League of Ireland and never experienced playing against Linfield, or Glentoran or

that. I remember the first couple of years it was very hostile and that, and we were going up to Windsor Park and there'd be loads of police about it and things like that, and we weren't used to it obviously at the Brandywell, but absolutely amazing games and the matches against them were so tight and they were a cracking team, Linfield and even Glentoran at the time were brilliant as well. But, yeah, it was a really, really good competition to be fair, so if it was to come back, yeah, it would be good to watch it again.

T IS FOR TALENT...
Who is the best player you've ever played with?
There were loads at Derry to be fair. Paddy McCourt springs to mind straight away! The you have Gary Beckett, Mark Farren... you know, there's some unbelievable footballers there. There were boys that I played with at Derby as well that were brilliant and went on to big things. But in terms of getting to play with them on a match day all the time, you'd have to say, Paddy McCourt.

U IS FOR UNPARALLELED...
Who is the best player you've ever played against?

I was quite fortunate when I was at Derby to be playing some really top players, so you had the likes of Fabregas, and Wayne Rooney and boys like that, but they were younger then. Boys like David Bentley as well, I always remember playing against him and he was unbelievable at the time. But, in the League of Ireland I came up against some unbelievable midfielders. There's the likes of Joseph N'Do, Keith Fahy, a guy called Kevin Hunt that

used to play for Bohs as well. Them three always spring to mind when I think about midfielders. They were top, top class. Different kinds of players as well, but they were always very difficult to play against. I enjoyed the battles with them.

V IS FOR VANITY...

Which team mate spent the longest in front of the mirror?
There was a few at Derry to be fair! Killian loved a wee look in the mirror! Deerso when he had hair always liked a wee look in the mirror too! Wee Eddie used to love it as well! Wee gorgeous Eddie! DK loved the sunbeds too!

W IS FOR WISHES...

Is there anything you'd change about your career if you could do it all again?
I always said, just belief! I was never an arrogant footballer or anything, but just probably having a bit more belief in my ability because I think it did hold me back a bit, but yeah, probably that be honest.

X IS FOR EXPERIENCE...

What's the best atmosphere you've ever experienced as a player?
Well, PSG was incredible like but I remember playing against Trabzonspor, away. That was unbelievable. Just the atmosphere at Turkish games in general, like. But there's this sort of ritual thing that Trabzonspor fans do every 61 minutes on the clock or something, the crowd just went mental! That was very unique when we played them out there like. It was a great experi-

ence, so, yeah, probably that one to be honest.

Y IS FOR YOUNG...

What is your earliest memory of going to a football match?
The 1995 FAI Cup Final. I remember travelling to Dublin to watch that. That was the first time really that I ever went to a match. I just remember my Da got me a ticket and put me on a bus with a load of his buddies from the pub and that, and I went down and watched that and that was the first football match I can remember going to and it was amazing. It was a great occasion.

Z IS FOR ZONE...

Did you ever have any pre-match rituals or superstitions to get you in the zone?
Not really to be honest. I just tried to have a bit of a routine, of like, eating at the right time and stuff like that, but I never really had a ritual or anything like that. But always remember in 2012 when we were playing a couple of games I had a sort of gym out in the shed and I used to go out and do a bit of a gym session beforehand and it worked for a while, but nothing major. But yeah, if there was anything in terms of routine, it would have been that.

KILLIAN BRENNAN

SPONSORED BY
BRANDYWELL PRIDE S.C.

A IS FOR ANNOYING...

Which of your former team mates was the worst to sit beside on the bus for long away journeys?

Kevin Deery! He'd probably never shut up! I can't think of anyone else that would be that annoying. Kevin would probably the most outgoing, you know!

B IS FOR BEHAVIOUR...

Which of your former team mates was always the most likely to get booked?

Apart from myself?! Oh... Probably, in the earlier days,

Doc. Eamon Doherty. Him or maybe Pizza or Clive Delaney. But, yeah, maybe in the earlier days when I was there, Doc.

C IS FOR CUP...

You played in the game voted the best ever FAI Cup Final, the 4-3 win in 2006, what are your memories of it?

The wind! Obviously we won the game but it was tough! It was a really cold game. I actually remember my Mam telling me in all the years that she followed me around watching games, she said that was by far the coldest she ever was! But I can just remember the ball

boy I think it was, holding the corner flag for Paddy McCourt! I remember as well I took a corner for the fourth goal actually and I started that at the 18 yard box and it's gone the whole way in. So I would say we won and it was great joy and everything else, but it's the wind that comes to mind. It was awful! Like, we'll take it and everything else because we got it over the line, but it shouldn't have been played. It wouldn't be played now.

D IS FOR DERRY CITY...

Do you remember the story of how you signing for Derry City came about?

145

Yeah, I just got a call off Stephen Kenny and he's obviously said that he's interested in signing me and he wanted to show me around and stuff. I remember playing in a friendly in the Brandywell and I scored two that night. But I do remember Decky Devine coming down and collecting me on deadline day to come up and sign. So that's a story for you! Decky collected me, because I didn't drive. I was only 18 or 19 at the time. And we'd agreed a deal and we had to get it over the line before the deadline, so Decky drove down to collect me from Drogheda and drove me to Derry so I could sign just before the deadline! I don't know if Decky will remember that story, but I can remember being told I would be collected by Decky and I didn't even know who he was at the time! But he made it to the house and raced me back up the road on time and we got the deal done!

E IS FOR EUROPE...

What are your memories of the European run that ended in the Parc De Princes?

Yeah, well, obviously we had Gothenburg, and then we had Gretna, which I wasn't involved in the two of them, because I'd done the remedial in my knee the Sunday before I think against Long-

ford. I think I'd done that and then actually my next game was then the home game against Paris St Germain! I hadn't even got to play a friendly or an underage game or anything to get back up to fitness! But I just remember the fans, as the run went on longer the more fans there where and the more noise they made. The Gothenburg game actually stands out more so than even PSG because that was brilliant and we really weren't expected to win over there. But the whole run and the whole journey from start to finish, obviously it would have been a massive achievement if we had got through against PSG, and obviously everyone was going on about me hitting the crossbar against PSG and stuff, but, no, I think just the whole adventure. I think

the whole Gothenburg experience of, you know, playing over there, seeing the fans and getting the win when we I think we were massive outsiders having a midfield as young as we did. Myself, Kevin Deery... I think Kevin played that day, and we were all like 19 or 20 years of age. But it's that that stands out and winning and just the fans and the whole buzz around the city.

Did you swap shirts with anyone?

I can't remember if the lads did at Gothenburg. We were probably told that we couldn't or we'd have nothing to wear the next week! I wasn't involved in the Gretna game, but I got the right back's shirt from PSG, Bernard Mendy. I still have that actually. I wonder if he still has mine!!

F IS FOR FUNNY...

What was the funniest thing you remember from your time in football? There must be a funny Stephen Kenny or Roddy Collins story?!

Yeah, well, the Roddy Collins one that comes to mind was at Dublin City and I remember we played a friendly. Roddy was only in, and I hit a free kick and it was about 30 yards over the bar, cleared the wall behind the net and into the graveyard next door! But the boys were all going 'What was that?!' like, and I turned around and kind of chuckled and laughed at how bad it was and the boys' reactions. It's probably something I shouldn't have done, but he's seen that and though 'this lad doesn't even care', but in truth I was having a laugh with the boys that it was a crazy bad free kick! But anyway, I arrived in to training on Monday to a letter that I got fined two weeks wages! He was obviously trying to cut the budget and he didn't know what players you want to keep and that, but I always remember that made me laugh because I knew that was my time up there and then!

There's plenty of Stephen Kenny stories as well! Like the time we all went for food and he got up and sang in the Chinese! And I was sitting right opposite him! The lads all had the girlfriends with him and I was a single man, so I was sitting facing Stephen Kenny, and then the man that ran the show. I think was Mandarin Palace, is it called? He got Steven up to sing 'Country Roads' and I never looked at him the same way again! I'll give you another one as well! When I was at Rovers, because he signed me at Rovers as well. So we were leaving the ground to travel to the AUL Complex, we trained at the AUL. So we stopped off to get diesel, me, Connor McCormack and Daryll Kavanagh, and we stopped to get whatever in the shop before we go the training. Anyway, Stephen was standing just beside the front door to go into the garage. So, I said 'everything alright Stephen?' and he goes, 'You won't believe what I'm after doing.' Turns out he'd put 80 quid petrol into a diesel car! So I said, you're not gonna be taking the training today then!

G IS FOR GOAL...

What was the best goal you've ever scored?

Do you know something, the one that always stands out for me, and it wasn't a great goal or anything, but the one against Finn Harps in the last minute down in Ballybofey. I think we were down to 10 men and Pizza missed 2 penalties! Like, that was carnage! That's going back nearly 20 years. I wouldn't say it was the best goal, but it was one of the most important goals I think I've ever scored. And best goal... I scored a couple of goals for Pats against Finn Harps in the semi-final of the FAI Cup. They would kind of stand out. But again, not really amazing goals, just important goals. I actually scored a really important goal against Derry for Pats, to keep Pats up. So,

yeah, that was a pretty important goal as well. If I was to put one down though, I'd put the Finn Harps one down.

H IS FOR HERO...

Who was your footballing or sporting hero growing up?

Roy Keane! Despite being a diehard Liverpool fan! It was the impact he had on the Ireland squad that caught my attention, but you can appreciate the way he goes about the game as well even at United.

I IS FOR IRELAND XI...

You played a game for League Of Ireland XI at the Aviva, what do you remember about the game and the call-up?

Yeah, we opened Aviva Stadium in a game against Man United. We were absolutely thumped as well to be honest! We started off really well, and to be honest with you, I shouldn't have played but obviously I really wanted to play because of the occasion, but I was definitely not fit to play the game. And then I had to chase back the likes of Valencia and all that and I was kind of like 'here, hold on a minute'! I seen the writing on the wall! I remember the physio came on at 3-0 down and I just said here, I'm coming off! I think I even got in injection so I could play, which obviously wouldn't have been the right thing to do because of my club, but as I say, I really wanted to play, but I knew I was only making myself and the team worse trying to keep up! But it started off really well and then obviously when they scored the

floodgates opened a little bit. It was a it was a good occasion though. I've never been on a team bus that got booed into the Aviva! You know, like, we were getting booed! I remember thinking how crazy this is! We're getting booed into the ground to play Man United! In our own country! Obviously we got tanked, think it was 7-1 or something was it? Yeah, Dave Mulcahy scored late in the game and he ran the length of the pitch celebrating like it was a last minute equalizer!

J IS FOR JOKER...

Who was the biggest practical joker you've met in football?

Hargy was funny. Sean Hargan. Even Paddy McCourt was actually very funny too. But I'd say Daryl Kavanagh. I played with him at Pats and Rovers. You wouldn't know what you'd get with him. You'd just have to be checking the whole time to see if he's around! Anything could happen with him, you know.

K IS FOR KIT...

What has been your favourite football kit that you've ever played in or owned?

I liked the Pats gear when I was when I was playing with Pats. I think when I look back then at photos of me in the Derry City kits, like, they weren't fitted kits in them days! Even at Bohs, the three or four years I played at Bohs, I just remember the jerseys swinging off me! I would say probably the Pats, the most recent year, probably just before I retired, maybe 2017, 2018, the last year probably was the nicest gear when fitted kits started to be a thing.

L IS FOR LIFE AFTER PLAYING...

Did you have a plan for after your playing career ended? Was management something you ever wanted to do?

It's something I never really thought about when I was playing football. Well, I'm actually still playing football. I'm playing and coaching at Glebe North. So I'm still playing away, for my sins! And doing a bit of coaching with Glebe North, but not something that I actually see myself doing full time. If I fall into it, then maybe, but obviously Ruaidhri and them have gone on to be successful and they're in around the same age as me. People always say to me, 'you know, you could do that!' and I'm saying, 'I don't know if I need the headache of all that kind of stuff'. I don't even know if I'd be any good at it if I'm being totally honest, but if it's something that happens down the line then so be it,

but it's not something that I've put in place for myself.

M IS FOR MEMENTO...

What is the one football memento you own that you'll never give away?

Well, obviously I've won a couple of cups with Derry. A couple of cups with Pats and Bohs and leagues, so I think they're all pretty much the same. I won't give any of them away and keep them all pretty close to me and anything that I win that you know, like, if it's worth winning obviously they'll stay close to me. They're the ones that stand out. I think any of the ones that have won at any of the places I've been will always be close enough to me, you know.

N IS FOR NIGHT OUT...

Which team mate was usually the first to initiate a night out?

Jesus, I'm just trying to think of my nights out at Derry! I

don't know if we had many nights in! In fairness though, we were that successful, we could go out all we wanted and we'd still get the job done. Like, I'd probably have to say Brian Cash for that one, because I lived with Brian for two years at Derry, and jeez I don't think there was very few nights he stayed in put it like that! But we just young, fit lads. We were able to do whatever we needed to do. Like if we were going out we'd go out, we'd get up for football training and there wasn't a problem. Nowadays, at my age you go for a few beers, you're in bed for two days, you know! Even with Stephen though, Stephen Kenny brought it in that if we had a long journey away, the boys could have a few beers on the bus on the way back. He knew there was professionalism in there that the boys wouldn't go mad. It's a long trip, especially when you're looking at a bottle of water! But a few cans can shorten the trip for sure. But that's just the professional way that things were done.

O IS FOR OPPOSITION...

Which opposition did you always look forward to playing the most in your career?

I think it's different whatever teams you're at. I think when I was at Derry we used to love playing against Shels and I used to revel playing against Shels as well. I used to get myself up an extra 10% as well because of the occasion. I think when I was at Pats the likes of the Dublin derbies obviously stand out. They're always ones you have to get yourself up for. Obviously you get yourself up from most games, but it just seems like you just roll your sleeves up a little bit

more when you're playing in them games. But overall, I'd say I love playing against Shels and the likes of Rovers..

P IS FOR PASSTIME...

Outside of football, what keeps you occupied now in your spare time?

Kids! And probably golf when I can get a chance to go golfing. Probably just my kids and golf!

Q IS FOR QUIZ...

Which former team mate would you definitely not want in your team if you were doing a quiz?

There's a few! It think it has to be Paddy McCourt! Paddy or Deerso!

R IS FOR RESULT...

Which result stands out or meant the most to you in your career?

I'd say the Gothenburg one. That game totally changed the way we thought we could play. And it gave us so much confidence going forward as a group and as individuals, thinking that we could probably, if we go to Europe next year or the year after, whether it would be with Derry or anywhere else, it gave us that much confidence that we thought we could just beat anyone to be honest. It made Europe definitely doable if that makes sense whereas Irish teams before kind of went with the mindset that we'll likely get beat. So, I'd say that one going forward gave me a lot of confidence. And then obviously playing against better players, knowing that you can hold your own against better players. So for me, the two Gothenburg games.

S IS FOR SETANTA...

What are your memories of the Setanta Cup? Linfield at the Brandywell was always an atmosphere to experience!

I remember my brother came up for that Linfield game. I actually can't remember the result that time, but I think we played them a couple of times in the Brandywell. I remember playing in the Setanta Cup with Bohs against Linfield. I actually missed a good few of the Setanta games when I was at Derry because I

was injured and at whatever stage I think that might have been around the time I was injured for the Gretna European one as well. I don't know if it was in around that same time, but I did miss a fair few games. Obviously it's a bit of carnage as well with a couple of buses getting windows put in on the way back. I can remember that alright! But, no, they were great occasions. Absolutely unbelievable occasions. I think they should bring them back. That needs to come back, in my opinion. Especially now that the League Cup has gone. If you take the top four from the Irish League, and the top four from our league, they'd have a massive following. You look at the likes of Rovers, Derry, Pats, Bohs or whoever. I think it would be just as exciting as it was in them days, probably even more so, especially since the games get more coverage these days than we got.

T IS FOR TALENT...

Who is the best player you've ever played with?
Undoubtedly Paddy McCourt

U IS FOR UNPARALLELED...

Who is the best player you've ever played against?
Paddy again!! I think it has

to be Paddy McCourt. We talked about European players, and I played against a couple of decent players in Europe and in my younger days and played against Iniesta and Torres when we played against Spain and stuff, but they were only young lads as well at that stage, So I'd say Paddy for both!

V IS FOR VANITY...

Which team mate spent the longest in front of the mirror?
Darren Kelly! He used to carry his own mirror around with him! In saying that, big Clive had his own sunbed! I'll go Darren though!

W IS FOR WISHES...

Is there anything you'd change about your career if you could do it all again?

I've been asked that a few times and it's so hard to answer them type of questions and because, like, the only thing that I would say I obviously was successful when I left Derry City, when I went to Bohs and Pats, but I kind of wish I'd stayed at Derry a little bit longer if I'm totally honest. Just to see which way it was going. Because Stephen Kenny was there when I signed, then it kind of all went a bit pear shaped when Pat Fenlon came in, and then Dave Robertson came in. So I wasn't sure which way things were going, but I think if he'd had a foundation there where he knew who was going to be there and stuff, I think I definitely would have stayed a bit longer and see what happened I think. But like I said, it's hard to turn around and leave a club and leave a city that you've been there for four years and go on to be successful. I think if I had gone and not been successful that definitely would have been the answer, you know?

X IS FOR EXPERIENCE...

What's the best atmosphere you've ever experienced as a player?

I'd say it would have to be PSG away. I know it wasn't full by any means, but it was still amazing. They had two sets of supporters at either side of the ground and they were shouting back and forth at each other and then obviously our own supporters as well. I can remember their right back, Mendy, and obviously they had the running track around the pitch at the time, and Hargy was playing left back and I was playing left wing. And I think he pushed the ball by me, but I thought was going out of play and Hargy was going to meet him. But he's kicked it round Hargy and I'm going 'That's going out of play. That's gone out for a goal kick.' And he's ran around Hargy, onto the track, and I could just hear the crowd going mad, and like, I'd pulled back at this stage. I was just going 'That's gone!', and he's come back off the track and on to the pitch again, and he's nearly got there! But how he's even managed to nearly get there I'll never know!

I remember Hargy looking at me then and going 'This is going to be a long night!' But yeah, the atmosphere was unreal. I remember even the bus when we arrived and you could even feel the crowd when they came out for their warm up, you know! It was crazy! I mean, I've played in bigger stadiums and that as well obviously, like the United one opening the Aviva was big as well, but the PSG one was brilliant.

Y IS FOR YOUNG...

What is your earliest memory of going to a football match?

Probably just going to see my dad. He played as well at decent enough level, so he used to bring me everywhere. So, yeah, just going to watch my Dad.

Z IS FOR ZONE...

Did you ever have any pre-match rituals or su-

perstitions to get you in the zone?

Plenty! One of the main ones anyway is that everything has to go from right to left for me. So if my left boot came off, I'd have to open my right boot, so I'd have to open my right lace, tie my right lace, and then put my left on. Same before the game I'd have to put my right shin guard on before my left shin guard, right boot before left boot and if I did manage to do the opposite, as in, if I put the left boot on before the right boot, then the left boot had to come off if I realised what I'd done! I'd always have to go from right to left. So yeah, that's a little bit of a weird one that! And that stands even to this day! Even the runners that I put on in the morning, I put on from right to left. Weirdo, I know! But I was lucky enough to be somewhat successful in my career, so if it works it works!

DARREN KELLY

SPONSORED BY
BRIAN DUNLEAVY

A IS FOR ANNOYING...

Which of your former team mates was the worst to sit beside on the bus for long away journeys?

I'm trying to think... You know something, it was probably me as weird as that sounds! Because I was always quite an annoying type! Me and Eddie McCallion, and I'll throw Eddie's name for that one too actually, we used to wind each other up! Who's the smartest between us and things like that! Because the thing about it is, me and Eddie go way back to primary school age. We were at primary school and secondary school together before he had his stints in England playing. But we always used to be the butt of the jokes! We'd always be asked 'Who's the smartest between you two?' and that would just start it all up! But I suppose we weren't so much annoying, but we always used to be in the same back and forth banter together. And because we were always in the same class we used to get the same banter that we were in the bottom group with all the simpletons and all that! But it was always good for changing room banter and good morale, and because we knew each other that long we enjoyed the craic that we were always the butt of the jokes! And I still maintain that I'm brighter! I've got a Masters and two degrees! I don't even think Eddie has any GCSEs! So, yeah, I would have said me because looking back now that I've matured through the years, there's times I even annoyed myself I was that annoying! But if it was anybody else, it wouldn't be so much Eddie, but the banter between us when we used to be at each other, in a good way!

B IS FOR BEHAVIOUR...

Which of your former team mates was always the most likely to get booked?

Hargy! Without a doubt! I mean there used to be a chant along the lines of

'Hargy's Gonna Get Ya!' But I'm just trying to think, because bear in mind, I was there from 1995! Heggsy as well. Heggsy was hard as nails, but he very rarely got booked! Paul Doolin was hard as nails and very rarely get booked as well. The thing about Hargy, he wore his heart on his sleeve. He'd go through a brick wall for you! So, Hargy is the first person that came to mind! But it's always probably defenders or defensive mids that are most likely to put in a hard tackle. Strikers in the era I was in weren't really hard players, you know, the likes of Liam Coyle, or Gary Beckett. You didn't have the likes of a Diego Costa or anything like that in them days really. A striker wouldn't be likely to get a booking or sent off. You know what I mean? Certainly no one that would bite you anyway!

C IS FOR CARLISLE...

What do you remember about getting your move to England with Carlisle United?

I can remember finding out on teletext! There's one for you! Showing my age! But, yeah I read it on teletext that Carlisle had tabled a bid. I didn't know anything about it at all. And at the time the club was struggling financially and I remember Jim Roddy and Kevin Mahon told me the next day that

they put in a bid and asked me what I thought. I agreed that I would be interested, but we said that it's got to be over £100,000. So that offer went back to them and Roddy Collins being Roddy Collins, another bid came back at £101,000! But there were sort of two stories going on at the time. The club were desperate to get money in. They were struggling massively financially and it was only a couple of years after that then that the scandal happened with the double registrations. To tell you the truth on it, I'm sort of going off on a side topic here, but I've always collected memorabilia from my career and I've always put it in scrapbooks. But I actually have the registration contracts as well! The sort of illegal ones! The club were found to be handing out two contracts! There was a contract that what you were actually getting, and then there was another sort of top-up contract if you like! A sort of 'This is what you're really getting!' contract, and I still have both! But anyway, getting back to the transfer... The club was struggling financially, they wanted a bit more because as I say, they desperately needed the money. And to be honest from my side, it was always a player's dream to move to the bigger leagues so to speak, so I was keen to make

that move to England. So the bid came back that they were happy with and I was happy to go and try my luck in the English Leagues and it just happened that quick after that. But, as I say, there was no social media or Sky Sports News, you're working with teletext! But the dream for every young lad was to go over to England and play. When I was younger I remember there was interest from the likes of Nottingham Forest, Port Vale, Liverpool, Celtic and all that, but nothing ever materialized, so it was always something I thought I missed the boat on. But John Cunningham was at Carlisle and when the second bid came in I was in touch with a few people at Carlisle, which was probably illegal! I can talk about it now, but you know, players aren't supposed to talk to a club without their own club agreeing to it first. But I was just keen for it to happen. And in fairness, the club was keen for it to happen as well because of the fact that they needed the money, you know. But yeah, it just happened that quick. Probably within a week. But the thing about it was, that year Derry went on and won the FAI Cup! So not only did I miss out on that that, but the club got money in anyway from the cup win!

D IS FOR DERRY CITY...

Do you still keep an eye on the Derry City results?

First one every single week! I watch the live games as well on the LOI streaming service. It's my hometown club, you know. I've always been a fan. I've even started now going on eBay, and collecting all the old match programmes and things like that. I remember going to the Brandywell from no age. I'm a Spurs fan, and I remember going to like the Spurs game at the Brandywell. I got the programme from that recently. I can remember even going back to the friendly games when they used to play likes of Crystal Palace and Man United. I actually remember a little letter I wrote out to give to the Man United keeper Jim Leighton, that was something along the lines of you're a great goalkeeper and things like that. I wanted to try and get his shirt. I had a notion of be-

ing a goalkeeper back then. And I remember I was ball boy when Derry played Nottingham Forest, if you can remember. Teddy Sheringham was playing that day. I was on the line just behind the net and Teddy Sheringham scored a diving header! I was right there actually beside it! You're bringing back fantastic memories! That's back when it was what I would say it was the proper Brandywell. I haven't been back to the new one in fairness! My last game, and Brian Dunleavy helped with this but because he done all my stats and everything, was around about August 17 years ago I think against Bray. It was my last game and then it was Pyunik in Europe before that and it's just absolutely flown by!

E IS FOR EUROPE...

What are your biggest memories of the European run that ended in the Parc De

Princes?

The best footballing memories of my life that nobody will ever take away from me! That whole European adventure! I think it was only one to play in every minute of every game. It was just... Even when I'm talking to you now it gives me goosebumps! The whole thing obviously started with Gothenburg, and they had the likes of Nicholas Alexandersson that played in the World Cup with Sweden that year, and everyone thought it was just a matter of them showing up and they were going to beat us. So, we knew that was a motivation in itself, and we went on and done what we done. The game itself, I remember the guy that was playing up front, I can't remember his name though to be honest with you, but he was like a Mido, if you can remember Mido that played with Spurs, and there was a lot of talk of him going to England at the time, but I was glad to play against him to be honest. When I played I enjoyed the big battles with the big, physical type of players rather than the fast skillful ones, and he was big and physical. But he was getting a lot of attention and I think there was talk that there was quite a few scouts watching him and I remember marking him out of the game. But also remember the corner in

155

the home game that ,if you see in the video, I was about to head it in before the guy handballed it! O'Flynn scored the penalty, but if you watch it back you'll see I'm right behind the guy ready to head it in! But yeah, I enjoyed those type of battles, and all three of those games had big physical attackers, like when we played PSG there was Pauleta and guys like that. But we had nothing to lose, so we went at them, and I don't think any of the teams expected that.

The other big thing about the experience as well was always the journey with supporters. I think that's why it's so memorable for all of us, because we all got to go to the Parc De Prince and we'll always have the videos and the pictures. As I say, I collect memorabilia, and I collected the memorabilia from them games. The cutouts and things like that. They're all in a scrapbook. But as I say, to be doing it with our supporters was amazing. It's like when we travelled to Gothenburg, or Paris or to Scotland there was always mingling with the fans and having a chat with them and it raised the morale a good bit, you know. I don't know what it's like now to be honest when the team travels now in Europe, but we enjoyed that we got out to wander about and chat to

the fans. They'd have been in bars and then you'd be going up the streets and you'd be singing with them and... just the best memories!

F IS FOR FAME...

Which would make the better TV show, DKTV or the Rod Squad?! And what ever became of those tapes?
DKTV! And I sort of had a gripe with this, and I kind of still have! But there's got to be a DKTV 2 because there's a lot of material that wasn't used and I think you could see probably a little bit more explicit things that wasn't used in the proper DKTV! So I think you could definitely make it a good DKTV 2! There's hilarious footage of when we were in Scotland when we were standing in the hotel and me and Steven O'Flynn glued a pound coin to the ground outside and just sat in front of all these glass windows and watched a load of people

trying to pick it up! It was all on DKTV, and we were just howling laughing. If you talk about team morale, team camaraderie, team togetherness and everything, it was just absolutely brilliant!

I'm pretty sure you featured in the Rod Squad TV show at Carlisle as well didn't you?

I did, yeah. It's still online somewhere. I'd occasionally drop in and watch it for a laugh. Again, I remember there was more explicit stuff that was shot there as well that didn't make it on TV, but I wasn't so much to do with it! It was obviously more about Roddy, but DKTV the unedited version would be better!

G IS FOR GOAL...

What was the best goal you've ever scored?
It's got to be the Gretna one, doesn't it? At Motherwell. Because of what it was, where it was, and then run-

ning the length of the pitch to our supporters who came in their thousands! I think there was about 3,000 or something that travelled. But scoring that goal that obviously levelled it up for us, and then just running to our supporters. So that was a no brainer really.

H IS FOR HAHA...

What was the funniest thing you remember from your time in football?
The funniest thing I remember, and I laugh about it now, was actually something that was done on me! It was when I first came on the scene, so I think it was about 1994/95 as a young whipper snapper, and Felix was the manager. We went down to the old Shamrock Rovers pitch and they were playing at the RDS at the time and if you remember they used to have a horse show on there. Kevin Mahon was the assistant manager at the time and they said to me before the game that I had to have tetanus jag. So I had to get on the physio bench before we went out to warm up. All the players looking on and everything and I had to whip my trousers down and get what I thought was a needle going into my backside was actually a pen! So when I think of that was they got me good that day! I was the butt of all jokes, but I never minded.

It'll bring memories back for the lads. I was caught hook, line, and sinker! Because I just presumed, you know, a tetanus jag to make sure we didn't catch any disease if there was a blood injury! But yeah, they got me good!

I IS FOR INTERNATIONAL...

What do you remember about getting your U21s international call-ups?
I remember everything! Luckily I have a good memory of them all. I remember the first one which, again, social media wasn't around then, but I was actually called up to play for the Republic of Ireland Under 18 against Northern Ireland, we won 4-0. I was in the Republic team with the like a Keith Doyle, Gary Doherty, Robbie Keane, Liam George, Richie Partridge, you had quite a few names in there. I remember I was to go and play the year they got into the quarter finals, and it was abroad but I'd lost my passport so I missed out! I actually found it about three years later! It was fully washed up lying under the washing machine! That's what stopped me from getting more caps for the U18s and U20s!

And was there ever a chance of a call-up to the senior squad?

No, I don't think so. The most senior I went was with the Northern Ireland U21 team. I was called up four times as standby. Two were against Malta, one was against Spain around the time that they had Raul and that. I think there was pressure from the media and the manager and the fans and that at the time for a call-up when we were doing well with the whole European thing, but nothing ever materialized from it. I've still got the stand by letters actually. Before anything was announced, you always get a letter to say if you were called up or not. But I've still got those letters in my scrapbooks.

J IS FOR JOKER...

Who was the biggest practical joker you've met in football?
Hargy! He loved to mess about! He used to make these noises, it was like a weird high pitched noise to try and put you off! But football can be intense sometimes and if you were just beaten or whatever and you needed something to give the mood a lift, Hargy would step in! But there was a good few in that 2006 squad. Stephen O'Flynn was another funny, funny guy! But we were all around the same age and we all hung about together. There were no cliques, we were all one big group. It was the best

157

changing room I've been in, for sure.

K IS FOR KIT...

What has been your favourite football kit that you've ever played in or owned?

The one I enjoyed the most was, and it was probably one of my first ones, but it was the Le Coq Sportif one. I can remember the ones that used to have the Smithwick's sponsor. They were always one that stands out. But certainly the ones I've got up on the wall in my, sort of, 'man cave' if you want to call it would be that Le Coq Sportif one, and the 2006 European one. They would have been the two favourites for obvious reasons because of how good that 2006 year was.

So you didn't swap a shirt in Paris or anything?

I didn't, no. I wouldn't have in fact. I always wanted to keep my European jersey to show my kids in future years. I speak all the time about my home town club because of how dear it is to me and the jerseys, as I say, are up in my mancave, which my kids see all the time, and the kids all have their own Derry tops and they're very proud of that and they always can't wait to get back to the Brandywell, so I'm glad I didn't swap it and give it away.

L IS FOR LIFE AFTER PLAYING...

Was management something you always wanted to do, or did you have a plan for after football?

I did, yeah. I always wanted to be in football. I done my B license when I was 19! I always had the vision that I wanted to stay in football when I finished playing. I knew the way the game was going because I was an old school, old style centre back. Coming for headers, go through a brick wall for the team type of player. Not necessarily the most technical player to get it, play it out from the back, play through the thirds and all that. But I knew the way the game was going because you had the likes of Rio Ferdinand and players like that coming through who were like the complete package as defenders and bringing a new style of play. So I trained to be a sports therapist after

I did my coaching badges, and got a masters and two degrees, and I then got my UEFA Pro Licence, so I'm qualified in every area now, and I've worked from being a head coach to what I'm doing now the last seven years being a sporting director. So I have a MSc masters in Sports Directorship, and I've done all that. But yeah, it was always the plan early on to stay in football because I knew the game.

It's funny you should ask that actually, because I do a lot with the FA and the PFA now where I'm putting on presentations and things, and a lot of that is based around getting players to plan and prepare for after football. Because it goes by in a flash really. I remember to this day making my debut against Sligo in 1996 like it was yesterday. I'm not even exaggerating. I remember getting an elbow right in the first 5 minutes from Ian Gilzean. I remember the

game clear as day. But now I try to pass that story on and some players I chat to take it on and some don't. It's mostly my level of players that I chat to, because obviously Premiership level players don't need to think of life after football money-wise, because let's be honest, if you're a Premiership player now, you don't need to work or worry financially after playing, so it's probably going to be punditry or media work or something like that that they'll do.

M IS FOR MEMENTO...
You were saying about your scrapbooks and you keep a lot, but if you were to give everything away but keep one item, what would you keep?
From football in general? I've got quite a lot. Obviously the FAI Cup medal would be one. You know, it was a bit of a running joke at the time, but I'd done my ligaments and my ankle just swelled up. But you know when you just run on adrenaline? If I'd been fit I would have played that game, but my ankle was swollen up. I remember Ruaidhri Higgins and Kevin Deery and them looking at me and laughing because I wanted to play so bad that I'm limping around training trying to show my fitness! And the reason was that going back to 1995 when we were beat by Shelburne

2-0 because I was in the squad for that game. That was the year sadly that Tony O'Dowd's brother died, but I had to watch it from the side and never go the chance to play. So when we got to the final again, that was my big chance. I couldn't wait to get an FAI Cup medal because growing up I always remember watching Derry in the Cup. Even as a young supporter, I remember my uncles Martin and Bill, taking me to the FAI Cup final in Lansdowne Road and I must have been about 12 or 13 and we were beaten, and it absolutely pissed down the whole day. But, yeah, I just couldn't wait to win an FAI Cup with my hometown club. And obviously the league as well. I was in the league squad when we won the league, but I was two appearances off getting a medal, so if I had have got them two appearances I would have probably said joint FAI Cup medal and the League Medal, but the fact that I've only got the one makes it all the more special.

N IS FOR NIGHT OUT...
Which team mate was usually the first to initiate a night out?
Killian Brennan or Stephen O'Flynn! Or in different eras, when Felix was manager that time we won the League in '95, we used to travel to Dublin in Ford Gal-

axies! Desmonds sponsored them. But we used to go in two Galaxies! Felix used to just drive one, and Kevin Mahon drove the other. But there was a number of times when you'd end up in Paul Curran's one and then you'd end up stopping off somewhere and just going clubbing! On the way back from somewhere! So from that era, it probably would have been Currny! In saying that, there were no protests from the likes of Peter Hutton and Sean Hargan either! But, yeah, we used to stop somewhere for a night out! Glencarn was usually the spot! In the later years then, depending what time the game finished up at, you'd end up with the likes of myself, Killian, Higgins, Deery, O'Flynn, and a few others, we would end up in Earth or something like that!

O IS FOR OPPOSITION...
Which opposition did you always look forward to playing the most in your career?
Team-wise, I loved playing against Shamrock Rovers. Because they were always one of the biggest clubs in Ireland at that time and they were always well supported and things like that so there was always a brilliant atmosphere between our supporters and theirs. Cork at the time as well were always 6 foot plus! But I would

always embrace them type of games. Playing against Rovers players like Stephen Grant and Tony Sheridan, that type of player because they were always really, really good players. But as I say, I always looked forward to playing against those type of strikers because you're playing against what they would say is the so-called best players in the League of Ireland.

P IS FOR PASSTIME...

Outside of football, what keeps you occupied now in your spare time?

Just family. I'll be honest, it's just family because that's what it's about. I'm in England here and I don't go out or anything like that, so I just support my kids with what they want to do. They obviously play football and my daughter, she horse rides, and just supporting with that really. So I'm probably one of those that don't really keep in touch with anyone in particular, just on the likes of Facebook or whatever, but, yeah any free time goes into being a devoted family man! That's away from football though because most of my time is taken up with that. Watching my kids' games, or watching Premier League with them, or watching Derry City in the League of Ireland with them. Trying to get them into Spurs and Derry City! It's always Derry

City first though and then work backwards from that!

Q IS FOR QUIZ...

Which former team mate would you definitely not want in your team if you were doing a quiz?

Eddie McCallion! Like I was saying earlier, the banter with me and Eddie used to go back and forth! He probably said me, did he?! As I say, we were always in the same class at school, but, yeah, I wouldn't want Eddie in my team! It's the only time I would want him to be in the opposition!

R IS FOR RESULT...

Which result stands out or meant the most to you in your career?

Yeah, most of my memorable results were with Derry. I have things that I've have done at Carlisle and at York, but when you're sort of clutching at the heartstrings and the best memories always come back to Derry. But the one game that always stands out, and I always remember the atmosphere was amazing, but one game that stands out for me would be the North West Cup Final against Sligo. Probably because we weren't expected to do anything. Sligo beat us 3-0. I didn't play in that game. I can't remember why, but we were beat 3-0 at the Sligo Showgrounds, but there was two legs in the final and

we played Sligo at home then the week after and we end up winning, if I'm right, 5-4! But the thing about it was, when we played them at the Brandywell, Sligo were three up from the first leg, but they scored early in the second leg to make it 4-0 and we ended up coming back. But what what was good about that journey was that I was only young, but there was a good mixture of players young and old. It was guys I played in the reserves with, the likes of Shaun Gallagher at left back, mixed with the senior players like Higgsy. Higgsy scored an absolute screamer as well from about 30 yards to win us the Cup final. But yeah, that's one game that really stands out. You had the likes of the League Cup game as well, which is probably level on par, where we beat Shelbourne. We were down to nine men and it went to extra time and then penalties. I remember scoring the winning penalty and then I ran off to our supporters, but I, and I don't know to this day, but apparently I was heading towards the Shelbourne supporters, but I ended up seeing somebody in the crowd somewhere else and I jumped in there instead! But if I had have went the way I was going to go first, I was running right into the middle of the Shelbourne supporters! I

don't ever remember away supporters being at the bottom end of the stand where usually Scaldy and them stand with the drums. But I remember somebody saying to me that they moved the away fans for that game and I was headed towards the Shelbourne fans! So that would have been funny! And I probably would have gotten a couple of digs to the jaw if I'd jumped in there celebrating!

S IS FOR SIGNING...

Do you remember the story of how you signing for Derry City came about? Both times!

Well, I can tell you a funny story for the second time! Well, the first time, yeah, I remember it as clear as day. I remember what I was getting and everything! But Felix signed me. Felix and John Cunningham signed me the first time. Just very straightforward, I was playing with

the reserves and doing well and I was asked to come along with the first team and made my unofficial debut, as such, against Ballymena in a friendly game at the Ballymena Showgrounds in 1994 I think it was. After that I was in and around the first team while training with the reserves and Bugsy was brilliant. I ended up making my real debut then against Sligo. Me and Tommy Mc-Callion, and Tommy scored a hat-trick! So, I made my debut and Tommy stole all the headlines! I remember though I was up against Ian Gilzean. I always remember Paul Curran saying when you go up for a header, protect yourself against these boys, but I didn't know what he meant, and lo and behold, in the first 5 minutes Gilzean must have saw I was only a young lad and he just threw his elbow and landed one right on me and gave me a black eye! Welcome to the League of Ireland type of thing! I remember then playing against Shamrock Rovers I think it was and I played right back beside God rest big Kevin McKeever! We ended up drawing one each. It wasn't long after that then that I signed my first contract. I signed for £45 a week. I think it was a five year contract. So I was sort of in and around the team from then on before, as you know, I was sold to

Carlisle. I had a couple of opportunities to stay in Ireland at that time. I remember even Shelbourne put a bid in for me. They put a £30,000 bid in for me and it was turned down wholeheartedly from the club. It was when Dermot Keeley was manager. I remember I was asked about it, but I said no, I don't want to go. They ended up signing Pizza then.

But I remember then the second time around there was a number of clubs looking to speak to me after Carlisle. Derry showed no interest at that time. Well, I spoke to Gavin Dykes when he was manager the year before I actually left Carlisle and said I'd be interested in coming back, but it ended up it didn't materialize for one reason or another. I think it came down to money maybe, but I ended up signing for Portadown a year later after I was released. But I remember then Stephen Kenny phoned me and he said 'I'd like to sign you' but I said I'd just signed for Portadown. So I phoned Ronnie McFall and pleaded with him to release me out of my contract because my hometown club wanted me, but he wouldn't do it, so I played with Portadown for about a year and a half because there's a cross of the seasons between summer football and winter football, but Stephen was true to his word and he made a note of when I was available and came in for me. He had signed a great defense then, Ken Oman, Clive Delaney, Pizza, so they were already there. So Stephen rang me when I became available and he said 'can you come and meet me?', so I said 'no problem at all'. Because Stephen always spoke highly of me going back to when I played for Derry City against Longford when Stephen was manager and I scored the goal that put them out of the FAI Cup, and I always remember I seen him a few times here and there and he always would come over and speak to me about things. Even when I was playing in England, he would have come over to a couple of games and things like that, you know? He wasn't manager of Derry, he was just always watching players.

I remember meeting him though and having this story in my head and thinking if I come back, I had an idea what players were on money wise and things like that. And even living-wise for me, it would just be simple going back to my mums for a while until I got somewhere or whatever. So I had it in my head when I was going to meet him that 'I'd be happy with this. That'll do me. It's all about coming home.' So I met him just chatting

small talk and he says, 'right, money wise, what are you looking for?' I said, 'make me an offer', so he made me an offer and I said straight away there and then 'I'll sign it!' It was double what I had in my head! So it was literally done in 5 minutes in the Everglades! I made my second debut against Drogheda in the League Cup and won 3-0, and we had such a good season!

T IS FOR TEAM MATES...

Who is the best player you've ever played with?

I have a few I'm thinking of. It's sort of how you break it down, if you know what I mean. Because you look at ability, skill-wise, and again I'm always biased towards Derry City! We had some fantastic players I played with at other clubs like Carlisle, you look at the likes of Leon Osman who went on to play Premier League and he was unbelievable. But at

Derry, I look from a centre back point of view, you look at the relationship I had with Peter Hutton as a centre back partnership. He, as a captain and as a leader, was brilliant. You look at Liam Coyle. You look at Paddy McCourt. So, yeah, it would be someone along them lines. To pick just one, somebody where you sit back and awe of, watching somebody who defied gravity almost, and all the odds of martial science it would be Liam Coyle. Because Liam shouldn't have been playing when he was. And what he was able to do with the ball at his feet when he shouldn't have been able to do it just defies the laws of science! He was unbelievable as a person as well. He's another funny character I put in there with Hargy and the others!

U IS FOR UNPARALLELED...

Who is the best player

you've ever played against?
I don't know. There's nobody that I've come off a pitch and thought, 'I never want to play against him again'. And I don't mean that in a cocky or arrogant way, it's just that there was nobody, even in England, that I wouldn't want to play against again. Nobody stands out.

What about some of the 'glamour friendlies' you played in?

No, because even when we played the likes in Real Madrid, they didn't have a lot of first team stars. Even playing against Celtic three times. I suppose the main memory I would have, but I don't know if he's the best player played against it as such, but I can remember when we played Celtic in that tournament in Lansdowne, you had the likes of DiCanio and Emerson Thom, Darren Jackson. But I loved playing against them. Even in the League Of Ireland, you had the likes of Glen Crowe who, kind of like Liam, you know isn't going to be the quickest, but his movement can trouble defenders. If I was to go for anyone in fact, there was one game where we played against Bohs and they beat us 3-1 and me and Peter Hutton and I remember Glen Crowe caused us problems a bit. Bohs had such a good year that year,

but there's nobody I've ever come off the pitch and thought I wouldn't want to play against him again.

V IS FOR VANITY...

Which team mate spent the longest in front of the mirror?
There's a few I have in mind! In fairness, I was one of the 'Tan-tastic' ones that went to the sunbeds, so I shouldn't talk about the others! I'm going to go for Eddie McCallion though! Because me and Eddie at that time were the Tan-tastic Two! Riviera Sunbeds was a regular stop for us! You had likes of Killian Brennan, and Stephen O'Flynn as well. They weren't so much on the sunbeds as much as me and Eddie! It wasn't just the two of us though! There would have been one or two more at that time, but me and me and Eddie got the grief! We could be spotted a mile off too! Bear in mind we live in Derry where you're lucky to get one day of sun a year never mind be glowing!

W IS FOR WISHES...

Is there anything you'd change about your career if you could do it all again?
No, I don't believe so. What I've done in football, I achieved pretty much the majority of it at Derry to be honest with you. I mean from a footballing perspective, I think every

young player wants to get to the high heights of the Premier League and things like that, but that was never really a goal for me. I knew my limitations and I knew that was it was never going to happen to be honest. I was always a realist. But I'm not ever one to look back and be annoyed about how anything turned out. I don't look back with regrets, I look back and be proud of the things I achieved with my hometown club. The supporters we had, the achievements we had, the success and the friendships we made. Off the pitch I focus everything on family and I'm not saying I left everything behind, but I wish I would have stayed in touch with people a lot more than what I probably have done. But again, as I say, I'm very much a family-man. But, no, I can't look back and say 'I wish...'! I'm happy with what I achieved. I think have done quite well, you know.

X IS FOR EXPERIENCE...

What's the best atmosphere you've ever experienced as a player?
There's one that I'm thinking of, when I was at Carlisle we got to the LDV Vans Trophy Final, or the EFL Cup as it is now, and we played at the Millennium Stadium in Cardiff. We were beaten by Bristol City and it was 50,000 there. That atmosphere was

unbelievable. The whole build up and everything was unbelievable even. But again if I go back to 2006 with the whole European run and going for the league, the Brandywell was bouncing at that time. The atmosphere for the European games especially, Paris St Germain, Gothenburg, and Gretna. Not so much Gretna at home, but Gretna away. But the PSG and Gothenburg games, because I think people probably thought we were dead and buried facing these teams and none of them could beat us at the Brandywell. I'll actually say Paris Saint Germain at the Brandywell as well as the LDV Final. Because of who they were and when we needed the 12 man, the supporters were right there with us. We achieved a 0-0 draw that night, and probably if it was against anyone else you'd have probably been a bit disappointed not to give the fans something to cheer about!

Y IS FOR YOUNG...

Where did you start your youth career, and were you always in the same position?
No, I started at Trojans as a centre forward! I was actually overall top goal scorer! I loved it there though. I always loved football, but Trojans would have been my first club under the guidance of Raymond Carton,

but then I was a striker and top goal scorer in the age groups that it was in, and overall top goal scorer. After that Dougie Wood took me into the Derry City youth team and then I played my first game for the reserves is against Enniskillen at St Julian's in Omagh, and then John Cunningham sort of took over the reserve side of things at the club, and then it just sort of happened quickly. Not like four or five years, it was almost like within a year that I was playing for the first team. Mostly because they no other centre backs, so they called me in! But I grasped it pretty quick, I wasn't intimidated or anything by it all. I always used the positives. And the crowd were very supportive. They knew I'm one of their own, so they got right behind me. I always remember a game I played against UCD. I was playing well against Jason Sherlock and I don't know why but Felix took me off after 60 minutes or whatever, but the crowd boo'd him! So I always knew I had all those people behind me. I always remember John Cunningham saying to me when you play for your hometown club, somehow you get an extra 20%! I always believed that! Because I think if I was to look back, I've had bad games like us all, but the majority were away from home. I very

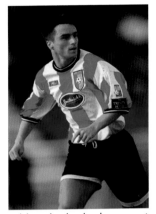

seldom had a bad game at home because of being a hometown boy and always knowing the supporters were right behind us.

Z IS FOR ZONE...

Did you ever have any pre-match rituals or superstitions to get you in the zone?
Sunbed the day before! No I'm only joking!! No, there was nothing I always had to do. The only thing I used to do when I was at Derry, because obviously I lived beside the Chapel in Creggan, I always used to go in for a bit of holy water and blessed myself before I'd head down. I'd be passing it anyway, because I lived Dunmore at the bottom of Creggan and I'd always have to go up Broadway, over past the chapel and down South Way. So I always used to call in and just bless myself with a bit of holy water and away I went to the game and that always helped me... I think!

THE A-Z OF... THOMAS STEWART

SPONSORED BY
BRANDYWELL PRIDE S.C.

A IS FOR ANNOYING...

Which former team mate was the worst to sit beside on the bus for long away journeys?

I've been pretty lucky to have good teammates throughout the years... but Michael Dougherty, who is now the goalkeeping coach with Derry City incidently, gets it because of the amount of times he played the song 'BELTER' by Gerry Cinnamon on repeat!!! Every time I hear it now it makes me laugh!

B IS FOR BEHAVIOUR...

Which of your former team mates was always the most likely to get booked?

Patrick Flynn at Shamrock Rovers! I think he got booked in warm ups and at half time!

C IS FOR CALIFORNIA...

How did your move to the USA come about with Sacramento Republic, and later in Canada with Ottawa Fury?

Yeah, I'd had a successful season at Shamrock Rovers and had won pretty much everything in Northern and Southern Ireland, so I wanted to test myself abroad. I had several phone calls with the owner and manager before flying out to California to sign. Ottawa just came

after that. I stayed out there to look for a club and Paul Dalglish, Kenny's son, was manager of Ottawa Fury at the time. Shane McEleney actually played at Ottawa with me as well for a while.

D IS FOR DERRY CITY...

Who is the best player Derry City have ever had?
Derry has been blessed with talent over the years and continues to produce the finest footballers...there are so many but I think Paddy McCourt was very special.

E IS FOR EUROPE...

What memories do you have of playing Juventus in Europe with Shamrock Rovers? Whose shirt did you get?
Probably the fans from both teams, Juventus had 40,000 in the stadium, and it just showed how huge a club they are. A fantastic experience to play in and I got two world cup winners shirts, Bonucci and Chiellini.

F IS FOR FUNNY...

Which former team mate was the biggest practical joker?
Eddie McCallion was always up to something!!

G IS FOR GOAL...

What was the best goal you've ever scored?
It's hard to say, I've scored some really good goals, but I always enjoyed the important goals that won us a title or cup so probably the goal that secured our glamour tie with Juventus.

H IS FOR HAHA...

What was the funniest thing you remember happening from your time in football?
I'd have to say the dressing room, with the players everyday there was always laughing and joking and stories being told. I think that's what all players miss when they retire.

I IS FOR IRELAND...

Do you still keep an eye on results of your former teams in the League Of Ireland?
Yes as a manager now I like to see how my ex teams are doing and always wish them well. I had a good relationship with all the teams I played for.

J IS FOR JOINING...

Do you remember the story of how you signing for Derry City came about?
Yeah, Stephen Kenny was monitoring my games and in my last 6 months of my contract at Linfield numerous conversations were had and the appeal of full time football under his leadership was important to me.

K IS FOR KIT...

What has been your favourite football kit that you've ever played in or owned?

I've kept jerseys from all my clubs and I really liked the gold and black kit from my time at Wolverhampton Wanderers.

L IS FOR LIFE AFTER PLAYING...

Did you have a plan for after football? Was management something you always wanted to do?

Yeah, I started my coaching badges when I was still playing and I was just trying to study the game as much as I could. I believe I've a lot to offer and football has been my life and will hopefully be a big part going forward as well.

M IS FOR MEMENTO...

What is the one football memento you own that you'll never give away?

Probably my international caps. They're very special to me.

N IS FOR NIGHT OUT...

Which former team mate was usually the first to initiate a night out?

We weren't allowed any nights out under Stephan Kenny! And he always knew if you did sneak out!

O IS FOR OPPOSITION...

Which opposition did you always look forward to playing the most in your

career?

Derby games were always good, and I've played a few in my career against West Brom, Glentoran, Finn Harps, Bohemians, LA Galaxy. They were always very exciting.

P IS FOR PASSTIME...

Outside of football, what keeps you occupied now in your spare time?

I like to cross country ski. That's on offer 5 months during the year here in Sweden. It's a good way to stay active and enjoy the outdoors. If it's indoors then darts. I have got myself into a bit of darts!

Q IS FOR QUIZ...

Which former team mate would you definitely not want in your team if you

were doing a quiz?

Ah, we were all a bright bunch at Derry!! I wouldn't want to drop someone in it!

R IS FOR RESULT...

Which result stands out or meant the most to you in your career?

There have been so many, but the result for Shamrock Rovers against Bray in 2010, winning the league again for the first time in 16 years would probably be the one that I celebrated most.

S IS FOR SWEDEN...

You manage in Sweden now, how did that come about?

I'd been getting some interest from abroad for a while but nothing that felt like it would really challenge me or help me grow. But then

I had seen a job advertisement that met my criteria and I quickly contacted the board, and they and the sportchief did the interview and they made me an offer and we got the deal done and I'm enjoying every second of it!

T IS FOR TALENT...

Who is the best player you've ever played with?
Jonny Evans. We played together on the youth team at Manchester United school of excellence and Northern Ireland U21.

U IS FOR UNPARALLELED...

Who is the best player you've ever played against?
Alessandro Del Piero. He was

a fantastic player and I grew up watching him and to get the chance to play against him in the Europa League was an amazing experience. You could probably name a few from that Juventus team though in fairness!

V IS FOR VANITY...

Which team mate spent the longest in front of the mirror?
Kevin Deery! He always tried to look sharp!

W IS FOR WISHES...

Is there anything you'd change about your career if you could do it all again?
No, I don't have regrets or anything, but it is such a short career and if I could go back and eliminate some of

the injuries that stopped me playing from time to time then I would! But I enjoyed my career as it was.

X IS FOR EXPERIENCE...

What's the best atmosphere you've ever experienced as a player?
The Juventus game out in Italy with 40,000 fans was incredible. The singing and chanting didn't stop all night!

Y IS FOR YOUNG...

What is your earliest memory of going to a football match?
My Dad brought me to watch Manchester United when they came to play my hometown team Portadown. Eric Cantona was there and he was definitely a hero of mine as a kid.

Z IS FOR ZERO CHANCE...

Was there ever a club that you would have refused to play for or support?
Being a Man Utd fan I couldn't support City, but that all changes when you start playing professionally. Football is the best game in the world and it has given me opportunities and the ability to perform and travel around the world, engaging with different people and cultures from all different backgrounds.

GER O'BRIEN

SPONSORED BY
GRAEME 'SCOOPS' TAYLOR

A IS FOR ANNOYING...
Which of your former team mates was the worst to sit beside on the bus for long away journeys?
I'm going to say... Gareth McGlynn! He'd just be talking about all his business interests the whole way there and the whole way back!

B IS FOR BEHAVIOUR...
Which of your former team mates was always the most likely to get booked?
Probably would have been Deerso I would say. Or Sammy Morrow, but I'd go Deer-

so. He liked to put himself about a bit!

C IS FOR CHAMPIONS...
It's more of a St Pat's question, but a big year for you personally. What are your memories of 2013, winning the league, you made it into team of the year, & won goal of the season?
Memories of the winning the league was that it started off quite slow. I remember actually getting thumped 3-0 in Tallaght by Rovers in our second game and probably that quickly we had a moment as a

group where we decided which way we wanted to go, and I remember, it might have been game 8, Sligo had won seven from seven and they won the league the previous year and people were saying they were going to walk it that year and we beat them 2-0, and that was probably the turning point for us. But that was that was a crazy season! It just felt easy that year. We were all just playing really, really well, all the lads. We could nearly name the team before the start of the game and we all came together really well as a unit.

D IS FOR DERRY CITY...

169

Do you remember the story of how you signing for Derry City came about?

Yeah, I got a phone call from Stephen Kenny. I was really surprised actually. He had made an approach to Rovers and Rovers were willing to accept it and let him to talk to me, so which to me sounded strange because I'd just got player of the year and Rovers and had a really good season, and was surprised that they'd just let me go. But Michael O'Neill had just come in as manager, and to be honest with you, he wanted to get Gary Twigg in and he needed finances to do that and I was probably one of the sellable people that could actually bring in some money at the time. So yeah, that's how it kind of came about. I drove to the City Hotel and met Stephen for probably 3 or 4 hours and had good chats. They actually

were going away on a pre-season trip, and me and him sat to about 1 in the morning before he left. He was to be in the airport for 5am the next morning going on a pre-season trip with the team. So, that's kind of my first memory of going up to Derry and the signing happened after that.

E IS FOR EUROPE...

Which team was your toughest European opponent? At any club.

I suppose... Like, I played around 24 or 25 times in Europe and had some really good performances, but the toughest game was probably was probably Široki Brijeg. Like, we played against Hanover and Legia Warsaw and teams like that, but that team in Bosnia, Široki Brijeg were tough. The travel was quote tough, the team were quite tough, but we ended up winning the game and the tie in the return leg at home. And that was in the days when away goals counted, so, yeah, that was probably the toughest.

F IS FOR FUNNY...

What was the funniest thing you remember from your time in football? There's usually a Stephen Kenny story!

Yeah, I'll give you a Stephen Kenny one! We're in Cork and we were down overnight

because of the journey. But at half time Stephen came in to do his team talk and he was walking up and down the dressing room and he slipped, went up in the air and fell on his on his head. He ended up having to go to the hospital and didn't make it out for the second half! I know it's terrible at the time, but funny when you look back!

G IS FOR GOAL...

What would you say was the best goal you've ever scored?

Probably... I scored one in Cork. We actually lost the game, so it was forgotten, but yeah, probably Cork. I got a couple of good ones from Bohs as well, one against Dundalk where I ran the length of the pitch and stuck one in the top corner. But, the Cork one stands out, because we won the league, even though we lost the game we won the league and it was just nice on the last game of the season to score one.

H IS FOR HERO...

Who was your footballing or sporting hero growing up?

Footballing hero growing up would have been probably... Well I was a big Liverpool fan, I was actually a huge St Pat's fan as well, so I would have been watching

Pats every week, but from a Liverpool point of view over the local, maybe someone like John Barnes. He was probably the big one for me that I used to love watching.

I IS FOR IT'S TIME...

What was your deciding factor in retiring as a player?

Injuries. Yeah, just constant niggles and issues from probably 2009 up in Derry, and then probably from 2009 to 2014, them five years I felt I was at the top of my game, I felt in my own head and with my performances, that I was probably the best full back in the league. And then I just started getting niggles towards the end of 2014. Groin issues and that, and it kind of continued in 2015 and then, 2016 was almost a write off where I was struggling to get up out of bed. I'd tried injections, I'd tried everything. You might get away with that from a centre forward's point of view where you can play half an hour or so. But for a full back, if you find that the winger's going at you and taking you on and stuff like that, it's just like you're actually probably hindering the team more than helping the team. So that was really the deciding factor.

J IS FOR JOKER...

Who was the biggest practical joker you've

met in football?
We had a good laugh and a really good group, no one was really a torture! Like, Mark Farren was a really good guy. A really, really funny lad. It was just a really good group of players, but from a joker point of view like, maybe Clive Delaney actually. Big Clive would have been a funny fella like. Clive had the ability to turn things on its head.

K IS FOR KIT...

What has been your favourite football kit that you've ever played in or owned?

I'm going to say the 'Patselona' one because we won the cup in it in 2014 against yourselves! It was the away kit we had that looked like the Barcelona shirt. Yeah, that's my favourite one. In fact all the cup wins since then 2014, 2021 and 2023 have all been in the away jerseys. But, yeah, definitely

the 'Pats-elona' one would probably be my favourite of them.

L IS FOR LIFE AFTER PLAYING...

Did you have a plan for after your playing career ended? Was management something you ever wanted to do?

Yeah, and ironically enough it was the time in Derry when everything from a financial point collapsed, it was that same weekend that I actually came home that I started on my youth cert, and then I did the B License, then A License. The plan was always to be involved in football full time after playing. Originally it would have been on the coaching side of things on the pitch, but then as things developed around the football in leagues and underage and academies I just found the niche and that and that's where it's kind of stood to

THE A-Z OF: GER O'BRIEN

me over the last number of years.

M IS FOR MEMENTO...

What is the one football memento you own that you'll never give away?

Definitely the cup final medal. I've been lucky enough to get a few caps as well and that, and the league wins are great and all, but there's something about a cup final that just makes it mean so much to everyone involved.

N IS FOR NIGHT OUT...

Which team mate was usually the first to initiate a night out?

Probably Higgy! He'll have a chuckle reading that, but yeah, I'd say Ruaidhri Higgins! Ah, in fairness, we had many good nights out there. We had a good crew where you know, if you preformed on the pitch on a Friday you could enjoy your weekend,

but yeah in my time up there it was definitely Higgy!

O IS FOR OPPOSITION...

Which opposition did you always look forward to playing the most in your career?

I suppose it changed as it goes on in the career because like in Ireland, players want to play in good facilities and you look at the likes of Cork, what they done at Turner's Cross, then Sligo put in the good stands and dressing rooms and stuff like that. But I suppose, you look at Tallaght now and be envious of the players playing in front of 10,000. But it's great, the league is growing, but I suppose for me, I played a lot of my time in Dublin where the Dublin derbys were always the best, so probably going to Tallaght and stuff like that.

Or when I was at Pats, bringing the local rivals to Inchicore. So probably playing a Dublin derby there would be my biggest one.

P IS FOR PASSTIME...

Outside of football, what keeps you occupied now in your spare time?

I suppose kids would be the big one. You turn into a taxi driver at night sometimes, you know, taking kids from one session to another session. But it's great, you know, that's what keeps me busy now is being able to kind of, stay on top of that. But I've not picked up the golf clubs just yet! And I was never into the computer! So it still just revolves around football!

Q IS FOR QUIZ...

Which former team mate would you definitely not want in your team if you were doing a quiz?

Let me see... I'm probably going to say James Doona for St Pats!

R IS FOR RESULT...

Which result stands out or meant the most to you in your career?

I'm gonna go back to the Cup Final again, probably because you have so many games in football, but in a cup final, when you get that relief more than anything. Which that cup final in particular in 2014 was! Yous had turned us over two years earlier, you know. And there was 53 years there that we just couldn't get close to it. So that was probably the best one for me.

S IS FOR STEPHEN KENNY...

What was Stephen Kenny like as a manager? Do you have any other funny stories involving him?

I could probably fill that whole alphabet with funny stories! But, no, Stephen was fantastic. I had known him from his time in Dublin and had plenty of chats with him, but Stephen is a proper football man and he gets the best out of his players and the best out of his group. He's very brave manager and I really enjoyed my time playing for him. I had the utmost respect for him and what he's done and he's gone on achieve at Dundalk and the senior team and

you know I think in years to come especially when those young players who did get the breakthrough under him end up going on and we do achieve an international tournament, whether that's the Euros or a World Cup, I think he'll get the credit he deserves. In terms of funny stories, ah listen, there's loads! But I think everyone knows that he's a quirky type of character in terms of, like, he can be tense. You know, when you walk into a room, you don't know whether you know you're going to get a smile or whatever. But I still have a laugh at the bottle caps! You know, the lads used to throw the bottle caps off the Lucozade out into the middle of the floor and he'd be walking up and down picking them up or kicking them out of the way and then he'd turn and more would be there and he'd be like 'I know what yous are doing!' But, yeah, there's loads of

funny stories, but he was so well respected, you know. One man's quirkiness is another man's genius, and he's definitely from a football perspective, a genius. He had a car as well when I was up there, it was obviously a company car. I think it was a Mondeo or something but he couldn't get the back window wiper to stop going! Even when he was like he was parked like the window wiper would be going, and even in the summer months when it's bone dry you could hear the wiper going and you knew Stephen was around! I don't think he ever figured out how to stop the wiper. God knows how he gave the car back!

T IS FOR TEAM MATES...

Who is the best player you've ever played with?

Probably Keith Fahy. Obviously he had been at another level and he'd come back here after he had a really good career in England in the Championship and in and in the Premier League as well. He won the League Cup over there with Birmingham. They beat Arsenal in the final. Keith was just on a different level you could see how good he was. I'm lucky, I played with Killian Brennan and Chris Forrester have had amazing careers here in Ireland, and one that would actually really sur-

prise a few people because when he was with Pats, he wasn't great because he had a lot of issues going on, but Keith Tracy was absolutely outrageous as well. Like his left foot, you know, and he was probably a stone and a half overweight at Pats, and was probably still the best player at the club. His fitness was an issue just, but I'd have to give it to Keith Fahy without a doubt.

U IS FOR UNPARAL-LELED...

Who is the best player you've ever played against?

Well, I was lucky enough to have played a lot of representative games for the League of Ireland XI against United and stuff like that so, you look at the likes of Rooney and people like that. I'm actually going to answer this question from a league point of view though. I think

Daryl Horgan. I used to have a good battle against Daryl and that's when he was kind of breaking into that Dundalk 2014-15 team. I didn't find any issues with him in them days, but the more I started struggling with injuries I found him to be top player, and again another one who went on to have a really good career in England. But, probably, yeah from a domestic point of view, I'd say Daryl Horgan.

V IS FOR VANITY...

Which team mate spent the longest in front of the mirror?

The boys nowadays are worse then when I was playing! Carrying hair brushes and all sorts with them! I say one in jest from a light hearted way because he'll probably read this and I'll go for Ciaran Martyn! Big John was a great looking fella, and a cool fella in fairness to

him, but yeah I'll pick him!

W IS FOR WISHES...

Is there anything you'd change about your career if you could do it all again?

I had a couple of opportunities to go away which I didn't take. One to America, and one to Scotland. They'd probably be regrets maybe, or more of a question of what might have happened if…, you know. But listen, I'm very proud to have played in the League Of Ireland for my whole career. It's given me so much and it's given me a full time job after playing now. You know, I know the league inside out and I'm delighted to see the growth in the league now. It's brilliant from the increase in spectators, to the stadiums being done up. I try not to have regrets because it's part of what makes you who you are and I'm not just saying it, but I actually loved my time up in Derry. I moved up there, I brought my dogs up there and I was all in on that three year deal, and I probably, looking at the group that we had coming through and some of the older players who were still playing really well, I think we could have achieved something and that's a regret in itself as well because there was such a good group in Derry and I committed myself to moving up and everything and I love the city, I love the place, and I still have a lot of people up there that I speak to regularly. So that's a regret in itself because of what turned out in the end about the club having to kind of restart again. That's the regret, not getting to see where that group could have got to. It's a great ground, and every Friday night it was absolutely jammers! And I had a bit of a time up there because obviously I joined late in the pre-season, and Stephen in fairness to him, put me straight into the team, and obviously Eddie was the right back for such a long time, and a local guy and a brilliant fella and a very good player. But it was great. Everyone welcomed me with open arms and I love going back up and seeing a lot of the same faces. So, you know, it's brilliant.

X IS FOR EXPERIENCE...
What's the best atmosphere you've ever experienced as a player?
Again, I'll probably go back to Pats here on this one. Probably like when Richmond was full, 5,000 people and you're playing Rovers and you're beating Rovers and stuff like that and that's probably the best. It's such a tight ground so it's quite close. Everyone feels like they're on top of you, so when you're winning it's absolutely brilliant. The other way though, when you're losing, it's not so good! But, yeah, definitely for me, Richmond, a full Richmond Park. And when you're winning is absolutely the best.

Y IS FOR YOUNG...
What is your earliest memory of going to a

football match?
Pats again! All my family are Inchicore, so that would be in the earliest football memory. I was lucky enough that my dad was a Liverpool fan and he would bring us over to watch Liverpool, maybe a couple of times a year and we used to go over on the boat. But certainly Friday nights in Inchicore standing in the shed where the Pats fans used to stand down there was probably the earliest memory.

Z IS FOR ZONE...
Did you ever have any pre-match rituals or superstitions to get you in the zone?
Yeah, it probably changed throughout my career though. I went through different phases where I felt a cold bath on the day of the game would probably do my legs and my body better, and I felt probably in my own head a bit better after that, and I think that's what a lot of those superstitions are, they're for your head more than anything. I didn't eat a whole lot on game days. I used to just eat a little sandwich or a bowl of cereal. That would have been about it. I used to look at lads eating a bowl of pasta and chicken and think how do they do it! A sandwich would do me. But, yeah probably the cold bath would be the main one.

175

EAMON ZAYED

SPONSORED BY
FURNITURE PLUS

A IS FOR ANNOYING...

Which of your former team mates was the worst to sit beside on the bus for long away journeys?

I'm just trying to think. I need to rewind back to that 2011 squad that we had and think of all the characters that we had! I'm going to say… and I wouldn't even call him annoying, but I would say James McClean because I didn't understand what he was saying most of the time! He spoke so bloody quick I never understood what he said! It took me a while to get used to him! And he was one of the guys that I hung out with the most out of the squad! But he spoke so quick with a really thick Derry accent that I never understood what the hell he was saying!!

B IS FOR BEHAVIOUR...

Which of your former team mates was always the most likely to get booked?

We had a couple! I'd say Kevin Deery probably! I mean, he was a moaner on the pitch! He was great to have as a teammate though. He would absolutely have your back, he'd battle it out for absolutely everything, but he'd be arguing every little decision with the ref! But you know, he was doing it to obviously try and get the upper hand and win. So, I would say probably Kevin Deery, yeah.

But as I say, we had a few like. We had Barry Molloy who wasn't afraid of a tackle either. Obviously going back to Ryan McBride as well. He was another one that again didn't hold back in a tackle, but I would say Kevin Deery for sure, yeah.

C IS FOR CHAMPIONS...

You've won almost everything possible in Ireland,

League, FAI Cup, League Cup, Setanta Cup, Golden Boot, Player Of The Year, Young Player Of The Year... Is there one that stands out over the others?

Yeah, I was fortunate. I think I won every kind of thing to win. I mean, they're all different for different reasons. Like, individually, for me, the final year with Derry City to win the Player Of The Year and the Golden Boot was a great achievement. I know it's an individual award and you know, I always say it to the lads here when I'm managing, obviously it's about the team. Obviously you can't win individual awards for me as a striker without the service that the team around you provides. So, I think that was definitely an individual award that stuck out.

In terms of trophies though, to complete the collection in 2011, when I was at Derry, I needed to win the League

Cup and we beat Cork City one nil, so that was the complete collection then, that was special.

I do think though, that 2011 season winning Player Of The Year, and Golden Boot; I won't say it was something that I chased, but it was definitely something that felt really, really, good and probably more so because in 2010 I had a shit year with Sporting Fingal and I didn't know where my career was going and then Steven Kenny obviously brought me back to Derry City and brought the confidence back in my game. So I would say because of that, being so low in confidence the year prior, then to reach those heights within a year was a great achievement for me.

D IS FOR DERRY CITY...

Do you still keep an eye on the Derry City results?

Yeah, all the time! Ah listen, you might jump on these interviews and everybody

says it to be nice, but truly ever since I left, I left a fan. I know for a fact that my best year in League of Ireland was that year with Derry. Not just on the pitch, even off the pitch. I just loved it. I had a lot of fun. I always remember the third game away to UCD, the Derry City fans started to call me Metro Man! They were singing 'Metro, Metro Man! Eamon wants be, a Metro Man'!! And then after the game Stephen Kenny saying 'What's all that about?', and it was obviously because I was in the the Metro all the time with the lads after a game!! You know, as you would after a game! Especially if we won! So I had a lot of fun. I loved it up there, so I always keep in touch with the results. And obviously now that Ruaidhri Higgins, an ex-teammate, is the manager as well. So, yeah, I left a fan for sure!

E IS FOR EUROPE...

Which team was your toughest European opponent? At any club.

I would have to say probably Dynamo Kiev. We played them at Drogheda united. They were probably the toughest. Athletically, they were just far superior to us. That was one thing that stood out. Obviously, we could play, they could play, but this was probably before strength and conditioning coaching really came into clubs in Ireland, and they were just athletically, miles ahead of us, so, yeah, they were tough, tough opponents.

F IS FOR FUNNY...
What was the funniest thing you remember from your time in football?
There's been loads! There's a good few Stephen Kenny moments as well. I remember being in the changing room, and Stephen Kenny was very particular in terms of his pre-match team talks. And listen, they were excellent. I loved them. I mean, they really got you going. They made you feel 10 foot tall. But he was very particular about the smallest things, especially cleanliness and tidiness. He always wanted your changing bags tucked under your seat, and he'd want a spotless floor when he walked into the locker room. But every now and again, Barry Molloy would purposely just put a little bottle lid, like a Lucozade bottle lid right in the middle of the floor and that would just throw Stephen off completely! Stephen would walk in and he'd just be doing circles in silence, staring at the at this little bottle cap, and he'd be fuming! And then he'd be like, 'who the fuck did that?!' And

then he'd have to walk back out, compose himself, and then come back in again!

G IS FOR GOAL...
What was the best goal you've ever scored?
I would say... I don't know if it's the best, maybe the most impactful, but for me, probably when I scored the third goal to complete a hat-trick when we beat our rivals Esteghlal 3-2 in the Theran Derby when I was with Persepolis, coming back from two goals down in the last 10 minutes and we were down to 10 men as well. The third goal was probably the most impactful. It was a nice goal. It was a nice strikers goal, but probably the most impactful rather than the best. But I mean it's hard for me to look back and say that another goal stands out more because that's the one I would think of. It was just real Roy of the Rovers stuff coming on as a sub on your debut and scoring a hat-trick in 10mins in the derby to win the game!

H IS FOR HANGING UP THE BOOTS...
Did you have a plan for after football? Was management something you always wanted to do?
No, it kind of just came to me. I mean, to be honest, in Ireland, I didn't see the career path in management.

It was a very difficult career path because if you're not coaching one of the full-time teams in the League of Ireland, or working with the FAI, you're pretty much a volunteer or part-time coach. But in terms of after football, it was a difficult one, but if I can rewind to when I was at Derry in 2011, I remember speaking to Mark Farren and he was obviously going through the issues that he went through and I think he had had his surgery and was trying to make a comeback in terms of playing that year. But I remember him telling me that he was coming near to the end of his career anyway, age-wise, and he was telling me that with the medical expenses that he was going through, he had to dip into savings, and sell the car and stuff like that and that was quite impactful, because I was thinking of when I hang up the boots. I mean, Mark Farren had everything. He had all the trophies you want and the individual awards as well and was one of the best strikers the League of Ireland had ever seen, but he was saying to me that at the end of it, what would he have? And he just he was telling me this in his words, like 'at the end of the day, when I quit football next year I won't have a lot to show for it, just trophies.' And those

took off. I probably had 6-7 years in terms of coaching and then I knew if I'm going to stay in the game I definitely want to be a head coach. I wanted to coach professional, competitive football, and yeah, it's been the best decision I've ever made to stay on in football because I really enjoy it so far. I've still got a lot to learn, but I'm doing alright I'd say.

I IS FOR INTERNATIONAL...

What do you remember about getting your first International call-up?

Yeah, my international call up was a game changer for me. I remember getting called up in 2010 again the year before I went to Derry, 2010, and that first call up just came out of the blue. I didn't expect it at all. But at that time I was kind of falling out of love with football if I'm being honest. I had a terrible year with Sporting Fingal and Liam Buckley and I just wasn't enjoying it and I wasn't playing well and in truth I was contemplating actually quitting football. But I got that chance to play international football and I remember jumping off the plane in Libya, that was where the first camp and first game was, and I remember being met with newspapers and the media with their cameras and

words kind of stuck with me and I always think about them when I think about Mark. Like, he had it all but he thought he didn't have much, and it made me think of when I hang up my boots, what do I want to show for it? Do I want individual awards and trophies or do I want to have something else that I can kind of hold on to? And I was thinking it would be great to have a deposit on a house or maybe buy a house or whatever the case is and be able to say 'my football career bought this house'. That's why I went from Derry City to play in Iran actually, because they offering me, financially, a really nice package and I genuinely just kept thinking of Mark and what he said and how life can just change like that for you.

So, I guess that was it, that's where I was thinking 'I'm just going to go with it for as long as I can and try to financially if I make some money in Iran, fantastic.' So kind of, that was it.

I finished my UEFA C license just before I came to the States to play, and I got involved in a little bit of coaching and really enjoyed it and that's kind of when it really

looking for interviews and that was the start of the experience. I just thought that week was unbelievable. It made me feel like a soccer player again and I wanted to experience it again. So that was it. I remember just the feeling that I got and I guess it was the feeling of importance or something, which sometimes you just need to feel like a proper soccer player again and I wanted to experience it again. And that's kind of what I took out of it. I just wanted to experience international football and being able to compete against another country, you know.

J IS FOR JOKER...

Which former team mate was the biggest practical joker?

Ah look, I had loads! I mean if I look back to the Derry City, we had a quite a few. I mean, both the McEleney brothers were jokers, we

had Danny Lafferty, even James McClean, but I think the biggest Joker was Barry Molloy! He was a clown like! Absolute joker! He was hilarious! The guys loved him. I mean, he was always doing some weird shit in the changing room before and after games. He used to do unbelievable impressions; I'm actually cracking up thinking about it! But he used to do unbelievable impressions of Steven Kenny! And he used to do it right before Stephen came in! So we'd be in the changing room and nearly every time he came in we were laughing! It was brilliant! Right before he came in, Barry would stand up and start doing these impressions of the team talk. And I mean it he nailed it! Like, it was perfect! And we'd be in stitches!

K IS FOR KIT...

What has been your favourite football kit that

you've ever played in or owned?

That's a tough one! I think the red kit that we have at Mansfield now is a beautiful kit. Honestly, a kit is a kit to me, but that one is a nice kit. I don't know, it has a bit of Man United in it or something.

L IS FOR LEAGUE...

You've experienced football in Ireland, England, Norway, Iran, Malaysia, and U.S.A, but is there a league that you preferred in terms of playing style?

Yeah, I mean, like, I played ten years in Ireland and loved it, but I wanted to experience new countries and so I started going a lot further. But, I'm going to call it more like a regret than anything else. I went over to Crewe Alexandra on loan and they were playing in the English Championship at the time and I remember going in there and training with the first team lads, and watching the games in the English Championship. I think it was 2004 or something. But I was on the bench for a game and I remember thinking, 'yeah, look, I can play in this level. I feel like I can do well in this level and score goals'. But I just wish I got more of a chance. There was a couple of lads playing ahead of me and I never got a chance to

get a proper run at it and my loan kind of came to an end after six months, but I just wished that I had gotten a chance. I mean, could have played in the English Premiership? Absolutely not. But was I as good as other lads who went over from Ireland, Kevin Doyle for instance, who was my age group, and Stephen Ward, who, growing up with them lads, I used to scored more goals then them. But I just felt, I could have done it in the English Championship, you know. I think I could have scored goals at that level and I think I could have done alright, you know.

M IS FOR MEMENTO...

What is the one football memento you own that you'll never give away?

Yeah, I have a few. I don't know if other footballers do this as well, but I collect all my trophies, I've kept them all. And the jerseys as well. I can't think of just one, but if I could just generalise it, I would just say the jerseys. I probably started collecting football jerseys a little bit later than I would have liked to though, so I have missed out on a few that I would have liked. But I still have to have most of the jerseys that I wore and I have a couple of them framed up in my office at home. I actually the Derry City one framed up. So yeah,

I would say football jerseys are the one thing that I like to keep and I want to frame as many as I can because yeah, I mean when I look at a football jersey, whether it's the team you played for, or whether it's from teams that you played against that you might have swapped, they make an impression on you and bring back memories straight away.

N IS FOR NIGHT OUT...

Which team mate was usually the first to initiate a night out?

We had a few! I would say the young Patrick Mceleney you know! I mean he's maybe settled down a little bit now the older he got, but man, he loved a night out! And I was right there with him!! And listen, we were good pros, don't get me wrong! Like, Monday to Saturday we were all about games and training and staying back behind and doing extra training and all that, but, we also like to have fun! But yeah, it was always me and Paddy McEleney who were always saying 'Right... night out!' and then 'Who's up for it?'! So, yeah, if I could say myself I would, but I'll say Patrick McEleney!

O IS FOR OPPOSITION...

Which opposition did you always look forward to

playing the most in your career?

Yeah, there was a couple. I loved playing against Shamrock Rovers. Partly because I just didn't like them! I like playing against him and trying to get the better of him just simply didn't like them! So yeah, they'd probably be the opposition in Ireland that jumps out at me as a team I liked playing against. But in terms of grounds in terms of grounds to play in, I really liked playing Saint Pat's in Richmond Park. I just liked it. It was a nice enclosed ground. So that was the other game that I always looked forward to playing away to St Pat's because the fans always seemed like they were on top of you.

P IS FOR PASSTIME...

Outside of football, what keeps you occupied now in your spare time?

That's an easy one... hiking! Yeah, I hike all the time. When I was at Derry I used to live down towards Fahan. I had a really nice apartment, I think it belonged to the chairman, maybe he still owns it, but I had an apartment there that I stayed at and it was just beautiful. The views were gorgeous overlooking the water. But yeah, I used to get out and hike as much as possible anywhere around that area, and I still do that now here in Colorado. I love hiking. It's kind of what clears the air. Especially after a game or a bad result when things don't go well for you, it's good to get out and clear the head.

Q IS FOR QUIZ...

Which former team mate would you definitely not want in your team if you were doing a quiz?

I mean like, I know there's a lot of former team mates I could go back to, and I'm not being funny, but I could go back to that Derry City team and name at least half of them!! Like, I mean, some of them were just not the most knowledgeable I'd say!! You can easily say James McClean or Paddy McEleney. They'd be up there. Danny Lafferty! I would not want him on my quiz team! No chance! Yeah, I mean, take your pick! There's quite a few from that team, honestly! Like, great lads! But

absolutely would fail miserably in a quiz! So from Danny Lafferty to James McLean and Paddy McEleney. And, actually, another one that was a bit of a space cadet, I remember we played with Micky Mc-Crudden that year, as well. He would have had no chance in a quiz! We were quite a young team and they were the youngsters in fairness to them!

R IS FOR RESULT...

Which result stands out or meant the most to you in your career?

I think it has to be a result that obviously means something, so maybe… I mean the result I spoke about earlier in Iran in the derby, that 3-2 win. That genuinely did change my career, so I would say that maybe, yeah. Obviously when you come to a new country, nobody knows who you are, and es-

pecially as a striker you have to score goals to make a name for yourself and if you don't score goals, nobody cares who you are or anything like that. Even when I came over to sign with Indy Eleven in America in 2016, I don't know if it was the 3rd or 4th game I played, but we played against New York Cosmos, who are obviously one of the most well-known teams in the States, but I scored two and we won 2-1. So I think that probably brought my name to the league, and on people's radar kind of like 'Who is that lad? He can score goals' and that kind of gave me the confidence as well to kick on. So, that would be another one that was 7-8 years ago and I'm still in the States working in football now. Maybe if I haven't scored those goals, you know, I might have been back in Ireland after a year, so that that probably sticks out as well.

S IS FOR SIGNING...

Do you remember the story of you signing for Derry City came about?

Yeah, you could fill a book with that story alone! Me signing for Derry City was one of the craziest stories of my career! I don't know if you want to call it fate, but it ended up working out in the end! I'll try and give you the brief version! So, long story

short, at the end of 2010, like I was saying before, it wasn't my best year in football to say the least. I was definitely leaving Sporting Fingal, and I had a couple of options. I was going to sign for Shels before an offer came in from Malta. So I eventually agreed to go to Malta and I was at home and I remember this like it was yesterday. I was at home on a Wednesday and they sent over a contract and I literally signed the contract there and then at home and I was up in my mum's office at home and she had a printer and scanner and I just scanned it and emailed it back to them and that was me signed. Literally as soon as I pressed send I got a phone call from Stephen Kenny! Completely unexpected! I hadn't talked to him in a long time. I mean, the last time I spoke to Stephen Kenny, he talked to me about signing when he was the coach of Bohemians, but it fell through. So he rang me anyway and said, would you, I like you as a player, and I haven't been looking for many players outside of the Northwest, but there could be an opportunity for you to come here. He was telling me that because Rafael Cretato, who he'd agreed terms with to sign from Sligo that year, his wife's mother, I think it was had just passed away and he was contemplating stay-

ing at Sligo now at the last minute and not signing for Derry. So I said, OK, what does that mean? So he said 'well, if he doesn't sign, I'd like you to sign. Hopefully we'll know in the next few days so and I'll let you know.' But he explained to me that I wasn't a second choice and all that and that it was just that he didn't want to sign two players who weren't local, and he really sold it to me. And I knew how good Derry City were at that time and the young talent they had was amazing. Like, James McClean, Patrick McEleney were all just youngsters at the time.

So, as soon as I jumped off the phone call, I knew I wanted to sign for Derry City. But, obviously, I'd just signed for a team in Malta! So first I was always thinking, well, hold on, I can't call off that move to Malta just yet because I need to wait and see if Raff is not going to sign or not going to sign, and then secondly, if

he doesn't sign and I end up signing, what the hell am I going to do about this team in Malta! So a couple of days passed. The Maltese team got me a flight for the Saturday morning and come the Friday, I was in contact with Stephen Kenny and he said 'Look it's not 100%, but it's 99% that Raff is not going to be signing for us', I think he found out that Raff had told Ruaidhri or Kevin Deery or someone, I can't remember who it was, that it wasn't looking good for signing, but nothing was confirmed yet with Stephen Kenny, so he still wasn't 100%, and he said 'I'm just waiting to hear it come from Raff himself, but we have a call tomorrow morning.' So I said, OK. I got off the phone with Stephen and now I hadn't told Stephen anything at all about Malta, because I didn't want it to ruin the deal to sign for Derry, and I didn't want him to think I was playing him, you know? So after hearing that the Cretaro deal was nearly off I contacted the Maltese team that night, just a few hours before I was due to fly and just said 'Listen, something's come up at home and I'm not going to make that flight tomorrow', and they were really nice about it. They were like, 'No, it's OK. Listen, we'll rebook and we'll get you on a plane next week.'

The next morning I got a call off Stephen Kenny and saying 'Can you get up to Derry today, and we'll get this deal signed? Raff just told me that he's not going to be able to sign'. So, I was really happy to be getting the move I wanted finally, so I drove up to Derry about ten minutes after I put the phone down, and signed as soon as I got there. I remember thinking great, this is exactly what I want to do. It feels right, I'm really happy, but what the fuck am I going to do with this Maltese team?!

So I contacted the Maltese team on the Monday and told them 'listen, something's come up' and I didn't tell them exactly what. I just said 'I'm not going to go to Malta'. And they were lovely. They were like, 'that's OK, no problem'. So I thought I got away with it and it was all sorted. But the following week, the Derry City office said, 'Hold on his IPC is in Malta. What the fuck is it doing there?! We signed

you from Sporting Fingal!' And I hadn't thought about that admin stuff! So, I had to obviously explain what happened and they said 'listen, if this team decide to want money from us for a transfer, which is well within their rights as you sign for them, it's going to have to come out of your salary.' So I said 'look, they've been really nice with me, so leave it with me and let me talk to them'. So I talked to the Maltese team and explained the situation and they then offered to double my salary! Which would have been more than double what Derry were paying me, but I'd already made me mind up, so it wasn't about money or anything like that. I think they thought it was. But as I say, it was more about Derry City and talking to Stephen Kenny and knowing that I'd be happier there. I came up on that Saturday to sign and Eddie McCallion and Barry Molloy met me for a coffee. I didn't know him, just from playing against them, but they met me for a coffee, and we had a good chat, so, no, I knew I wanted to sign for Derry, and the Maltese team agreed to tear up the contract.

I do believe in some things happening for a reason, and fate stepping in sometimes. You know, I wouldn't wish it on anybody, but had it not been for Raff's mother in

law passing away, he would have been at Derry, and I would have went to Malta, and I wouldn't have won the player of the year and golden boot and everything that year, and I wouldn't be in the states right now probably. So, yeah, it's of bizarre how it happened, just kind of out of nothing, but I'm really glad it all worked out.

T IS FOR TEAM MATES...

Who is the best player you've ever played with?
There's a lad over in Iran, Ali Karimi. Him or Ali Daei, who every Iranian will say is the best player that's ever come out of Iran. He was a wizard with his feet. So he was definitely one that stands out.

In Ireland, I think of Derry City in 2011, because when you look at that squad, I mean, there's some talent in there. I played with Stephen McLaughlin, Gareth McGlynn, Ruaidhri Higgins, Kevin Deery as well. I think talent-wise, obviously the most naturally talented players where the young lads at the time, like Patrick McEleney. He's definitely up there. When I think of talented players, I like to think of players that can produce that X Factor moment. But another young lad as well, because of what he did in his career, it's genuinely hard to bypass James McClean. It suppose it comes down to how you define

talent. I mean, is talent hard work? Because James Mc-Clean was potentially the most hard working player I've ever played with. His will to work and want to succeed was by far more than any other player I've ever seen and I think that's what got him to where he is. I mean, 100 caps for Ireland is no joke, you know. So, I guess my answer. Would be how do you define talent, but, because I can define it as a coach now, I mean you need to work your balls off and have that commitment and obviously have end product and he had it. In terms of natural talent, you might look at somebody like Patrick McEleney as one of the most kind of gifted. Jason Byrne would be an-other one I would think of as maybe the most talented goal scorer I've played with. But, yeah, I'd have to say,

talent can be defined dif-ferently. Some players are born with it and waste it, others like James work hard to get it. I mean, how many football players got over 100 caps for Ireland and played Premiership football and still playing at 35 or 36. Look, you can say what you want about him, hate him, love him, but he's a brilliant professional. So, yeah, I'll say him.

U IS FOR UNPARAL-LELED...

Who is the best play-er you've ever played against?

I've played against some re-ally good players, so that's a tough one! If I go local, as in, players in Ireland, it's a toss-up. It's hard actually to differ-entiate who's a better player between Joey N'Do, Wes Hoolihan, and Paddy Mc-

Court? I can't differentiate between the three of them. They were all unbelievably talented. I remember play-ing against Paddy McCourt when he had a brief stint with Shamrock Rovers, and he scored potentially the best hat trick I've ever seen against us! It was an outra-geous hat trick! I mean, typi-cal him, he was dribbling past players for fun! And the finishes for each goal were unreal! I mean, Wes Hooli-han was phenomenal as well, as is Joey N'Do! So, any of them 3 in terms of League of Ireland.

Outside of that, I played an international for Libya against Cameroon in 2013. They qualified for the World Cup in 2014. I'm looking at their team and Samuel Eto'o was their captain at the time, so, yeah maybe outside of Ireland I would say him.

V IS FOR VANITY...

Which team mate spent the longest in front of the mirror?

I'll pick somebody from that 2011 team. I mean, I know Paddy McEleney loved him-self. I mean, he really loved himself, you know?! He was young and he though all the girls in Derry were after him! He played up to it as well! He always made sure that his hair was on point and he was going out dressed well.

So, yeah, I would say him.

W IS FOR WISHES...

Is there anything you'd change about your career if you could do it all again?

Yeah. I mean, you look back at experiences in your career and think were any of the experiences a waste, or were they needed to get you to where you are today? The only one I'd say that probably sticks out to me, and this probably ties into my answer earlier, would be signing for Shamrock Rovers. That was a waste. Absolute waste of a year. I came back from Iran and had options. I actually was about to sign for Sligo at the time. And I should have went to Sligo. Yeah, I feel like I wasted 18 months of my career in 2013 until the kind of middle of 2014 signing for Shamrock Rovers. It never felt right. You should trust your gut instinct. I held up the Shamrock Rovers flag for a photo shoot when I signed and I knew even then, like, 'this doesn't feel right', you know? That's kind of the one that I look back on and think I should have made a better choice, because Iran full of confidence, still with plenty in the locker to kind of make an impact in Ireland again and try to do well and, yeah, that was probably the biggest kind of regret that I

look back on.

The other one I think of, but it's not a regret, it's more of a 'wonder what…', but I signed for Leicester City when I was 17. Obviously most players in Ireland go to England when they were 16. I had an opportunity to go to Arsenal. They offered me a three-year deal. I would have been playing with quite a good team. David Bentley, Steve Sidwell, Rohan Ricketts, Jermaine Pennant… There was a lot of really talented players there and they saw me as one of them and had potential. Liam Brady was the director there at the Academy and he told me they really had high hopes for me and I probably should have signed there. I only stayed back because I wanted to finish school, but I kind of look back at that now and go 'what if' like. 'What would have happened?'

You know, that's the only thing. Because out of that team I would have been playing with, they all, if they didn't make it with Arsenal, they all went on to decent championship teams and other Premiership teams and did quite well. So, yeah, that's always had me wondering what would have happened.

X IS FOR EXPERIENCE...

What's the best atmosphere you've ever experienced as a player?

The best atmosphere, I'm probably giving the same answer for a lot of them, but it would be the Iranian derby. It was outrageous! We had 96,100 and something at the game I think was what was put up on the screen. So, yeah, I mean it's hard to look past that. International games come close, but, no, that derby game was louder because of the local rivalry.

Y IS FOR YOUNG...

What is your earliest memory of going to a football match?

I can't remember what age I was, maybe 8 or 9, but it would have been going to a St Pat's game. Now listen, was I a St Pat's fan? No, I wasn't! But we did the school thing. It was like a football training thing in the school for a week or so and it was down out of St Pat's and we did a little skills competition at Richmond Park and we got tickets to the game then at the end of the week. That's probably my earliest memory of going to a proper game and I loved it. Again though, I'll go on record, I'm not a St Pat's fan at all!! But I loved the atmosphere and the occasion of it all just.

Z IS FOR ZONE...

Did you ever have any pre-match rituals or superstitions to get you in

the zone?

Yeah. I have shit loads! Like, I have these old, and I mean really old, Batman boxers, like boxer briefs that you'd wear in games and, listen, there's holes in them and everything at this stage! At least I'm not still playing! Yeah, I'm really superstitious in terms of them and I wear them all the time if there's a game. Even recently, I got into coaching maybe 2 years ago now and results at the start weren't going the way I wanted and I even put them on to see if they would give me a bit of luck!

So, yeah, I do have a few strange things. I mean, everyone has their own rituals, I guess. I like to get up in the morning, go to the gym and have a stretch, and I started getting into yoga the older I got as well. So I have that routine and I would have always done that before a game.

But I would say, yeah, Bat-man stuff. Even to this day, I have Batman socks, Batman boxers that are newer boxers, but they don't have the same effect as the old ones! I keep them around though just in case results aren't going my way! So, yeah, finish the interview with me looking weird!!

Yeah, well that's all the questions! Thanks for taking the time Eamon!

No, not at all. I mean, I've always said it, and it's not because I know Derry City fans are reading or anything, but I think I played 10 years in Ireland, and that time at Derry City was definitely the best year I ever had in Ireland. Actually, it was probably my favourite year ever playing full stop. I mean, I remember just going across the bridge into the city on my first day and I just loved it. It's just a working class city. Even the team, the lads that we had in the Derry City team as talented

as some of them were, we had no prima donnas, nothing like that. And obviously some of them have gone on to do big things in England, but everybody just so down to Earth. Even walking around the streets, getting people stopping you for a chat about football. Derry's a proper football city, so you know, if you did well they would let you know, and if you didn't do well they'd let you know as well! But, yeah, I just loved it that year. I still try to keep in contact with people from back home and the lads who we played at Derry with. It wasn't that long ago I spoke to Danny Lafferty actually, I'd message James McClean as well, you know. Barry Molloy would have been somebody who I was quite close to when I was playing there as well, and I lived with Stewart Greacen there as well. I try to stay in contact with the lads from back home as well. It's good to kind of reminisce about those times and I'm sure if we'd talked for a few more hours I'd start remembering more things! But yeah, it was it to think back on it there. I enjoyed that! It was a great year. Unbelievable year. And honestly, the best year I've had in football, so that's why I still watch games when I can and keep up with the team today as a fan still you want them to do well.

THE A-Z OF...

STEPHEN McLAUGHLIN

SPONSORED BY
The Horseshoe Organisation
www.horseshoe.tv

A IS FOR ANNOYING...
Which of your former team mates was the worst to sit beside on the bus for long away journeys?
If I was to go back to my Derry City days, I'd say Barry Molloy!!

B IS FOR BEHAVIOUR...
Which of your former team mates was always the most likely to get booked?
Well, here at Mansfield it's definitely Ollie Clarke! To pick a former Derry City team mate, I'd have to go for Kevin Deery!

C IS FOR CUP...
What are your memories of that F.A.I Cup Final in 2012? What were the feelings when Patterson's goal went in?
When the goal went in? Relief! Pure relief just! A mixture of relief and excitement and just waiting for the final whistle!

D IS FOR DERRY CITY...
Do you still keep an eye on the Derry City results?
I do, yeah, of course. I keep an eye on the League Of Ireland every Friday night.

E IS FOR ENTERTAINMENT...
It's your choice to pick a movie and the music for the team bus, what do you pick?
Something funny anyway if it's for the team bus to keep it light hearted. Inbetweeners or something maybe. It would have to be country music then for the music choice! It's the Donegal man in me!

F IS FOR FORREST...

Do you remember the story of how your move to England with Nottingham Forrest came about?

Yeah, I went for a trial just and it went form there. Alan Hill spoke to me after the FAI Cup final in Dublin in the hotel and said he was impressed and he spoke to Derry City and I went for a two week trial and Alex McLeish liked me and then they signed me after that.

G IS FOR GOAL...

What was the best goal you've ever scored?

The most memorable goal for Derry anyway would be the Linfield goal that I scored I would say. But the best goal I scored overall would probably be one when I was at Southend against Bury away.

H IS FOR HOME...

Have you ever consid-

ered coming back to play League Of Ireland football before you retire?

I'd hope so, yeah. I don't think too much about the end of my career, but yeah it's in the back of my mind that it would be good to come back. Things don't always plan out the way you want sometimes, but I would like to, yeah, at some stage.

I IS FOR INFLUENCE...

Who would you say was the biggest influence on your footballing career?

It's probably my dad to be honest, yeah. He always says it straight, which I like.

J IS FOR JOKER...

Who was the biggest practical joker you've met in football?

I'd probably say Shane McEleney for that one. He was always at some sort of

prank!

K IS FOR KIT...

What has been your favourite football kit that you've ever played in or owned?

That's a tough one! I think the red kit that we have at Mansfield now is a beautiful kit. Honestly, a kit is a kit to me, but that one is a nice kit. I don't know, it has a bit of Man United in it or something.

L IS FOR LIFE AFTER PLAYING...

Do you have a plan for after football? Is management something you would ever want to do, or is it a case of when it's over, it's over?

No, I will do something, yeah. I think I might do some coaching maybe. I would like to anyway.

M IS FOR MEMENTO...

What is the one football memento you own that you'll never give away?

Probably... well there's a few, actually! Obviously, my F.A.I. Cup medal, the EA Sports Cup medal, and my League Two Playoff Final medal that I won with Southend as well.

N IS FOR NIGHT OUT...

Which team mate was usually the first to initiate a night out?

It's between two! It's between Rory Patterson and Barry Molloy! I've had a few nights out with Rory Patterson, so I'd say Rory!

O IS FOR OPPOSITION...

Which opposition did you always look forward to playing the most in your career?
In the League Of Ireland?
Anywhere.
I used to always look forward to playing against Gillingham when I was at Southend.

P IS FOR PASSTIME...

Outside of football, what keeps you occupied now in your spare time?
My two kids! I have no time for anything else now really! No golf or anything!

Q IS FOR QUIZ...

Which former team mate would you definitely not want in your team if you were doing a quiz?
I don't think a quiz team would get very far with Davy McDaid in it!

R IS FOR RESULT...

Which result stands out or meant the most to you in your career?
It's got to be that FAI Cup win in 2012.

S IS FOR SIGNING...

Do you remember the story of you signing for Derry City came about?
Yeah, Stephen Kenny came down to my house. The Finn Harps manager came down first and then Stephen Kenny came down later on the same day. After speaking to him then I made my mind up. Stephen said he wanted me at Derry and he was building a great team at the time, so, yeah, that was it, really. He's a really nice man and I was looking forward to working with him.

T IS FOR TEAM MATES...

Who is the best player you've ever played with?
That's a tough one, there's been a lot! The one that comes to mind would be Michail Antonio. I played with him at Forrest. It's a tough one though because there has been a good few players that I could name.

U IS FOR UNPARALLELED...

Who is the best player you've ever played against?
That would have been Harry Kane when Forrest drew Spurs in the FA Cup. He's just different class.

V IS FOR VANITY...

Which team mate spent the longest in front of the mirror?
At Mansfield it's Jordan Bowery! Don't have to think about that one! At Derry City though, I'd say Fats, Patrick McEleney. Always liked to look sharp!

W IS FOR WISHES...

Is there anything you'd change about your career if you could do it all again?
I would, yeah. Bits of it anyway, not massive parts.

The main thing though, I wouldn't care too much about what other people were thinking or saying. That's probably one of the things I would have changed when I first came over, definitely.

X IS FOR EXPERIENCE...

What's the best atmosphere you've ever experienced as a player?

That 2015 League Two play-off Final against Wycombe Wanderers. It was amazing getting to play at Wembley, and then winning it was just unreal.

Y IS FOR YOUNG...

What is your earliest

memory of going to a football match?

Just going to watch my dad and my uncles play, really. Just Sunday league teams. I used to love it! I would just stand behind the goal Whatever side they were shooting in to and swap at half time! They played for Rashenny and Clonmany Shamrocks.

Z IS FOR ZONE...

Did you ever have any pre-match rituals or superstitions to get you in the zone?

Not really, I just keep the same routine, you know, what I eat the day before the game and just, my routine in

the morning, lay my clothes out and my gear so I don't forget anything, I would eat at the same time, shower at the same time, different things like that, and just keep a routine, yeah.

STEWART GREACEN

SPONSORED BY

JIM SHOVLIN

A IS FOR ANNOYING...

Which of your former team mates was the worst to sit beside on the bus for long away journeys?

I'd say big Gerard Doherty! Gerard was always up to something like taking the lid off the salt for pre match meals!

B IS FOR BEHAVIOUR...

Which of your former team mates was always the most likely to get booked?

It's got to be Rory Patterson hasn't it!

C IS FOR CUP...

What are you memories of that famous FAI Cup Final win in 2012?

It just remember it being a scrappy kind of first half, but the second half kind of opened up and then obviously they get their like goal. We managed to pull one back through myself, which was a bonus to equalise. But I remember the tale of two halves! First half has cagey, second half we both opened up a bit, but then just the relief of getting over the line like you know, it's just it's a great feeling. Always good to get a goal, but also the the main thing

was winning the cup and it was just a great Cup Final. I don't think you get to probably enjoy the game all that much when you're playing in it, but the relief of winning after is what it's all about!

D IS FOR DERRY CITY...

Do you still keep an eye on the Derry City results?

I do, yeah. I keep an eye every Friday. Good to see them going well!

E IS FOR EUROPE...

Which team was your toughest European opponent?

I played against Trabzonspor. That was an amazing

experience going out there and experiencing Turkish football was amazing. That was my first experience of playing in Europe, so I couldn't have asked for much better really, and we managed to keep the tie reasonably alive at 4-2 because away goals counted at that time, so to bring it to the Brandywell with a fighting chance was brilliant.

F IS FOR FOOTBALL FRIENDS...

Are there any of your former team mates that you keep in touch with?

Yeah, I still keep in touch with Higgy, Ruaidhri Higgins. Great to see him doing well. Barry Molloy too from time to time. A couple of other people as well. We had a great squad. Great, great bunch of lads. Absolutely love them all like, you know. Great, great bunch of lads.

G IS FOR GOAL...

What was the best goal you've ever scored?

I think it has to be the Cup Final goal! It was definitely the most important anyway! But, yeah, hands down, that would be my favourite goal.

H IS FOR HAHA...

What's the funniest thing that you remember from your time in football?

I can't think of something just now! There's been a lot of laughs though! Especially at Derry!

I IS FOR IDOL...

Who would you say was your biggest footballing idol growing up?

When I was growing up it was Maradonna that was the best played in the world. All the kids wanted to play like him!

J IS FOR JOKER...

Who was the biggest practical joker you've met in football?

I'd probably go Barry Molloy or Gerard Doherty!

K IS FOR KIT...

What has been your favourite football kit that you've ever played in or owned?

I had a few from Italia '90! I had a Holland one and an Italy one I think. One of those. It was my first memory of a World Cup.

L IS FOR LIFE AFTER PLAYING...

Did you have a plan for after your playing career ended? Was management something you ever wanted to do?

No, I didn't have any plans at all. I think, you always know that football's not going to last forever. But in reality when the end does strike, it comes fast! I had six months as an assistant manager at Stenhousemuir. I finished off my playing career there. I had to give it up because of my knee at that time, unfortunately. I was six months as assistant manager then, but as much as I enjoyed that, it probably wasn't a path that

I was all that struck on going down, but it's good to get a wee flavour of that to see how it works. How the dark side works! You know, you see the effort and the time that goes into actually being a coach or a manager or whatever, but as much as I love football, it's just probably something that wasn't for me.

M IS FOR MEMENTO...

What is the one football memento you own that you'll never give away?

Probably my FAI Cup final medal. Probably all my medals. When I won the league at Morton as well, so yeah, probably my medals. Not that I look at them much! They're probably up in the loft somewhere! But, yeah, medals are something you can never take away from somebody. Really, no matter what level you play at you remember those wins, you know.

N IS FOR NIGHT OUT...

Which team mate was usually the first to initiate a night out?

That'd by Barry Molloy for that one!

O IS FOR OPPOSITION...

Which opposition did you always look forward to playing the most in your career?

I enjoyed the games against Bohemians. Always enjoyed going down to Dalymount. Probably because I had a good record there is the main reason. I enjoyed going to some of the bigger Dublin clubs, the Shamrock Rovers and that as well, but I enjoyed Bohemians with Pat Fenlon and that. They were always good competitive games.

P IS FOR PASSTIME...

Outside of football, what keeps you occupied now in your spare time?

I like golf. I took up the old man sport, golf! It gives you a good balance of exercise and that competitive spirit again and that as well so, the football has been traded in for a golf ball on a Saturday!

Q IS FOR QUIZ...

Which former team mate

would you definitely not want in your team if you were doing a quiz?

I don't know, we were quote an intelligent bunch at Derry! I think maybe wee Tommy McBride had a few silly moments when I was there! I'll go Tommy!

R IS FOR RESULT...

Which result stands out or meant the most to you in your career?

Probably... not to state the obvious about cup finals and stuff like that, but probably the one game that I really enjoyed I think was when we beat Shamrock Rovers 3-1 away from home one night and we were absolutely brilliant. I think it was 3-1 going on 5 or 6, and Shamrock Rovers were a very good side at the time. That's probably the one I can think of the now in terms of actual performance.

S IS FOR SIGNING...

Do you remember the story of you signing for Derry City came about?

Aye, pretty much. Stephen Kenny had managed at Dunfermline and I'd played against Stephen's teams when I was at Morton so he'd seen me play and I must have made a decent enough impression. But I'd left Morton at the time, I'd managed to get myself out of a contract in a mutually consented sort of thing, so I could sign with other clubs and Stephen had phoned, I think it was through Derek McInnes, and Derek had said that I was a free agent, so Stephen phoned me and that was it, the rest is history as they say. So as soon as Stephen phoned me, it was something intriguing for me

and as I say, it's probably one of the best decisions I made in my life. I absolutely loved my three years in Derry.

T IS FOR TEAM MATES...

Who is the best player you've ever played with?

I would probably go with James McClean there on that one. He was a cracking big player when he burst on the scene and he's had a great career since.

U IS FOR UNPARALLELED...

Who is the best player you've ever played against?

I'd say Scott McDonald. I played against him maybe three times before he got the move to Celtic.

V IS FOR VANITY...

Which team mate spent the longest in front of the mirror?

That'd be Barry Molloy again!

W IS FOR WISHES...

Is there anything you'd change about your career if you could do it all again?

Probably avoiding injury a bit more. I had a bad injury when I was 18 and I've had a few knee operations throughout my career, but I lasted until 33!

X IS FOR EXPERIENCE...

What's the best atmosphere you've ever experienced as a player?

Definitely Trabzonspor away! That famous Turkish atmosphere. At the Brandywell, probably the Linfield games!

Y IS FOR YOUNG...

What is your earliest memory of going to a football match?

My uncle was the manager at Albion Rovers back in 1986, so probably going to see him.

Z IS FOR ZONE...

Did you ever have any pre-match rituals or superstitions to get you in the zone?

Not really, I wasn't too bad that way!

SIMON MADDEN

SPONSORED BY
MARTIN GORMLEY

A IS FOR ANNOYING...
Which of your former team mates was the worst to sit beside on the bus for long away journeys?
At Derry? Probably Thomas Crawley! Remember him? He never shut up!

B IS FOR BEHAVIOUR...
Which of your former

team mates was always the most likely to get booked?
Kevin Deery I'd say! Yeah, or Patterson! For different reasons though! Patterson for mouthing off, Deery just for the way you played I'd say.

C IS FOR CUP...
What are you memories of that FAI Cup Final in 2012? How did you feel

when Patterson's goal went in?
It was unbelieve! Unbelievable! Just elation I suppose! I remember Patterson was on the bench as well from the start and he came off the bench and scored. So yeah, just pure elation and joy I suppose when the winner finally went in in extra time.

D IS FOR DERRY CITY...
Do you remember the

story of how you sign-ing for Derry City came about?

Yeah, I was actually in my sit-ting room, and I was talking to Ian Foster, who was Dun-dalk manager back then and he said Stephen Kenny is going to ring you. So I spoke to Stephen on the phone and we had a good chat and he sold the club to me and I agreed to sign and was looking forward to it, but then it all fell through when he left to go to Rovers! But then Decky rang me back a couple of days later when he got the job, so it all moved pretty fast after that, like. I already wanted to go there, so Decky didn't have much convincing to do!

E IS FOR EUROPE...

Which team was your toughest European op-ponent? At any club.

The team we played from

Turkey, Trabzonspor! They were tough to hold off. I re-member the first leg away from home in front of 25,000 over there was unbelievable with the atmosphere that Turkish games get. I think Florent Malouda was in the hotel we were in. He was just after signing from Chel-sea, but he couldn't play in the game though. But that was the kind of players they were attracting!

F IS FOR ST FRANCIS...

You're involved at St Francis FC now, how did you get involved and what do you do?

Yeah, I'm currently, the Di-rector of Football and the first team coach of the sen-ior team, so I'm kept quite busy!

G IS FOR GOAL...

What was the best goal you've ever scored?

Probably one I scored for Rovers against Finn Harps. I think it was 2-2 and then last few minutes I came in off left side and I just pinged it back across into the corner. I lobbed the keeper from about 10 yards however that happened, I don't know! But, yeah, it was against Finn Harps to win 3-2.

H IS FOR HAHA...

What's the funniest thing that you remember from your time in football?

It was probably at Rovers again. We had we used to change in the rugby club across the road from where it is now. But we used to have a pool table in there. So the lads would have to be in for like 10 o'clock and we'd have to be on the pitch and training for 11. But lads would get up for 9:15 just to play games of pool and there'd be some serious competitions going on! So, yeah, if I was to remember funny times it would just be the craic around the pool ta-ble I'd say.

I IS FOR IDOL...

Who would you say was your biggest footballing idol growing up?

Peter Schmeichel!

A goalkeeper?

A goalkeeper, yeah! I always wanted to be a goalkeeper at the start, and then things didn't turn out that way so

I started playing outfield! But yeah, United were always winning in the 90s, and it was always Peter Schmeichel that I liked. I'd have loads of his jerseys and stuff like that.

J IS FOR JOKER...

Who was the biggest practical joker you've met in football?
Probably... Well Barry Murphy would be one, and Robert Bayly, if you remember Robert Bayly? He'd be one as well!

K IS FOR KIT...

What has been your favourite football kit that you've ever played in or owned?
It was probably a Schmeichel jersey years ago that I had, a white Umbro one with a big black collar on it back when 'keepers had them big jerseys!

It was white with, like, bits of yellow and blue going through it and a big black collar. And I actually got it in town! This is nearly 30 years ago when you couldn't really get that many jerseys around Ireland, especially not goalkeeper ones, and you certainly couldn't order them online, but I actually got that one in town here in Dublin I remember, and I was delighted to get it!

L IS FOR LIFE AFTER PLAYING...

Did you have a plan for after your playing career ended? Was management something you always wanted to do?
Yeah, I think it started when I was young. I used to always play Football Manager and since then I always wanted to be a coach or manager. So I started coaching when I was 26 and I think that's why I haven't really missed the playing side of football now, because I was coaching while I was playing, so it was an easy transition when I retired from playing. It was like I never stopped really.

M IS FOR MEMENTO...

What is the one football memento you own that you'll never give away?
Probably the FAI Cup winners medal with Derry. That was such a huge moment to win it playing in the Aviva in

front of family and friends, and especially just the way we want it as well. We had a great bunch of lads and staff, so that was huge for me. I'll never give that away.

N IS FOR NIGHT OUT...

Which former team mate was usually the first to initiate a night out?
Probably David Webster! He likes a gargle! Fond of a Guinness!

O IS FOR OPPOSITION...

Which opposition did you always look forward to playing the most in your career?
I liked playing against Bohs. Always good playing against Bohs when I was playing for Rovers. Probably UCD as well. I used to always like playing against UCD down at the Bowl. It was a huge pitch and they always give you a game. They never really changed. You knew what you were getting with UCD. But, yeah, UCD and Bohs.

P IS FOR PASSTIME...

Outside of football, what keeps you occupied now in your spare time?
Well, I have two jobs, two kids, and one wife as well! And they're all brilliant, which is great. So yeah, I'm always, always busy.

Q IS FOR QUIZ...

Which former team mate would you definitely not want in your team if you were doing a quiz?

James Doona! He hasn't got a clue! Him or Darren Meenan! Used to play for Dundalk and then he was at Rovers for a couple of years. Madman!I don't know if he'd be smart or not for a quiz, but just experiences I've had, he's a madman like!

R IS FOR RESULT...

Which result stands out or meant the most to you in your career?

Maybe the Cup Final again you know. 3-2. Yeah, that one or I remember the semi-final, I think we drew with Shels 1-1 at home on the Sunday, and I think we played them on the Wednesday and we won two or three one I think or whatever it was. That result there was huge, like. That could have been a tough one for us in Tolka Park, but we did it.

S IS FOR SETANTA...

You'd played in the Setanta Cup before, but surely nothing beats scoring a goal against Linfield in the 94th minute?

Oh yeah, yeah, that was brilliant! Those Stenata games used to be brilliant to play. We actually played really well in that Linfield game as well. It ended up 3-1 I think late on? Yeah, but I remember, we battered them for 90mins. I think it was 1-1 in the 85th minute or something and we got two late ones. Actually, I think it was a decent goal I scored as well if I remember? I don't think it was my debut, but it was near enough, wasn't it? For some reason I think I was playing right wing, or maybe I started right wing. Yeah, I don't know what happened there, but yeah, the Setanta Cup was always good. Especially against the teams in the north, but I think I lost two cup finals as well in that tournament, so that wasn't great!

T IS FOR TEAM MATES...

Who is the best player you've ever played with?

There's a few! The one maybe that had the most impact on a game, and I remember playing against him as well, was Kevin Deery, because when we was on it he was horrible! He'd be standing on your toes and all sorts of tricks! But when he was on your team, I think it was great just to have that kind of presence that would upset the opposition and get around the pitch. He wasn't as fit as he used to be when I was there like, so he didn't play many games, but when he did play he was excellent.

U IS FOR UNPARALLELED...

Who is the best player you've ever played against?

That's a tough one... Who

gave me a nightmare… James McClean actually! I mean, he was pretty tough as well, sticking to the League of Ireland. That was a good Derry side when I went up with Dundalk and drew 0-0, but you had James McLean on the wing, Eamon Zayed up front, so I think that was one of the better Derry teams that I've played against. And Mark Farren of course. That midfield though with Molloy, Higgins and Deery. It was a really good side, but yeah, McClean was tough. I was at Rovers when we played against Real Madrid as well with Ronaldo and Benzema and them, but I didn't play, so to stick to the League Of Ireland it was definitely James McLean.

V IS FOR VANITY...

Which team mate spent the longest in front of the mirror?

Probably James Doona again! I don't know why because he has the worst hair in the world! Straw hair!

W IS FOR WISHES...

Is there anything you'd change about your career if you could do it all again?

I would usually say no regrets, but probably when I was younger when I was over at Leeds. Maybe you think with more dedication and hard work could I have stayed there. But you're really quite naïve you're young, and if you could have that experience when you're 30 it would be different. But, yeah, probably just better decision making when I was younger. I think most people may say that though!

X IS FOR EXPERIENCE...

What's the best atmosphere you've ever experienced as a player?

Probably that Trabzonspor game away. The Turkish crowd were mad! Or I played against Liverpool in the Aviva and I think it was nearly full. 50,000 or 55,000 or whatever it holds for Rovers

vs Liverpool and that was a great atmosphere as well

Y IS FOR YOUNG...

What is your earliest memory of going to a football match?

I didn't actually go to many games when I was younger in the League of Ireland. Probably getting a backer, or getting a lift off my brother on the bike. Do you know how you used to sit on the handlebars and get a lift? Yeah, that always sticks out in my mind going to training or to play a match with my brother. It was only like a 10 minute walk away! You hardly see that anymore now, lads getting a lift on bikes!

Z IS FOR ZONE...

Did you ever have any pre-match rituals or superstitions to get you in the zone?

Yeah, I had a couple. It's been that long now, I can't remember! I used to always wear bottoms warming up. I never used to wear the shorts or socks. I wore my own socks and bottoms and t-shirt warming up and then get completely changed then for the game when I went back in. So yeah, that would be the main one that people would probably have seen me doing. I never used to wear the shorts or socks.

RYAN McBRIDE

SPONSORED BY
THE RYAN MC BRIDE FOUNDATION

(This A-Z interview is the only one in the book that has been re-used. It was first published in the Derry City vs Dundalk match programme on Friday 1st July 2016, but a book of club legends wouldn't be complete without Ryan)

A IS FOR ANNOYING...
Which player past or present would you hate to sit beside on the bus all the way to Cork and why?
Eddie McCallion! He just talks too much!

B IS FOR BOX...
What is your favourite TV show? Either at the minute or of all time.
At the minute it's Suits. I enjoyed Game Of Thrones as well though, so either one of them two.

C IS FOR CHILDHOOD...
Who were your favourite team as a boy and what got you into them?
Derry City and Manchester United were my favourite. And only because my father supported Liverpool!

D IS FOR DRESS SENSE...
Which team mate has the worst fashion sense?
I'd like to say Aaron McEneff

because the boys always say him, but I like his a bit, so I'll say.... Na, I'll still say Aaron!!

E IS FOR ENTERTAIN-MENT...
What CD and DVD would you play on the bus to Dublin if it was your choice?
CD would be something like Kings Of Leon.
DVD would be an action

movie, maybe Taken.

F IS FOR FUNNY...
What's the funniest thing you've seen happen in your time in football?
The funniest one actually happened to me!! The Irish Daily Star were at a game and used a photo of me going in for a sliding tackle, but whether they seen it or

203

not I'd come free at the side of my shorts lets just say!! And they printed it!! Bit of a wardrobe malfunction!! I still have it in the house!!

G IS FOR GOAL...
What's been the best goal you've ever scored?
I don't really score that many goals, but I scored one direct from a free kick at underage level for Tristar back when I played centre mid! I think most goals since then have been headers or tap-ins, so nothing really spectacular!

H IS FOR HOLIDAY...
What is your favourite holiday destination? Or where would you like to go no expense spared?
Favourite holiday I've been on would be Las Vegas! I'd love to go to somewhere

like Bora Bora though!

I IS FOR IDOL...
Which footballer did you idolise as a boy?
It was always Roy Keane! He was just a great player with hard tackles, and a great attitude towards the game!

J IS FOR JOKER...
Who is the biggest practical joker in the team?
Wardy enjoys a god laugh! Keith Ward! He just keeps the dressing room going!

K IS FOR KIT...
What has been your favourite football kit that you've ever played in or owned?
Has to be that United reversible one that was out a few years ago! White on one side and gold on the other! They don't make them like that

any more!

L IS FOR LIFE AFTER PLAYING...
Do you see yourself staying in football when your playing career is over?
Definitely not coaching! I wouldn't be into setting out cones and all! I would like to have a go at management maybe, but I suppose to be a manager you have to coach first!

M IS FOR MEMENTO...
What is the one football memento you own that you'll never give away?
I got Gary Hooper's top from that Airtricity League Select game a few years back against Celtic. He scored two that day as well.

N IS FOR NEXT BIG THING...
Which young team mate do you think could be the next to make a move overseas?
I think Josh Daniels is a great player that has what it tames to make it in England. I think it's only a matter of time for him to be honest.

O IS FOR OPPOSITION...
Which opposition do you look forward to playing the most? Either this year or every year?
I like the big games. Every year it's usually Shamrock Rovers. This year it's Dund-

alk!

P IS FOR PASSTIME...

Outside of football, do you have any hobbies in your spare time?

Nothing at all really. Just working in the bar at Peadar O'Donnell's! That's takes up most of my time when I'm not training!

Q IS FOR QUIZ...

Which team mate would you definitely not want in your team if you were to do a quiz?

I'm not a great quizzer myself, so I'm not sure! I'd say Jordan Allen if I can't say myself!

R IS FOR RESULT...

Which result meant the most to you in your career?

Probably the 2012 FAI Cup Final. It's a great feeling at the end of the season to be lifting the cup.

S IS FOR SKILLS...

Who has the best skills in the team?

Josh Daniels has some good skills!

T IS FOR TEAM MATES...

Who is the best player you've ever played with?

Probably James McClean. He's just gone from strength to strength now!

U IS FOR UNPARAL-LELED...

Who is the best player you've ever played against?

I'd say Gary Hooper or Victor Wanyama when I played in that Airtricity League Select game against Celtic at the Aviva a few year's back.

V IS FOR VEHICLE...

What car do you drive now, and what would you drive if you were in the Premiership?

Don't drive at all now, but if I was in the Premiership I'd drive an Audi Q7.

W IS FOR WHILE AWAY THE TIME...

How do you stop from getting bored travelling to away games?

Netflix just. I'm always watching Suits on Netflix.

X IS FOR EXCHANGE...

If you could change places with someone in another sport for a day, who would it be?

Conor McGregor! Love the UFC! Wouldn't be bad to have that money for a day as well!

Y IS FOR YOUTH...

Where did you start your youth career, and did you always play in the same position?

I actually started off in centre midfield with Tristar and then played centre half with Brandywell Harps and then Brandywell Celtic and then that was me on to Derry City then.

Z IS FOR ZERO CHANCE...

What club would there be no chance of you ever playing for or supporting?

Finn Harps!

DANNY VENTRE

A IS FOR ANNOYING...

Which of your former team mates was the worst to sit beside on the bus for long away journeys?

Young Roddy! No, let me see... We had Rory Patterson, Barry Molloy, big Shane McEleney, Fats... I'm going to say Jarvis you know! He's quite a lively lad isn't he?! I think he's still playing isn't he? He was with Larne, but I think he's moved. Coleraine is it? Yeah, he's a sound lad, but yeah, I'll go Dean Jarvis!

B IS FOR BEHAVIOUR...

Which of your former team mates was always the most likely to get booked?

Rory Patterson! Easy one that! Well, in fairness, it could be Barry Molloy either!

C IS FOR CHAMPIONS...

What do you remember about the season you won the league with Sligo in 2012?

Yeah, obviously the actual day of winning it against St Pats is the day that stands out, because I actually got sent off that game myself, talking about bookings! So I think we won it with two games to go, so the game at the Showgrounds and we played St Pats, and they were sitting in second place so it was kind of a must win game for them and a not lose game for us and I think we won due to a dubious penalty if I remember correctly. I got sent off just afterwards as well, but we won 3-2, yeah. So it will be that one that I would remember most.

D IS FOR DERRY CITY...

Do you remember the story of how you signing for Derry City came about?

Yeah, it was obviously Roddy that signed me. Roddy actually got in touch me earlier in the year to sign for

Athlone. I was out injured at Sligo at the time and I was just coming back playing and he asked me to go to Athlone and I said no, but he was saying 'I'll sign you eventually wherever I go!' And then obviously at the end of the year in December he got the job at Derry, and he got back in touch and I think I was his first signing.

E IS FOR ERA...

Money and technology included, would you prefer to have played when you did, or in modern football?

Now for a bit more money! Na, well they say the referees are harder and the game getting a bit more stricter every year, isn't it? So for my style of play I'd probably be happier to just play when I did!

F IS FOR FAI CUP...

You won the FAI Cup 3 times with Sligo, is there one that stands out over the others?

Yeah, the Derry one when we lost it! When I made the mistake on the back post and I couldn't sort my feet out! So, it's not the ones I've won, it's the ones I've lost that I think about more! And that one in particular for Derry, I thought I'd let everyone down, all the fans and my team mates, and just all the people of Derry. So yeah, even though I have good memories of winning them with Sligo, the one that sticks out is the one that I never won!!

G IS FOR GOAL...

What was the best goal you've ever scored?

You know something, it was probably against Derry! It was in one of the cups, I think it was the League Cup. Sligo played in a light blue away jersey. I remember Eoin Doyle pulling the ball back to me on the edge of the box and I took a touch, pulled it back, and curled it into the bottom corner. I don't score many outside the box, or I didn't anyway. I just didn't always used to love playing in the Brandywell, so to score there was great I think. Someone got sent off in that game as well. I think I got Danny Lafferty sent off in that game late on. But, yeah, that was the one I'd remember.

H IS FOR HAHA...

What was the funniest thing you remember happening from your time in football?

I can't think you know! There's been a lot of funny lads and funny moments over the years, but there's not one individual one that's jumping out at me just now.

I IS FOR IRELAND...

Do you still keep an eye on results of your former teams in the League Of Ireland?

I do, yeah. Derry and Sligo. So, yeah, been keeping up with that. I know there's big things expected of Derry this year. I still know some of the lads playing there like Fats, Micky Duffy, Shane and them, so yeah, I keep an eye on it all.

J IS FOR JOKER...

Who was the biggest practical joker you've met in football?

I want to say... Gary McCabe when he was at Sligo. Gary McCabe and Derek Foran! They were like a tag team! They were always up to no good playing tricks on people. Leaving fish in cars… all sorts of stuff!

K IS FOR KIT...

What has been your favourite football kit that you've ever played in or owned?

Favourite kit that I've ever owned would be the Italy 1994 kit when they played in the World Cup in the USA. I had the home and the away one as well! I liked the white one, but it didn't stay white for too long when I was out and about playing football when I was younger. How old would I have been then, 8!

L IS FOR LIFE AFTER PLAYING...

Did you have a plan for

after your playing career ended? Was management something you ever wanted to do?

Yeah, I'm on my coaching journey now at the minute. I've just been at Bristol Rovers for the last 18 months or so. I've just come out of it actually. I'd like to be a manager, but the game's changing, so I'm thinking some sort of role in football now, but that might be off the grass so, I think, yeah, you know the way Sporting Directors and all that stuff going now they might be a little bit safer jobs than being a manager!

M IS FOR MEMENTO...

What is the one football memento you own that you'll never give away?

Probably just the medals that I've achieved. Yeah, the medals you've won I'll never give away. Well, when I die they'll be given away, obviously! You get that much

stuff sometimes it's hard to keep it all. I don't keep much stuff, really. Yeah, I don't think I've never had anyones shirt or anything. Like you think 'Oh, he's a top player, I might swap his shirt', but I have nothing like that, no.

N IS FOR NIGHT OUT...

Which team mate was usually the first to initiate a night out?

At Derry it would have been Rory Patterson!

O IS FOR OPPOSITION...

Which opposition did you always look forward to playing the most in your career?

Yeah, well the reason I signed for Derry was that I loved playing against them. The bigger teams in Ireland really were the ones I enjoyed, so it was always Shamrock Rovers and Derry. When I was at Sligo I always seemed to play well and get

a result at the Brandywell, that's why I liked playing there. It was always a great atmosphere. It just felt a bit like home.

P IS FOR PASSTIME...

Outside of football, what keeps you occupied now in your spare time?

Three children! All under the age of 7! And one's running around mad here now! So, yeah, that's what keeps me going! Now I'm going to their football practice. Mine kind of finished and theirs is just starting, so I enjoy that.

Q IS FOR QUIZ...

Which former team mate would you definitely not want in your team if you were doing a quiz?

Fats! Or Micky Duffy either in fairness!

R IS FOR RESULT...

Which result stands out

or meant the most to you in your career?

I could say one of the three FAI Cup wins, but two of them were 0-0 and we won on penalties, and then it would have been the last one against Drogheda I'd say when the game was dead for 80 minutes and then there was four goals within the last 10! I think Danny North scored two to go 2-1, but they scored an equaliser in the last minute, but then I think big Anthony Elding scored the winner in the 95th minute or something! Yeah, so probably that one.

S IS FOR SLIGO ROVERS...

What was it that made you leave England and move to Sligo Rovers?

Paul Cook the manager. Yeah, because I played with Cookie at Accrington and then he went into manage-

ment and then he ended up at Sligo and then I probably followed him over maybe a year or so later when he gave me a call.

T IS FOR TEAM MATES...

Who is the best player you've ever played with?

That I've ever played with like from schoolboys right the way up? It'd probably be Wayne, yeah. Wayne Rooney. He used to be in my class in school. So we played in all the school teams together, through school boy teams and stuff, yeah.

U IS FOR UNPARALLELED...

Who is the best player you've ever played against?

Yeah, Wayne again! He used to destroy us all at football many times, every day actually in school! So yeah, Wayne for that one as well!

Are you still in touch with him?

No, not really. He obviously went on his own thing, didn't he? I don't think he looked back at any of us! But, yeah, that would be before professional football, but then when you say played again in professional football, and particularly in Ireland, probably Joseph N'Do. Again, one of the best I've played with and against.

V IS FOR VANITY...

Which team mate spent the longest in front of the mirror?

No one loved themselves really. Well, maybe Richard Brush at Sligo. He had the long hair at the time and then he ended up shaving it all off, but he's got the tattoos and all that. Ross Gaynor was another one actually!

W IS FOR WISHES...

Is there anything you'd change about your career if you could do it all again?

Yeah, practice more and get more money! Na, well, maybe sometimes a couple of decisions along the way like. Maybe being too loyal sometimes when I could have moved or whatever, but it's always hindsight isn't it when you think, 'If I'd

made that decision, where would I have been?'. I'm happy for what I've done, but there's always that in the back of your mind, 'what if I'd have moved then'. Probably maybe making a bit of a different decision along the way just. Taking a phone call from Roddy might have been one of them! Na, he was alright Roddy. Well, you know, he treated me alright. I think it was just the whole situation up in Derry and maybe some of his actions killed him a little bit with the fans and that.

X IS FOR EXPERIENCE...

What's the best atmosphere you've ever experienced as a player?

One would have been a European trip for Sligo, I think we played in Slovakia against Spartak Trnava. They were a very good team. And

the stadium was good because it was quite close and, like, the stands were quite close to the to the pitch and that, and it was quite high, so it was a little bit intimidating. But it was good even though we lost 3-1. That game as a player. in terms of like as a fan obviously Anfield on a Champions League night!

Y IS FOR YOUNG...

What is your earliest memory of going to a football match?

My earliest memory of going to a game, yeah, would have it have been Anfield, because it was the last day of the Kop. You know you used to be used to be able to stand in the Kop and they played Norwich and they got beat 1-0. By Norwich! That would be like the earliest memory of going to a game. That might have been 1994 actually! Yeah, the last day of the standing Kop!

Z IS FOR ZERO CHANCE...

Was there ever a club that you would have refused to play for or support?

It's gotta be Man U hasn't it!

Not even Everton?

No, you know what I don't even mind Everton! But I hate Man U! Well, I wouldn't support them, but I'd play for them if I get paid right!!

HAVE YOU JOINED
**THE DERRY CITY F.C.
MONTHLY DRAW?!**

YOU COULD WIN £850 IN THE

**DERRY CITY F.C.
£850
MONTHLY DRAW**

**PLUS A SECOND PRIZE OF
£300 EVERY MONTH!! AND
EXTRA DRAWS AT CHRISTMAS!!**

THAT'S OVER £13,000 IN PRIZES EVERY YEAR!!

Playing could not be easier!
Each entry costs just £10 per month to win £850!
See the website for full details!

To join the Monthly Draw contact the Derry City Office on:
Telephone no. (028) 71373 111,
or by email at office@derrycityfc.net

AARON BARRY
SPONSORED BY
DERRY CITY
DEVELOPMENT COMMITTEE

A IS FOR ANNOYING...
Which of your former team mates was the worst to sit beside on the bus for long away journeys?
At Derry? Well Keith Ward was there for a year and he's the liveliest man I've ever known! He's just a chatterbox! So if you were beside him you wouldn't get a minute's rest!

B IS FOR BEHAVIOUR...
Which of your former team mates was always the most likely to get booked?
Big Ryan! Has to be! Has to be Ryan McBride! Or Patterson either! Rory did a lot of giving out to referees!

C IS FOR CORK CITY...
You had the opportunity to join the team that won the double the year before you went there. Do you remember the transfer?
They'd won the double, yeah. That was the year I'd left. I kind of just felt that the time was right to leave. I think a good bit went on at the time at Derry and stuff especially, you know, with Ryan passing and that. I think a few things like that happened. Mark Farren passed away, and Josh's family had a tragedy. I was actually due to go to Cork the year before to be honest, but I'd had surgery on my hip and basically, that's eventually what made me retire, it just got worse and worse. But, yeah, I suppose I just felt like I kind of had to move on from a Derry perspective, and I wasn't sure where I'd go, but as you say the chance came in from the club that won the double the year before and I thought it would be a great opportunity for me before I retired. So, yeah, it wasn't any bad reason I left Derry, it was just with injuries and that I knew I wasn't going to

have much longer to play.

D IS FOR DERRY CITY...

Do you still keep an eye on the Derry City results?

I definitely do, yeah. In the League of Ireland I'd consider myself to be a Derry City fan. I played over 100 games there I think. I would still be very good friends with Barry McNamee as well and we'd often chat football, and mostly Derry City you know. I'd be very hopeful that we have a have a bit more success in the league this year. That'd be great to see. Myself and my wife just had a little girl there, so her first kit could well be a Derry jersey!

E IS FOR EUROPE...

What are your memories of the European nights in Wales and Belarus?

Yeah, Wales and Belarus. I think in Wales, I don't think they were what we expected. Like, we were at a kind of a different level, but then likewise we found ourselves at a bit of a different level after that tie, especially getting drawn against Midtjylland and teams like that, you know, whereby you know they're a serious team! You know, you need everybody firing at the top of their game, but I think we were missing a few lads and it didn't go our way. But I always enjoyed the European games. Probably just wish that we constantly got through a tie or two. That would have made a big difference, you know. Because when you hear about other European nights that the club had, like the year with Gothenburg, Gretna, you know, the run that ended up with Paris St Germain and stuff like that, you think it would have been nice to have a bit more success like that. Those are the ties

you dream of when you get through a round in Europe.

F IS FOR FAI CUP...

What are your memories of that FAI Cup Final in 2014?

Yeah, that was my first year at the club and we got straight into the final! Not that I took it for granted, but when you're just in the moment you don't really think about it, but it was a big occasion. I was playing with an injury. That tends to be the theme of my career! I had surgery after that final I had some issues with my knee that needed looked at. But, yeah, I enjoyed it regardless of the result. I think we always did well in the FAI Cup, but I'd have loved to have gotten to a few more finals. We reached a few semi-finals and lost out and obviously that final we lost out in as well, but, yeah, definitely, especially with Derry's cup pedigree. But, no it was a great experience.

G IS FOR GOAL...

What was the best goal you've ever scored?

I was much better at stopping them to be honest!! I think I scored mainly headers, so I don't know if one stands out! I can't even think if I ever scored with my foot in the League Of Ireland! Yeah, just one of the headers!

H IS FOR HAHA...

What was the funniest thing you remember from your time in football?
There's a lot like!

There must be a Roddy Collins story?!
Ah Roddy! I came to the club under Roddy and I think I was his only signing that stayed beyond a few months! To be honest, there's so many funny moments. I've been away from football a few years now, but that's one of the main things you miss, you know. You do miss just the bit of craic and stuff like that. I would say, at Derry, played under Roddy and then Kenny Shiels, and they were both big characters in totally different ways! I can't think of one particular story off the top of my head though!

I IS FOR IDOL...

Who would you say was your biggest footballing idol growing up?
I was a Liverpool fan so Steven Gerrard, and then I always liked the Italian defenders. I always thought they were class, like Maldini, Nesta and those lads. Especially Maldini as a left footer. Just a class act.

J IS FOR JOKER...

Who was the biggest practical joker you've met in football?

I would have said Keith Ward. He was funny, but he was just constant banter. But there was a guy Tobi Adebayo-Rowling. I played with him at Cork. He signed for Cork from Sligo, but that lad was just a different character altogether! He was at Cork under John Caulfield. John was a certain type of character and how in under God he ended up signing Toby I don't know! They were polar opposites! Toby was a bit of a lunatic like! He was actually in the house with myself, Barry McNamee and Keiron Sadlier. He left after a few months like, but he was a character!

K IS FOR KIT...

What has been your favourite football kit that you've ever played in or owned?
I liked the Derry kits in fairness. The Derry kits were always nice. I would say probably the Bohs kits were

actually nice as well, you know the way they do those kind of special ones every now and again. Cork actually had a special edition kit as well for a hospital down there that we wore for a one off game and the kits went to charity then after, that was a nice kit. But I would say one of the Derry ones. I have them all in the house, I must have a root through them. I have the turquoise one, and I think there was one with a little bit of a collar on it as well?

L IS FOR LIFE AFTER PLAYING...

Did you have a plan for after your playing career ended? Was management something you ever wanted to do, or was it more when you're done, you're done?
Yeah, a bit of both. Obviously I was all in on the football, but I had surgery on

my hip when I was at Derry and I was only about, I'd say maybe just turned 25. Micky Hegarty, who's still there, very sound man! Micky was working night and day on me for a couple of years, and then eventually I had surgery. When I woke up from the surgery, the surgeon came in and the first thing that I remember him telling me was that I need to plan for a new career. I just turned 25! So I was like, 'ah shit', you know. That kind of shaped my career from the age of 25 onwards. So yeah, immediately that kind of kicked me into gear, but I suppose I've always been bright enough, so I wanted to have a have a career after football, so I studied. I did an online degree in sports business management and then since then I've done my chartered accountants

exam, and that's what I do now, I work as a chartered accountant. And that's like the academic stuff, but in terms of coaching and stuff, yeah, definitely always interested in coaching and maybe managing. I kind of played like that. I would have been organizing and just thinking about the game. But I don't know. I wouldn't take management on as a career in Ireland. You know yourself, it can be fairly volatile! I would imagine if there was a League of Ireland team on my doorstep I would definitely go into an underage setup or something like that, but no, I'd imagine maybe coaching my kids' teams or something like that in the future. I might do a few badges now when I settle in. I just got a new job and stuff like that. But in the next few years I'll probably

do my badges, yeah.

M IS FOR MEMENTO...

What is the one football memento you own that you'll never give away?
Not sure. Like I have my old jerseys and things like that. Maybe one of the jerseys after Ryan passed. One of the embroidered ones I suppose. Because I would say Derry was one of my favourite times in my career. I have very good memories. But then everything just sort of felt like I needed to move on. To be honest with you, with my injury as well and the surgery and stuff like that, I got a full season under my belt post-surgery at Derry and I had a very good year, so, yeah, maybe that jersey in my last year there just after Ryan passed.

N IS FOR NIGHT OUT...

Which team mate was usually the first to initiate a night out?
There's a few like! We had young squads at Derry at that time. Conor McCormack enjoyed getting out. He was a sensible enough lad though. He wouldn't go out mad on the booze or anything, he just liked to get out of the house! I would say it was a group effort though, and it was always on the cards but we never went too mad!

O IS FOR OPPOSITION...

Which opposition did you always looked forward to playing the most in your career?

Team-wise, I'd say Rovers. Home or away. I enjoyed playing them away as much as anything. Just, you know, probably the most professional set up in the league just terms of facilities and stadium. I know they've increased it now, but they're probably the blueprint of what other clubs hope to achieve, stadium-wise with a 12,000 seater stadium or whatever it is. Not that would I look forward to playing tougher opponents because, as a defender if you make one mistake, you could ruin it for everyone. But guys like Christy Fagan, Seanie Maguire, Pat Hoban, Rory Patterson, you know, those guys were always the toughest in the league.

P IS FOR PASSTIME...

Outside of football, what keeps you occupied now in your spare time?

Well we had our first child there, me and my wife, so that's what keeps me busy now! But before that I was doing my accountancy exams for three and a half years, so I'd been working full time in an accountancy firm and doing exams at the same time! For two of

the years I was even playing for Bray as well! It was kind of like, I think I left Bohemians and then I wanted to start work, so I went into the job. But I was offered the Bray thing and I didn't even know if it would work type of thing, but it did. I made it work for a couple of years, but to be honest, that was a very busy time!

Q IS FOR QUIZ...

Which former team mate would you definitely not want in your team if you were doing a quiz?

I'd say… Skinny! Nathan Boyle! Maybe even Ronan Curtis! They were all great lads, but maybe as you say, no use in a quiz!

R IS FOR RESULT...

Which result stands out or meant the most to you in your career?

With Derry in the first year,

when we beat Rovers in the FAI Cup semi-final replay. That was a great result. Yeah, maybe that one to be honest with you. There's a few results as well that year that Ryan passed in 2017 as the season went on that we came back together and got some great results again and I think we even qualified for Europe. I think we came third or something. The were a few there were like, you know, we really came together and got through some tough times.

S IS FOR SIGNING...

Do you remember the story of you signing for Derry City came about?

Yeah, so I was at Sheffield United and then a new manager came in. I was on loan in Scotland at the time with Dumbarton and my loan was due to be up, so I came back and I was like 19 or 20,

217

but like I realised quickly enough that I wasn't going to feature in his plans, you know, I wasn't going to get game time, so I kind of just made a judgement call and went to the manager and asked could I look for a different club. I was probably going to pursue something in England, you know, to try and go on trial for a couple of clubs there because I was already living there. But then the captain of Sheffield United at that time Micky Doyle, somehow he knew Roddy Collins and it just sort of happened. I think I just came home from Sheffield for a while and Roddy just got in contact, so I said I'd call up to Derry for a while and see how it goes sort of thing, so I spent a few days training, and yeah, that was sort of it. The Rod Squad!!

T IS FOR TALENT...

Who is the best player you've ever played with?

In the League of Ireland, probably Fats would top the list, Patrick McEleney. But there'd be a great shortlist of names I was lucky enough to play with like Fats, Micky Duffy, Ronan Curtis, Keiron Sadlier, Danny Mandroiu. Yeah, they're all, like, not too dissimilar type of players. All players that are really good and went on to achieve great things.

U IS FOR UNPARAL-

LELED...

Who is the best player you've ever played against?

In the League of Ireland, again, there's probably about a three man shortlist! Seanie Maguire at his peak just before he left for England. Jack Byrne was always excellent as well. And maybe Keith Fahy. I know in the League Of Ireland he was kind of nowhere near his peak, but he was top class. Outside of the League Of Ireland, probably Pogba, or Ravel Morrison.

V IS FOR VANITY...

Which team mate spent the longest in front of the mirror?

Aaron McEneff! I didn't have to think about that one!

W IS FOR WISHES...

Is there anything you'd change about your career if you could do it all again?

Yeah, I would have got a new hip! Na, I think just if I'd have been a bit more experienced I maybe would have seen the signs that injuries needed looked at. You tend to just play on when you're younger and think it'll sort itself out by tomorrow. But, yeah, if I had the benefit of hindsight I would ease off on myself. I think definitely that a bit of it was a predisposed, but I think I could

have had a longer career if I'd have managed myself better in the gym and stuff like that.

X IS FOR EXPERIENCE...

What's the best atmosphere you've ever experienced as a player?

We played Legia Warsaw away with Cork. It wasn't a full packed house, but it still had that kind of Eastern European atmosphere, you know. It held 30,000 or something, and although it wasn't full it was an amazing experience.

Y IS FOR YOUNG...

What is your earliest memory of going to a football match?

I would have went to a few Liverpool games when I was younger, so they'd be the ones that would stand out in my mind.

Z IS FOR ZONE...

Did you ever have any pre-match rituals or superstitions to get you in the zone?

Yeah, well, maybe not so much superstition, but I would have a specific routine and I would get everything ready in a certain way and then get the body ready as well. As I went on, I couldn't walk on to the pitch without doing about an hour's worth of stretching and rolling!

STEPHEN DOOLEY

A IS FOR ANNOYING...

Which of your former team mates was the worst to sit beside on the bus for long away journeys?

He's probably not too bad, but I'll go for Philip Lowry. He was always a bit big-time! He's probably not the worst, but I'll go for Philip.

B IS FOR BEHAVIOUR...

Which of your former team mates was always the most likely to get booked?

I'm struggling to think early doors here! Most likely get booked... Maybe I'll go for Rory Patterson! Just because he's always giving off the referee and that. I think

he'd end up picking up the most cards, so, yeah, he's probably the most likely. He's got to be up there at least!

C IS FOR CORK CITY...

Do you remember how your move to Cork City came about?

Yeah, well, actually, I was coming off a terriblly in-jury hit campaign for Derry, where I just couldn't get my body right, and I was living at home. It was a re-ally tough campaign, that 2015 one, which was really disappointing. It was really disappointing for me per-sonally, and then I just re-member John Caulfield kind

of talking to me at the end of the season. Obviously, Peter Hutton had just left Derry, so I was kind of a lit-tle bit in limbo just before Kenny Sheils came in, and John Caulfield offered me a chance to go to Cork, and it was just a chance to kind of get away from home for a bit as well. Derry was great, but I just wanted maybe to move away from home a bit after being used to my own space from living in America. So I was was look-ing to not be at home, get a change of scene and take every minute to kind of go through that process again and just kind of get back to doing things and focusing on football. So it wasn't anything against Derry, it was just more a lifestyle thing for me, and John gave me the chance to do it.

D IS FOR DERRY CITY...

Do you still keep an eye on the Derry City and League Of Ireland or Irish League results?

Yeah, I definitely check the results. I don't get to as many games as I would like, but I was rooting for Derry last year, and I was hoping they would beat Shamrock Rovers to the title, unfortunately it wasn't to be, but hopefully this year they can get there.

E IS FOR ENTERTAIN-MENT...

It's your choice to pick a movie and the music for the team bus, what do you pick?

I'd pick something like NFL related, maybe like Any Giv-en Sunday, or Friday Night Lights, something like that. I'm a big fan of them kind of movies. And music then, I'm going for country music, like a Luke Combs or something, that's my kind of thing!!

F IS FOR FUNNY...

What was the funniest thing you remember from your time in football? Was it Roddy Collins that signed you? There must be a Roddy story!?

No, it wasn't actually. It was Peter Hutton. Roddy had literally just left, so I didn't know Roddy at all. I've heard great stories, as you say though, but they're not mine! There's a ton of things in football that happen, but I do remember something about Galway United away, someone kind of like fell through the changing room ceiling! There was just a pair of legs kind of like dangling about! We were trying to

get changed and ready for a match! It's just kind of a thing that would only happen in the League of Ireland!

G IS FOR GOAL...

What was the best goal you've ever scored?

That's an easy one for me, because there's not too many goals to my name! I'll say probably the one for Cork against Dundalk. I kind of picked it up at the halfway line on a kind of a counter attack. I mean, it just lined up on the edge of the box, a little step over and straight in at the far post. Nothing crazy about it, but probably the best one I've scored.

H IS FOR HOME...

Have you ever considered coming back to play League Of Ireland or Irish League football again before you retire?

Yeah, I mean, absolutely would like to play in either or again, but it's just, you know, when you get older, life happens and it's kind of harder to do it then if you know what I mean? If you live in England for six, seven years, and then you have a life here, and people here, it's hard to then just pack up and go back. I'll never say never, but it's probably unlikely.

I IS FOR INFLUENCE...

Who would you say was the biggest influence on your

footballing career?

I mean, there's various footballers and all out there that I could name, but when I think about it, it's probably my Dad.

J IS FOR JOKER...

Who was the biggest practical joker you've met in football?

Again, many, many practical jokers throughout my career. Stephen Beatty was great at Cork for an honourable mention! For Derry though, I'd go for Shane McEleney. He's always joking about! Really good laughs in that team though.

K IS FOR KIT...

What has been your favourite football kit that you've ever played in or owned?

Played in is hard because it's kind of like which team you like the best. Owned though... I remember when I was younger, I got this Man United gold and white reversible kit. That was by far the best kit ever produced! They don't make them like that anymore!

L IS FOR LIFE AFTER PLAYING...

Do you have a plan for after football? Is management something you ever wanted to do, or is it a case of when you're done, you're done?

Well I'm currently doing some coaching badges. I don't really see myself as

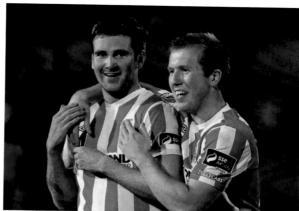

a great coach though to be honest! I have a degree which I did obviously went to America for and haven't done much with it, could potentially look at something there. But I'm very interested in, like, the strength and conditioning, sports science side of things in football. I'd really like to do something there. I think injuries have kind of plagued my career a little bit, so it'd be good to understand the body a bit more. Something along those lines I would really like to do, but we will see.

M IS FOR MEMENTO...

What is the one football memento you own that you'll never give away?

I've got a few medals here and there. I have one that was like the County Player Milk Cup award. I was like 16 at the time. I guess it was for the Derry, or County Derry, or whatever side. A few of

the lads I would have played with at Coleraine and Derry would have been in there as well. We did quite well. We lost out to Hearts on penalties in the end up. I missed a pen! But, yeah, I've got the Players Player kind of award of the county squad. We didn't win the tournament, but that was a nice one to get at that age.

N IS FOR NIGHT OUT...

Which team mate was usually the first to initiate a night out?

Who could I say for this one?! To be fair, there's too many to name! Well, that Derry team, or any League Of Ireland team in them days, there were any amount of guys who would initiate a night out! So, I think there's no shortage of players that I could name!

O IS FOR OPPOSITION...

Which opposition did you

always look forward to playing the most in your career?

I think I enjoyed the Cork City vs Dundalk battles a lot. You know, when we were kind of going head to head for a couple of years, and they always kind of sold out because obviously the grounds are fairly small, Turners Cross and Oriel Park. And the games always ended up being, kind of, league deciders those years between the two sides. Yeah, I really, really enjoyed those games.

P IS FOR PASSTIME...

Outside of football, what keeps you occupied now in your spare time?

I get out golfing as much as I can. I think that's very stock answer for footballers! But, yeah, I got the golf bug, which everyone seems to have. So yeah, I love it.

Q IS FOR QUIZ...

Which former team mate would you definitely not want in your team if you were doing a quiz?

I'm going to say Mickey Duffy just because I know he's back there right now! I remember from before he was not much of a quizzer! A fantastic footballer! But I don't think he's going to help you too much on a quiz team!

R IS FOR ROCHDALE...

What were your thoughts when the offer came in to play football in England? Every player's dream surely?

Yeah, I mean, Rochdale were in League One the time. I had just finished another injury hit campaign with Colraine and I just got an offer. Luckily I was 26, so I was like, you know, it's now or never. I just thought, why not give

it a go and see. I mean I've always wanted to try stepping up in terms of football pyramids, so give it a go and see what happens. That was it, I just got lucky I suppose.

S IS FOR SIGNING...

Do you remember the story of you signing for Derry City came about?

Yeah, I played two games with Colraine over the Christmas period and I scored in both of them and I think it kind of maybe put me back on the map a little bit in terms of when I was coming back. This was like in the Christmas I still had one semester left to do at Uni. I was kind of set to move back and maybe sign with Coleraine, but then as I got home, in the August, I got a call from Peter Hutton. He had just taken the Derry job and he was talking about the Derry and what they were doing and all, and the fact Derry was full time and the league was ready to go because of the summer football thing, so it suited me and felt better timed as well. I was like, it's just the full time aspect and I really wanted to make football my life. That kind of swayed me towards Derry City in the end up and that was it.

T IS FOR TALENT...

Who is the best player you've ever played with?

This is a tough one! I got a

play with a lot of great players who went on to do big things in the game. Like, Robert Sánchez came in on loan at Rochdale as the goalkeeper and now he's the Chelsea number one! You know, you got team mates like that, which is good. But I'd say, Patrick McEleney maybe. He's honestly, and that's not just because he's now back at Derry, but he's as good as any of them, football ability wise. I've always said that.

U IS FOR UNPARALLELED...

Who is the best player you've ever played against?
Played against Man United a bunch of years back. Pogba was playing. So I'll go Pogba just because of that. He didn't really have to do much! So it wasn't his finest performance, but we'll go for Paul Pogba.

V IS FOR VANITY...

Which team mate spent the longest in front of the mirror?
Oh, let me see... I'll go with... I'll go Seanie Maguire at Cork! He's always styling the hairstyle! Loves his hair! To be fair to him, it was his standout feature and he was scoring a lot of goals, so whatever worked for him!

W IS FOR WISHES...

Is there anything you'd change about your career if you could do it all again?
I would definitely want to learn more about just like strength and conditioning, and the biomechanics side of the game. And I'd read a lot more. I'd learn a lot more before going straight into things. I think just being injured and stuff is really curtailed if you look after yourself. So, yeah, I'd like to learn a lot more.

In terms of the teams I signed for and all that, I enjoyed playing for each team and every team had a, you know, a different part that I really, really liked. It was just, I think I could have done a bit better for each of them maybe.

X IS FOR EXPERIENCE...

What's the best atmosphere you've ever experienced as a player?
There's a few in England when you play some of the big teams. It's good. It's tough, but it's good. But, again, the League of Ireland, I did like when the likes of Dundalk came to Turners Cross. Or there was one night for Derry that stands out, I remember when we beat Shamrock Rovers at the Brandywell to get to the FAI Cup Final. It was 2-0. It was Patterson and Mickey and Duffy. I remember that atmosphere being, being really, really good! It was one of the first times that I'd experienced an atmosphere like that.

Y IS FOR YOUNG...

What is your earliest memory of going to a football match?
Irish Cup 2003, Coleraine 1-0. Jody Toland goal. I remember that was the first, or one of the first games that my family brought us to. I can't really remember all the play in the game, but I can remember the winning goal and everyone just... yeah! It was such a good game!

Z IS FOR ZONE...

Did you ever have any pre-match rituals or superstitions to get you in the zone?
I think all players do. Slightly anyway. We all try and just, you know, do the exact kind of same things if we win. If we lose, we don't do what we did previously. I just usually listen to the same songs and I'll do a few nonsense things. But no, I try not to have rituals. Not too many anyway!

ACKNOWLEDGEMENTS

Thanks for buying and reading the book! It's been a lot of work carried out over the stage of about a year. I started with the ones that I thought would be very hard to get, and I'm glad to say that I actually did achieve some of them! Trying to find a contact for the likes of Dennis Tueart was difficult, but I found one that I thought might be a long shot, and to my surprise, I recieved a reply immediately with his contact details and a message saying 'Dennis said he's really looking forward to your call'!

Some others were just as hard to track down, but even harder to arrange a time for a phone call to get the interview done! There have been some very late nights working on the book due to time differences around the world, but all worth it. Clive Delaney in Australia, Thomas Stewart in Sweden, Eamon Zayed in Colorado, USA, Russell Payne in Illinois, USA, Tommy Dunne in Finland, and of course Owen Da Gama being in South Africa being among some of the furthest away, but with a bit of back and forth arranging times, we managed to make it work!

Of course, even the former players based in Ireland and the UK still have their own jobs and work to be at during the day, and they have families to get home to in the evening, so thanks to them as well for giving me some of their spare time.

I'd like to say a word of thanks a few people who helped me along the way in different capacities. Kevin McLaughlin, Lawrence Moore and Gary Ferry for the player contacts that they had, Brian Dunleavy for the stats, my other half Nicola for giving me the time most evenings to work on the book or type up an interview, my father Sean who is the reason I remember all of these legends playing due to taking me to the Brandywell with my grandfathers Paddy and Jack since I was no age, to City Print who printed the book and helped me out with advice for my first self-published book along the way, all the players who took part, the current clubs of some players for allowing me to speak to them, all the player sponsors, and sponsors who took an ad, I couldn't have had the book published without yous.

I've massively enjoyed making this book and chatting to the players involved. We've had some great laughs during the calls, and I consider myself really lucky to be able to chat to them all and lucky to know that I'm the only one who got the 'full' version of the book, including the stories that the players would tell me followed by '...don't print that though'!! Calls ranged from 25mins to over an hour, and I've tried to include as much as I could from the interviews.

I've been very lucky over the last 10 years to have been the editor of the famous CityView Derry City match programme and have access to chat to every player who has put on the Candystripe jersey during that time. But thanks to this book, I've also been very lucky to pick up the phone and chat to players that I grew up watching at the Brandywell, and who I missed out on getting interviews with for our match programme.

Thanks again for your continued support of the club, of the match programme, and of this labour of love that you've just finished.

Andrew Cassidy